CHOCOLATE
BIBLE

180 RECIPES FROM THE FAMOUS
FRENCH CULINARY SCHOOL

This English language edition published in 2019 by
Grub Street
4 Rainham Close
London
SW11 6SS

Email: food@grubstreet.co.uk
Web: www.grubstreet.co.uk
Twitter: @grub_street
Facebook: Grub Street Publishing

A CIP catalogue record for this book is available from the British Library.

ISBN 978-1-911621-85-0

Printed and bound in Slovenia

LE CORDON BLEU®

CHOCOLATE
BImageE

180 RECIPES FROM THE FAMOUS
FRENCH CULINARY SCHOOL

GRUB STREET • LONDON

Preface

Le Cordon Bleu is proud to present this collector's edition of its famous Chocolate Bible, a reference book that brings together the culinary and educational expertise of Le Cordon Bleu.

With more than 120 years of history, Le Cordon Bleu has always been faithful to its philosophy of excellence. The institute has amassed a world-leading network of culinary arts and hospitality management institutes, with 35 establishments in 20 countries. Le Cordon Bleu offers a large range of training programmes, from initiation right through to university curricula in the restaurant, wine & beverage, hospitality and tourism sectors.

Le Cordon Bleu has brought a high level of culinary and hospitality training to all four corners of the globe. We are committed to ensuring our training programmes are outstanding.

The institution prides itself on constantly developing new programmes and updating those already in existence. In recent years, Le Cordon Bleu has partnered with educational and industry leaders, including local authorities, universities and prestigious establishments. These internationally recognised partnerships ensure the content of the programmes are continually improving and providing world-class teaching experiences to students, as well as supporting local gastronomies.

The mission of Le Cordon Bleu is to impart the skills and knowledge passed down from the great masters of French cuisine. Today, Le Cordon Bleu institutes train over 20,000 students with 100 different nationalities every year in cuisine, pastry, bread-making, wine and beverages, nutrition and hospitality management.

Le Cordon Bleu institutes teach French culinary techniques, and beyond. Indeed, using the same teaching method and the same practical approach as our classic diplomas, some institutes propose training programmes dedicated to Mexican, Peruvian, Thai, Japanese and Spanish cuisines. Some of these have been commissioned by local governments who wish to preserve their own gastronomy and heritage.

While excellence in education is the essence of Le Cordon Bleu's mission, the teaching has never been limited to the lessons and training given by Chef Instructors, industry experts and lecturers. More than 14 million books have been published by Le Cordon Bleu, and many of these are acclaimed throughout the world, with some considered reference books for culinary training. Which seems fitting, since Le Cordon Bleu was born out of a Parisian magazine created by the journalist Marthe Distel in 1895. Readers were offered cooking lessons by the chefs whose recipes were featured. The magazine reflected the most refined French cuisine of its time and was already opening up to the cuisines of the world, eventually being published in a number of different languages.

This collector's edition of Le Cordon Bleu Chocolate Bible illustrates the institution's mission to pass on expertise and promote contemporary gastronomic styles, both in France and around the world.

We are delighted to share with you our experience, our vision and our passion for the culinary arts. We hope that we can help contribute to your success.

AMITIÉS GOURMANDES,

André Cointreau
President

Le Cordon Bleu around the world

LE CORDON BLEU PARIS
13-15 Quai André Citroën
75015 Paris, France
T: +33 (0)1 85 65 15 00
paris@cordonbleu.edu

LE CORDON BLEU LONDON
15 Bloomsbury Square
London WC1A 2LS
United Kingdom
T: +44 (0) 207 400 3900
london@cordonbleu.edu

LE CORDON BLEU MADRID
Universidad Francisco de Vitoria
Ctra. Pozuelo-Majadahonda
Km. 1,800
Pozuelo de Alarcón, 28223
Madrid, Spain
T: +34 91 715 10 46
madrid@cordonbleu.edu

LE CORDON BLEU ISTANBUL
Özyeğin University
Çekmeköy Campus
Nişantepe Mevkii, Orman Sokak, No:13,
Alemdağ, Çekmeköy 34794
Istanbul, Turkey
T: +90 216 564 9000
istanbul@cordonbleu.edu

LE CORDON BLEU LEBANON
Burj on Bay Hotel
Tabarja – Kfaryassine
Lebanon
T: +961 9 85 75 57
lebanon@cordonbleu.edu

LE CORDON BLEU JAPAN
Le Cordon Bleu Tokyo Campus
Le Cordon Bleu Kobe Campus
Roob-1, 28-13 Sarugaku-Cho,
Daikanyama, Shibuya-Ku, Tokyo
150-0033, Japan
T: +81 3 5489 0141
tokyo@cordonbleu.edu

LE CORDON BLEU KOREA
Sookmyung Women's University,
7th Fl., Social Education Bldg.,
Cheongpa-ro 47gil 100, Yongsan-Ku,
Seoul, 140-742 Korea
T: +82 2 719 6961
korea@cordonbleu.edu

LE CORDON BLEU OTTAWA
453 Laurier Avenue East
Ottawa, Ontario, K1N 6R4, Canada
T: +1 613 236 CHEF (2433)
Toll free +1 888 289 6302
Restaurant line +1 613 236 2499
ottawa@cordonbleu.edu

LE CORDON BLEU MEXICO
Universidad Anáhuac North Campus
Universidad Anáhuac South Campus
Universidad Anáhuac Querétaro Campus
Universidad Anáhuac Cancún Campus
Universidad Anáhuac Mérida Campus
Universidad Anáhuac Puebla Campus
Universidad Anáhuac Tampico Campus
Universidad Anáhuac Oaxaca Campus
Av. Universidad Anáhuac No. 46, Col.
Lomas Anáhuac
Huixquilucan, Edo. De Mex. C.P. 52786,
Mexico
T: +52 55 5627 0210 ext. 7132 / 7813
mexico@cordonbleu.edu

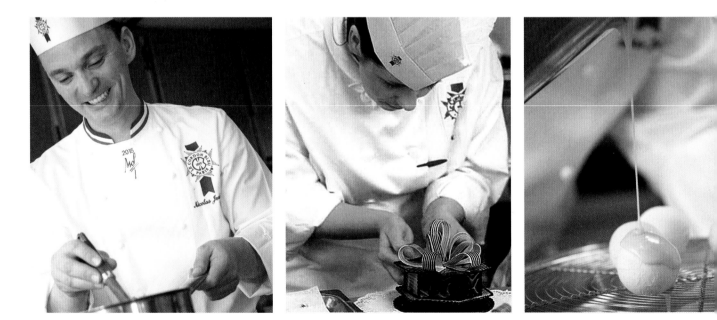

UNIVERSIDAD LE CORDON BLEU PERU (ULCB)
Le Cordon Bleu Peru Instituto
Le Cordon Bleu Cordontec
Av. Vasco Núñez de Balboa 530
Miraflores, Lima 18, Peru
T: +51 1 617 8300
peru@cordonbleu.edu

LE CORDON BLEU AUSTRALIA
Le Cordon Bleu Adelaide Campus
Le Cordon Bleu Sydney Campus
Le Cordon Bleu Melbourne Campus
Le Cordon Bleu Perth Campus
Le Cordon Bleu Brisbane Campus
Days Road, Regency Park
South Australia 5010, Australia
Free call (Australia only): 1 800 064 802
T: +61 8 8346 3000
australia@cordonbleu.edu

LE CORDON BLEU NEW ZEALAND
52 Cuba Street
Wellington, 6011, New Zealand
T: +64 4 4729800
nz@cordonbleu.edu

LE CORDON BLEU MALAYSIA
Sunway University
No. 5, Jalan Universiti, Bandar Sunway,
46150 Petaling Jaya, Selangor DE,
Malaysia
T: +603 5632 1188
malaysia@cordonbleu.edu

LE CORDON BLEU THAILAND
17th-19th Floor, Zen Tower,
Central World Center,
Ratchadamri Road, Bangkok 10330
Thailand
T: +66 2 237 8877
thailand@cordonbleu.edu

LE CORDON BLEU SHANGHAI
2F, Building 1, No. 1458 Pu Dong Nan Road,
Shanghai China 200122
T: +86 400 118 1895
shanghai@cordonbleu.edu

LE CORDON BLEU INDIA
G D Goenka University
Sohna Gurgaon Road
Sohna, Haryana
India
T: +91 880 099 20 22 / 23 / 24
lcb@gdgoenka.ac.in

LE CORDON BLEU CHILE
Universidad Finis Terrae
Avenida Pedro de Valdivia 1509
Providencia
Santiago de Chile
T: +56 24 20 72 23

LE CORDON BLEU RIO DE JANEIRO
Rua da Passagem, 179, Botafogo
Rio de Janeiro, RJ, 22290-031
Brazil
T: +55 21 9940-02117

LE CORDON BLEU SÃO PAULO
Rua Natingui, 862 Primero audar,
Vila Madalena, SP, São Paulo 05443-001
Brazil
T: +55 11 3185-2500

LE CORDON BLEU TAIWAN
NKUHT University
Ming-Tai Institute
4F, No. 200, Sec. 1, Keelung Road
Taipei 110, Taiwan
T: +886 2 7725-3600 / +886 975226418

LE CORDON BLEU KAOHSIUNG
No.1, Songhe Rd
Xiaogang Dist., Kaohsiung, 81271,
Taiwan
T: +886 (0) 7 801 0909

LE CORDON BLEU, INC.
85 Broad Street – 18th floor,
New York, NY 10004 U.S.A.
T: +1 212 641 0331

www.cordonbleu.edu
e-mail: info@cordonbleu.edu

Contents

A few tips before starting…

CHOOSING INGREDIENTS

All the ingredients listed in this book are the ones used in the testing of the recipes. The majority are easily found in your local supermarket; only a few will be available in speciality stores. The basic ingredients include plain flour (not self-raising), whole milk, baking powder, 50 g (small/medium) eggs, whipping cream (35% butterfat) and unsalted butter, unless indicated otherwise. Use "dessert" chocolate if available; if not, use good-quality dark, milk or white chocolate. However, when tempering and/or glazing, professional couverture chocolate would be the best choice. For this process, always use chocolate containing at least 31% cocoa butter.

SPECIFIC EQUIPMENT

The recipes generally use equipment and tools found in most kitchens. Some of the recipes, however, require specific items such as: a fine-meshed sieve or strainer, pastry piping bags fitted with round or star nozzles, different sized dessert or tart rings, a digital or sugar thermometer (an electronic one with a temperature probe is ideal for tempering chocolate) and, last but not least, a kitchen scale.

OVEN TEMPERATURES

The oven temperatures and cooking times indicated in the recipes can vary slightly depending on your oven (see p.416).

Temptingly
rich cakes

The best way to make a basic ganache

In this recipe, equal amounts of chocolate and cream are used to produce a creamy chocolate mixture suitable for filling, glazing or coating cakes. If the quantity of chocolate is increased, the ganache will become firmer – perfect for preparing truffles and other sweets. Some of the recipes in this book use an adapted form of this basic version.

(1) Coarsely chop 300 g dark chocolate and place in a large bowl.

(2) Heat 300 ml cream in a saucepan until simmering, and pour it over the chocolate.

(3) Stir the cream and chocolate until evenly combined. Continue stirring until the mixture has cooled and is smooth and glossy. Let the ganache rest at room temperature until it can be easily spread.

The best way to make a rolled sponge

Cook the sponge and prepare the filling as indicated on pp.18 or 76.

① Put the cooked sponge on a piece of baking parchment (or a clean tea towel), crust-side down.

② Using a palette knife, spread the filling evenly over the sponge leaving a small border along the outside edges uncovered.

③ Start rolling on one of the long sides; fold approximately 2 cm of the sponge over tightly. Using the baking parchment as a guide, slowly pull up the edge to form the sponge into a roll. Finish with the seam underneath and cut a small piece off each end to even the roll.

The best way to glaze a cake or entremets

Prepare the cake or entremets and the glaze. Let cool and prepare the glaze indicated in the recipe of your choice, for example, on pp.32 or 44.

(1) Place the cake on a rack over a hotel pan.

(2) Pour the glaze over the entire cake including the sides.

(3) Use a palette knife to spread the glaze evenly over the top of the cake and around the sides. To set the glaze, refrigerate for 30 minutes before serving.

The best way to glaze a cake in dark and white

Prepare the cake or entremets and the glaze according to your chosen recipe (for example, see page 32 or 44). Use the glaze warm. Combine 30 g of melted cocoa butter with 30 g of clear glaze.

① Place the cake on a rack and place this over a large hotel pan. Pour the warm dark chocolate glaze over the cake in one go, letting it run down the sides. Next, pour in the centre a little of the cocoa butter-clear glaze mix.

② Use a palette knife to spread the cocoa butter-clear glaze mix across the top, then smooth. The glaze should have a stripy appearance. Leave to firm up in the refrigerator for 30 minutes.

Chocolate Christmas Log

SERVES 10–12

DIFFICULTY ★ ★ ★

PREPARE: 1½ hours

COOK: 8 minutes

REFRIGERATE: 1 hour

Almond Sponge
- 150 g almond paste
- 60 g icing sugar
- 3 egg yolks
- 2 egg whites
- 60 g caster sugar
- 100 g flour, sifted
- 50 g unsalted butter, melted

Ganache
- 200 g dark chocolate
- 250 ml whipping cream
- 75 g soft unsalted butter
- 50 ml rum

Rum Syrup
- 120 ml water
- 100 g caster sugar
- 1 tsp coffee extract
- 40 ml rum

Coffee Buttercream
- 1 egg
- 2 egg yolks
- 160 g caster sugar
- 80 ml water
- 250 g soft unsalted butter
- Coffee extract, to taste

◊ See p.13: Making a rolled sponge.

Preheat the oven to 180°C (350°F). Line a 30 x 38 cm oven tray with baking parchment.

Almond Sponge: Place the almond paste in a bowl and add the icing sugar; beat until the mixture resembles fine breadcrumbs. Whisk in the egg yolks one at a time. In a separate bowl, whisk the egg whites until frothy; add 20 g of the sugar a little at a time, whisking until the egg whites are smooth and shiny. Gradually add the remaining sugar, whisking until stiff peaks form. Fold 1/3 of the whisked egg whites and 50 g of the sifted flour into the almond-icing sugar mixture; carefully fold in another 1/3 of the egg whites and the remaining flour. Fold in the rest of the egg whites and the melted butter. Pour a 5 mm layer of batter into the prepared tin. Bake about 8 minutes, or until the surface of the sponge is firm but springy to the touch. Cool on a rack.

Ganache: Coarsely chop the chocolate and place in a bowl. Heat the cream in a saucepan until simmering then pour over the chocolate; stir until smooth. Add the butter and the rum. Set the ganache aside at room temperature until it can be spread easily.

Rum Syrup: Place the water and sugar in a saucepan over low heat; stir until the sugar is completely dissolved then bring to the boil; cool. When the syrup is cold, add the coffee extract and the rum.

Coffee Buttercream: Beat the whole egg and egg yolks in the bowl of an electric mixer until well combined. Place the sugar and water in a saucepan and stir over low heat until the sugar is completely dissolved. Bring to the boil and cook (do not stir) the syrup until it registers 120°C on a sugar thermometer. With the mixer running, gradually pour the syrup in a thin steady stream down the inside of the bowl; continue beating until cool. Add the butter and coffee extract.

Peel off and discard the baking parchment used to cook the sponge. Place the sponge on another piece. Brush with the rum syrup and spread with a layer of coffee buttercream. Start rolling one long side and fold approximately 2 cm of the sponge over tightly. Using parchment as a guide, slowly pull up the edge, forming the sponge into a roll. Finish with the seam underneath; cut a small piece off each end to even the roll. Coat with coffee buttercream and refrigerate for 1 hour. Before serving, spread ganache over the coffee buttercream, using a palette knife.

Fresh Fruit Christmas Log

SERVES 10–12

DIFFICULTY ★ ★ ★

PREPARE: 1½ hours

COOK: 8 minutes

REFRIGERATE: 1 hour

Chocolate Sponge
- 3 egg yolks
- 75 g caster sugar
- 3 egg whites
- 70 g flour, sifted
- 15 g unsweetened cocoa powder, sifted

Chocolate Cream
- 40 g dark chocolate
- 1 leaf gelatine
- 150 ml milk
- 2 egg yolks
- 50 g caster sugar
- 20 g cornflour
- 200 ml whipping cream

Chocolate Syrup
- 100 ml water
- 100 g caster sugar
- 10 g unsweetened cocoa powder

Fruit
- 200 g strawberries, diced
- 1 pear, diced
- 100 g raspberries
- 100 g blackberries
- 1 kiwi, diced

Decoration
- Kiwis, pears, raspberries, strawberries, blackberries
- Icing sugar

Preheat the oven to 180°C (350°F). Line a 30 x 38 cm oven tray with baking parchment.

Chocolate Sponge: Combine the egg yolks and 25 g of the sugar; beat until pale yellow and creamy. In a separate bowl, whisk the egg whites, gradually adding the remaining sugar until stiff peaks form; gently incorporate the egg yolk-sugar mixture. Fold in the sifted flour and cocoa powder. Pour the sponge batter into the prepared tin and smooth with a palette knife. Bake for about 8 minutes, or until firm but springy to the touch. Cool on a rack.

Chocolate Cream: Chop the chocolate and set aside in a large bowl. Soften the leaf gelatine in a bowl of cold water. Bring the milk to the boil and remove from the heat. Whisk the egg yolks and sugar until pale yellow and creamy; add the cornflour. Slowly whisk in half the hot milk then add the remaining milk; return the mixture to the saucepan and stir continuously over low heat until thickened. Continue stirring and boil for 1 minute; remove from the heat. Squeeze the excess water from the leaf gelatine and add it to the hot milk mixture. Pour over the chopped chocolate and stir until smooth; cool. Cover the surface with cling film, stir from time to time and set aside to cool. Beat the whipping cream until firm and gently fold into the cooled chocolate cream.

Chocolate Syrup: Place the water, sugar and cocoa powder in a saucepan and stir over low heat until the sugar is completely dissolved then bring to the boil; cool.

Finishing: Fold the fruit carefully into the chocolate cream. Line a 35 cm log mould with a piece of baking parchment larger than the mould. Cut the chocolate sponge into 2 rectangles, 13 x 35 cm and 5 x 35 cm. Place the larger rectangle in the mould (it will come up the sides) and brush with chocolate syrup. Fill with the chocolate-fruit cream, mounding the cream towards the top. Brush the smaller rectangle with chocolate syrup and place on the top log. Refrigerate for 1 hour then carefully invert the log and tip it out onto a platter. Decorate with fruit and dust with icing sugar.

Fruit and Nut Chocolate Loaf

SERVES 8–10

DIFFICULTY ★ ★ ★

PREPARE: 25 minutes

COOK: 50 minutes

- 150 g dried apricots
- 40 g glacé cherries
- 50 g candied orange peel
- 50 g sultanas
- 50 g hazelnuts, toasted
- 30 g pistachios
- 100 g mixed glacé fruits
- 300 g soft unsalted butter
- 250 g icing sugar
- 5 eggs
- 300 g flour, sifted
- 30 g unsweetened cocoa powder, sifted
- 1 tsp baking powder, sifted

Preheat the oven to 180°C (350°F). Butter a 28 x 10 cm loaf tin.

Cut dried apricots, glacé cherries and candied orange peel into small pieces, then mix them with sultanas, hazelnuts, pistachios and glacé fruits; set aside.

Place the butter in a bowl and beat with a spatula until creamy. Add the icing sugar and beat until the mixture is soft and light. Beat in the eggs one at a time and add the sifted flour, cocoa and baking powder. Gently fold in the reserved dried fruit and nuts.

Pour the batter into the prepared loaf tin and bake for 50 minutes. Cool in the loaf tin for about 15 minutes, before turning out onto a rack.

CHEF'S TIP: The cake can be kept refrigerated for several days or wrapped in cling film and frozen for several weeks.

Chocolate-Raspberry Square

SERVES 8–10

DIFFICULTY ★ ★ ★

PREPARE: 1 hour

COOK: 15 minutes

REFRIGERATE: 15 minutes

Chocolate Sponge
- 75 g dark chocolate
- 50 g unsweetened cooking chocolate
- 125 g soft unsalted butter
- 3 egg yolks
- 100 g caster sugar
- 4 egg whites
- 50 g cornflour, sifted
- ½ tsp baking powder, sifted

Chocolate Mousse
- 110 g dark (55%) chocolate
- 25 g unsweetened cooking chocolate
- 250 ml whipping cream
- 4 egg yolks
- 60 g caster sugar

Raspberry Syrup
- 50 ml water
- 50 g caster sugar
- 100 ml raspberry juice
- 40 ml raspberry eau-de-vie

Raspberry Glaze
- 65 g raspberries
- 1 or 2 tsp mild honey
- 60 g caster sugar
- 4 g pectin

Preheat the oven to 180°C (350°F). Line a 17 X 17 cm square cake frame with baking parchment.

Chocolate Sponge: Melt the chocolates over a bain-marie. Remove from the heat and mix in the butter, egg yolks and 50 g of the sugar. In a separate bowl, whisk the egg whites, gradually adding the remaining sugar until the whites are smooth, shiny and stiff peaks form; gently fold onto the chocolate mixture. Add the sifted cornflour and baking powder and mix to combine. Pour the batter onto the prepared cake tin and smooth with a palette knife. Bake for about 15 minutes. Let cool and remove from the cake tin.

Chocolate Mousse: Roughly chop the chocolates and melt over a bain-marie. Remove from the heat and cool. Whisk the cream until firm. Combine the egg yolks and sugar and whisk until pale yellow and creamy. Using a spatula, mix in the chocolate a little at a time. Fold in the whipped cream.

Raspberry Syrup: Place the water, sugar and raspberry juice in a saucepan over low heat, stir until the sugar dissolves then bring to the boil; let cool. Add the raspberry eau-de-vie to the cold syrup.

Raspberry Glaze: Put the raspberries, honey and 30 g of the sugar into a saucepan and bring to the boil. Combine the pectin with the remaining sugar and add to the raspberry mixture; bring to the boil again. Set aside to cool.

Place a 17 x 17 cm pastry frame on a baking tray lined with a clean sheet of baking parchment. Cut the chocolate sponge horizontally into 2 even layers. Place the first square in the bottom of the cake tin, brush it with syrup, then spread over the chocolate mousse. Place the second square of sponge on the chocolate mousse, brush it with the syrup and cover with a thin layer of mousse. Use a spatula to spread the raspberry glaze over the surface of the sponge. Refrigerate for 15 minutes, then unmould and even the sides of the chocolate raspberry square with a sharp knife dipped in hot water.

CHEF'S TIP: If desired, other berries, such as blackberries, could be used to prepare the glaze. If you cannot find cocoa paste, use chocolate with a high percentage of cocoa, 72% for example. And, if you do not have pectin, you can replace it with 2 gelatine leaves.

Genovese Almond Cake

SERVES 4–6

DIFFICULTY ★ ★ ★

PREPARE: 20 minutes

COOK: 25 minutes

- Flaked almonds
- 60 g unsalted butter
- 4 eggs
- 200 g almond paste (33% almonds)
- 20 g flour, sifted
- 10 g unsweetened cocoa powder, sifted
- ½ tsp baking powder, sifted

Preheat the oven to 160°C (325°F). Butter an 18 cm square cake tin and sprinkle it with flaked almonds.

Melt the butter in a saucepan and set aside.

Beat the eggs into the almond paste, one at a time. Continue whisking for 5 minutes, or until the mixture is pale and thick and falls from the whisk in a ribbon without breaking. Fold in the sifted flour, cocoa and baking powder; add the melted butter.

Pour the cake batter into the prepared cake tin, to come $^2/_3$ up the sides. Bake for 25 minutes. Turn out onto a rack and cool.

Chocolate Heart

SERVES 8–10

DIFFICULTY ★ ★ ★

PREPARE: 1½ hours

COOK: 40 minutes

REFRIGERATE: 50 minutes

Chocolate Cake
- 140 g unsalted butter
- 225 g dark chocolate, chopped
- 4 egg yolks
- 150 g caster sugar
- 4 egg whites
- 50 g flour, sifted

Ganache
- 250 g dark chocolate
- 250 ml whipping cream

Decoration
- Raspberries, strawberries, blackberries, blueberries

◊ See p.14: Glazing a cake or entremets.

Preheat the oven to 180°C (350°F). Butter and dust with flour a heart-shaped cake tin (or a 24 cm round cake tin).

Chocolate Cake: Melt the chocolate and the butter over a bain-marie; stir until smooth. Beat the egg yolks and 75 g of the sugar until they are pale and thick. In a separate bowl, whisk the egg whites, gradually adding the remaining sugar until they are smooth, shiny and stiff peaks form. Fold the sifted flour into the egg yolk-sugar mixture and combine with the melted chocolate-butter mixture. Whisk $1/3$ of the egg whites into the chocolate mixture to lighten it; carefully fold in the remainder in two separate batches. Rest the batter for 5 minutes before pouring it into the prepared cake tin. Bake for 40 minutes. Cool on a rack before turning the cake out; refrigerate for 20 minutes.

Ganache: Coarsely chop the chocolate and place in a bowl. Heat the cream in a small saucepan until simmering and pour over the chocolate; stir until smooth. Set the ganache aside for about 10 minutes at room temperature, until it can be spread easily.

When the chocolate cake is cold and fairly hard, cut a thin slice from the top to level it; use a long serrated knife and cut in a sawing motion. Spread the ganache evenly over the entire surface of the cake; refrigerate for 30 minutes until firm. Decorate with berries.

CHEF'S TIP: The cake can be kept refrigerated for 2–3 days. It can also be served with a crème Anglaise or whipped cream.

Meringue Nests with Spiced Pears in a Chocolate and Wine Sauce

SERVES 6

DIFFICULTY ★ ★ ★

PREPARE: 1½ hours

COOK: 35 minutes approx

REFRIGERATE: 30 minutes

Meringues
- 4 egg whites
- 50 g caster sugar
- 70 g ground almonds, sifted
- 75 g icing sugar, sifted
- 30 g flour, sifted

Ganache
- 90 g dark chocolate
- 100 ml whipping cream
- 15 g mild honey
- 35 g soft unsalted butter

Spiced Pears
- 6 pears
- ½ lemon
- 30 g unsalted butter
- 40 g mild honey
- Ground cinnamon
- Cloves
- Ground nutmeg
- Ground pepper

Chocolate and Wine Sauce
- 100 g dark chocolate
- 375 ml red wine
- 3 star anise
- 20 ml water
- 30 g caster sugar

◊ See p.210: Shaping quenelles.

Preheat the oven to 170°C (335°F). Trace six 8 cm circles on baking parchment and turn the marked side over onto one or more baking trays, depending on the oven size.

Meringues: Whisk the egg whites, gradually adding the sugar until stiff peaks form. Carefully fold in the sifted almonds, icing sugar and flour. Fit a piping bag with a medium-sized round nozzle and fill with the meringue mixture. Start piping in the centre of the circles, working outwards in a spiral until filled. Pipe a raised border on the edge of each circle to form a nest. Bake for 20 minutes. Remove the nests from the hot baking trays to avoid drying; cool on a rack.

Ganache: Coarsely chop the chocolate and place in a bowl. Heat the cream and the honey in a small saucepan until simmering and pour over the chocolate; stir until smooth. Add the butter and stir until well combined. Refrigerate for 30 minutes.

Spiced Pears: Peel and cut the pears in half and core, leaving the stalks in place for presentation, if you like. Rub with the lemon to prevent discolouration. Place the butter, honey and spices in a large frying or sauté pan and bring to the boil. Lower the heat, arrange the pear halves in a single layer and cook gently for 15 minutes; turning the pears over after approximately 7 minutes.

Chocolate and Wine Sauce: Coarsely chop the chocolate. In a medium saucepan, heat the wine and the star anise over medium heat. Then raise the heat and boil until the liquid is reduced by 1/2. Add the chopped chocolate, water and sugar, bring to the boil again. Cook until the chocolate is completely melted. Using a fine-meshed sieve, strain the sauce; cool.

Place a dacquoise on 6 plates. With 2 tablespoons, form quenelles of ganache and put one on each dacquoise. Top with half a hot pear and decorate the plate with chocolate and wine sauce.

Chocolate Hazelnut Square

SERVES 8

DIFFICULTY ★ ★ ★

PREPARE: 1 hour

COOK: 20 minutes

REFRIGERATE: 1 hour

Cake
- 60 g unsalted butter
- 6 egg yolks
- 130 g caster sugar
- 4 egg whites
- 60 g flour, sifted
- 30 g unsweetened cocoa powder, sifted
- 50 g ground hazelnuts or almonds

Chocolate Glaze
- 100 g dark chocolate
- 100 ml whipping cream
- 20 g mild honey

Decoration
- 150 g chocolate sprinkles

Preheat the oven to 180°C (350°F). Butter an 18 cm square cake tin and dust it with flour.

Cake: Melt the butter; set aside. Beat the egg yolks and 100 g of the sugar until pale and thick. In a separate bowl whisk the egg whites, gradually adding the remaining sugar, until they are smooth and shiny and stiff peaks form. Gently fold into the egg yolk-sugar mixture. Combine the sifted flour and cocoa powder in a bowl; add the ground hazelnuts. Fold 1/3 of this mixture into the egg white mixture; carefully fold in the remainder in 2 separate batches; add the melted butter. Pour the batter into the prepared cake tin. Bake for 20 minutes, or until a knife inserted into the centre of the cake comes out clean. Cool before turning out onto a rack.

Chocolate Glaze: Finely chop the chocolate and place in a bowl. Heat the cream and the honey in a small saucepan until simmering and pour over the chocolate; stir gently until smooth. Set aside to cool. Use a palette knife or spatula to spread the glaze evenly over the entire surface of the cake; press the chocolate sprinkles around the sides. Refrigerate for 1 hour, or until the glaze is firm.

CHEF'S TIP: This cake is even more delicious when served with an orange sorbet.

Chocolate Walnut Cake

SERVES 8–10

DIFFICULTY ★ ★ ★

PREPARE: 1¼ hours

COOK: 40 minutes approx

COOL: 2 hours

REFRIGERATE: 1 hour

Chocolate Cake
- 190 g dark chocolate
- 125 g soft unsalted butter
- 125 g dark brown sugar
- 2 egg yolks
- 90 g chopped walnuts
- 40 g ground almonds
- 2 egg whites
- 40 g caster sugar

Chocolate Glaze
- 100 g dark chocolate
- 100 ml whipping cream
- 20 g mild honey

Decoration
- 50 g white chocolate
- Walnut halves

◊ See p.14: Glazing
a cake or entremets.

◊ See p.329: Making a paper
piping bag.

Preheat the oven to 160°C (325°F). Butter a 20 cm round cake tin.

Chocolate Cake: Finely chop the chocolate and set aside. Place the butter in a bowl and beat until smooth. Add the dark brown sugar and continue beating until creamy. Blend in the egg yolks, then the chopped chocolate, walnuts and ground almonds; set the mixture aside. In a separate bowl, whisk the egg whites until frothy. Add 15 g of the sugar a little at a time and continue whisking until the egg whites are smooth and shiny. Add the remaining sugar, whisking until stiff peaks form. Whisk $1/3$ of the egg whites into the chocolate mixture to lighten it; carefully fold in the remainder in 2 separate batches. Pour the batter into the prepared cake tin and bake for approximately 40 minutes, or until a knife inserted into the centre of the cake comes out clean. Cool for at least 2 hours before turning the cake out onto a rack.

Chocolate Glaze: Finely chop the chocolate and place in a bowl. Heat the cream and honey in a small saucepan until simmering and pour over the chocolate; stir gently until smooth. Set aside to cool. Use a palette knife or spatula to spread the glaze evenly over the entire surface of the cake. Refrigerate for 1 hour, or until the glaze is firm.

Decoration: Make a small paper piping bag. Melt the white chocolate, cool and pour it into the piping bag; snip off the tip. Decorate the surface of the cake with geometric designs and walnut halves.

CHEF'S TIP: The cake can be kept refrigerated for 2–3 days or, if carefully wrapped in cling film, it can be frozen for several weeks.

Autumn Leaf Gateau

SERVES 6

DIFFICULTY ★ ★ ★

PREPARE: 1½ hours

COOK: 1 hour

REFRIGERATE: 1 hour

Almond Meringue
- 4 egg whites
- 120 g caster sugar
- 120 g ground almonds

Chocolate Mousse
- 250 g dark (55%) chocolate
- 4 egg whites
- 150 g caster sugar
- 80 ml whipping cream

Decoration
- 250 g dark chocolate
- 40 g icing sugar, sifted, or unsweetened cocoa powder

◊ See p.211: Shaping meringue, batter or pastry discs.

Preheat the oven to 100°C (210°F). Trace three 20 cm circles on baking parchment and turn the marked side over onto one or more baking trays, depending on oven size.

Almond Meringue: Whisk the egg whites, gradually adding the sugar, until the whites are smooth and shiny and stiff peaks form; gently fold in the ground almonds a little at a time. Fit a piping bag with a plain round nozzle and fill it with the almond meringue. Start piping in the centre of each traced circle, working outwards in a spiral until filled. Bake for 1 hour. Cool on a rack until required.

Chocolate Mousse: Chop the chocolate and melt in a bain-marie over low heat. Remove from the heat and stir until smooth; cool. Whisk the egg whites, gradually adding the sugar, until they are smooth and shiny and stiff peaks form. Whisk the cream until firm and clinging to the whisk. Quickly whisk $1/3$ of the egg whites into the chocolate mixture to lighten it. Use a spatula and carefully fold in the remainder in 2 separate batches; fold in the whipped cream. Refrigerate until firm.

Preheat the oven to 50°C (125°F) and put two baking trays into it. Chop the chocolate for decoration and melt over a bain-marie; set aside.

Put a meringue disc on a plate and spread it with a layer of chocolate mousse. Place the second meringue disk on top and spread with another layer of chocolate mousse, reserving some mousse for later use. Finish with the remaining meringue disc and refrigerate for 30 minutes.

Remove the baking trays from the oven and spread with a thin layer of melted chocolate. Place in the bottom of the refrigerator for 10 minutes. Spread the top of the cake with the reserved chocolate mousse and smooth the surface using a palette knife; refrigerate for 20 minutes. When the chocolate on the baking trays begins to harden, remove from the refrigerator and bring to room temperature. Use a broad flat scraper to scrape up a wide rectangle of chocolate. Wrap it around the gateau, carefully folding it over the top. Scrape the remainder, in smaller rectangles, bending them gently until wavy; use to decorate the top of the cake (see photo opposite). Dust lightly with icing sugar or cocoa powder.

Chocolate-Pistachio Opera Cake

SERVES 8

DIFFICULTY ★ ★ ★

PREPARE: 1 hour

COOK: 20 minutes

Pistachio Sponge
45 g caster sugar (+ 35 g)
45 g ground almonds
45 g coloured pistachio paste
2 egg yolks
1 egg
20 g plain flour, sifted
20 g unsalted melted butter
3 egg whites

Syrup
120 ml water
100 g caster sugar
20 ml Kirsch

Ganache
200 g dark (54%) chocolate
200 ml whipping cream
20 g unsalted butter

Pistachio Chantilly Cream
150 ml whipping cream
15 g icing sugar
20 g coloured pistachio paste
1 tsp dessert jelly

Decoration
Icing sugar
20 pistachios

Preheat the oven to 200°C (400°F). Line two 30 x 38 cm baking trays with baking parchment. Place three 17 x 17 cm baking frames on the trays.

Pistachio Sponge: Mix together the 45 g of sugar in a bowl with the ground almonds, pistachio paste, egg yolks and the whole egg. Fold in the flour and lukewarm melted butter.

In a separate bowl, whisk the 3 egg whites until slightly frothy. Gradually add the 35 g of sugar, continuing to whisk the egg whites until smooth and glossy. Gently fold in the remaining sugar and mix until the egg whites are fairly stiff. Fold the meringue into the mixture. Distribute the batter among the three baking frames. Bake individually for around 10 minutes. Leave to cool on a rack, then remove from the frames.

Syrup: Bring the water and sugar to boil in a saucepan, then leave to cool. Add the Kirsch.

Ganache: Chop the chocolate and place in a bowl. Bring the cream to a boil in a saucepan, pour over the chocolate and gently stir with a flexible spatula. Add the butter. Set aside.

Brush the pistachio sponges with syrup. Put the first sponge in the baking frame and put half of the ganache over it without working it. Place a second sponge on top and add the remaining ganache. Cover with the last sponge. Set aside.

Pistachio Chantilly Cream: Whip the cream in a bowl with the icing sugar, pistachio paste and dessert jelly until firm and clings to the tip of the whisk. Transfer the pistachio Chantilly cream to a piping bag fitted with a 6 or 8 mm nozzle and pipe over the sponge using a back and forth movement. Remove the baking frame (gently heat with a blow torch to make this easier). Sprinkle the Opera cake with icing sugar and decorate with pistachios before serving.

Chocolate Almond Kugelhopf

SERVES 8

DIFFICULTY ★ ★ ★

PREPARE: 30 minutes

COOK: 40 minutes

REFRIGERATE: 30 minutes

Cake
- 150 g dark chocolate
- 170 g soft unsalted butter
- 115 g soft dark or light brown sugar
- 3 egg yolks
- 175 g ground almonds
- 3 egg whites
- 35 g caster sugar

Chantilly Cream
- 250 ml whipping cream
- 2 or 3 drops vanilla extract
- 25 g icing sugar

Decoration
- 2 tbsp sliced almonds

Preheat the oven to 150°C (300°F). Butter a 22 cm diameter bundt tin or Kugelhopf mould.

Cake: Chop the chocolate and melt in a bain-marie over low heat. Remove from the heat and cool. Place the butter in a bowl and beat until smooth. Blend in the brown sugar and continue beating until creamy. Add the yolks, one at a time, to the butter-sugar mixture, beating well after each addition. Fold in the ground almonds and the melted chocolate; set aside. Whisk the egg whites, gradually adding the sugar, until they are smooth and shiny and stiff peaks form. Add $1/3$ of the egg whites to the chocolate mixture to lighten it then gently fold in the remainder. Pour the batter into the prepared mould and bake for 40 minutes, or until a knife inserted into the centre of the cake comes out clean. Cool before turning out onto a rack.

Chantilly Cream: Combine the cream and vanilla extract and whisk until the cream begins to stiffen. Add the icing sugar and continue whisking until the cream is firm and clings to the whisk. Fit a piping bag with a star nozzle, fill it with the Chantilly cream and decorate the top of the cake; sprinkle with sliced almonds.

CHEF'S TIP: Instead of soft brown sugar, Demerara sugar could be used. When making Chantilly cream, use a deep bowl; chill it and the cream 15 minutes before whisking or beating.

Bitter Chocolate Cake

SERVES 8

DIFFICULTY ★ ★ ★

PREPARE: 35 minutes

COOK: 45 minutes

REFRIGERATE: 30 minutes

Cake
- 125 g soft unsalted butter
- 200 g caster sugar
- 4 eggs
- 150 g flour, sifted
- 40 g unsweetened cocoa powder, sifted

Ganache
- 200 g dark (55–70%) chocolate
- 200 ml whipping cream

Decoration
- 150 g chocolate sprinkles

◊ See p.12: Making a basic ganache.

Preheat the oven to 180°C (350°F). Butter a 20 cm round cake tin.

Cake: Place the butter in a bowl and beat until smooth. Blend in the sugar and beat until creamy. Add the eggs, one at a time, being careful not to over mix. Gently fold in the sifted flour and cocoa powder. Pour the batter into the prepared tin and bake for 45 minutes, or until a knife inserted into the centre of the cake comes out clean. Turn out onto a rack and cool.

Ganache: Coarsely chop the chocolate and place in a bowl. Heat the cream in a saucepan until simmering and pour it over the chocolate; stir until smooth.

Use a long serrated knife to cut the cake horizontally into two even layers. Place one layer on a rack and spread it with a thin layer of ganache, using a palette knife. Top with the remaining layer and refrigerate for 30 minutes.

Glaze the entire surface of the cake with the remaining ganache; press the chocolate sprinkles around the side using a palette knife. To decorate, dip a serrated knife (or a fork) in hot water and make wavy lines in the top.

CHEF'S TIP: If the cake is too dry, brush or sprinkle with the syrup of your choice, before applying the ganache. It could also be decorated with Chantilly cream rosettes.

Chocolate-Cherry Cake

SERVES 8

DIFFICULTY ★ ★ ★

PREPARE: 2 hours

COOK: 30 minutes approx

REFRIGERATE: 1½ hours

Sponge
- 20 g unsalted butter
- 4 eggs
- 125 g caster sugar
- 90 g flour, sifted
- 30 g unsweetened cocoa powder, sifted

Syrup
- 100 ml water
- 80 g caster sugar

Chocolate Mousse
- 200 g dark (55%) chocolate
- 400 ml whipping cream

- 25 bottled cherries, stoned

Preheat the oven to 180°C (350°F). Butter a 20 cm round cake tin.

Sponge: Melt the butter in a saucepan over low heat; set aside. Place the sugar and the eggs in a heatproof bowl; whisk to combine. Stand the bowl over a bain-marie and whisk continuously for 5–8 minutes, or until the mixture becomes light and doubles in volume. Do not allow it to become too hot. Remove the bowl from the bain-marie and continue whisking quickly by hand, or with an electric beater on high speed, until cool and the batter falls in a ribbon from the whisk or beater. Gently fold in the sifted flour and cocoa powder, adding it in 2 or 3 batches. Quickly add the melted butter. Pour the batter into the prepared tin, bake for about 25 minutes, or until the surface is firm but springy to the touch.

Syrup: Place the water and sugar in a saucepan over low heat, stirring until the sugar dissolves, bring to the boil; cool.

Chocolate Mousse: Roughly chop the chocolate and place it in a bowl; melt over a slowly simmering bain-marie until the temperature reaches approximately 45°C on a digital thermometer. Beat the cream until firm peaks cling to the whisk. Whisking quickly, add about 2/3 of the whipped cream to the hot chocolate. Pour the mixture over the remaining cream and fold in gently with the whisk or a spatula to blend the ingredients evenly. Cover with cling film; refrigerate for 30 minutes.

Using a long serrated knife, cut the sponge horizontally into two layers of equal thickness. Place one layer on a rack, brush or sprinkle with syrup and spread with a thick layer of chocolate mousse. Reserve some bottled cherries for decoration and scatter the remainder over the mousse. Brush the other sponge layer with syrup and place it on top of the cherries; refrigerate for 1 hour. Decorate with the remaining chocolate mousse and cherries.

CHEF'S TIP: For a professional touch, fit a piping bag with a star nozzle, fill with the chocolate mousse and decorate the cake.

Chocolate-Raspberry Cake

SERVES 8–10

DIFFICULTY ★ ★ ★

PREPARE: 2½ hours

COOK: 8 minutes

REFRIGERATE: 1 hour 10 minutes

Sponge
- 4 egg yolks
- 125 g caster sugar
- 4 egg whites
- 90 g flour, sifted
- 30 g unsweetened cocoa powder, sifted

Raspberry Syrup
- 100 ml water
- 50 g caster sugar
- 50 ml raspberry liqueur

Chocolate Mousse
- 250 g dark (55%) chocolate
- 500 ml whipping cream

Chocolate Glaze
- 140 g dark chocolate
- 200 ml whipping cream
- 25 g mild honey

Decoration
- 350 g fresh raspberries

◇ See p.211 Making pastry, batter or meringue discs.

◇ See p.14 Glazing a cake or entremets.

Preheat the oven to 180°C (350°F). Prepare one or more baking trays, depending on the oven size. Trace 3 circles (20 cm) on baking parchment and turn the marked side over onto the baking tray(s).

Sponge: Combine the egg yolks and 60 g of the sugar; beat until the mixture is pale yellow and creamy. In a separate bowl, whisk the egg whites, gradually adding the remaining sugar, until the whites are smooth and shiny and stiff peaks form. Gently fold in the egg yolk-sugar mixture, then the sifted flour and cocoa powder. Fit a piping bag with a plain round nozzle and fill it with the sponge batter. Start piping in the centre of the traced circles, working outwards in a spiral until filled. Bake approximately 8 minutes; set the discs aside until required.

Raspberry Syrup: Place the water and sugar in a saucepan over low heat, stirring until the sugar is dissolved then bring to the boil. Remove from the heat; cool. Add the raspberry liqueur to the cold syrup.

Chocolate Mousse: Roughly chop the chocolate and place it in a bowl and melt over a slowly simmering bain-marie until the temperature reaches approximately 45°C on a digital thermometer. Beat the cream until firm peaks cling to the whisk. Whisking quickly, add about 1/3 of the whipped cream to the hot chocolate. Pour the mixture over the remaining cream and fold in gently with the whisk or a spatula to evenly blend the ingredients.

Chocolate Glaze: Finely chop the chocolate and place in a bowl. Heat the cream and honey in a small saucepan until simmering and pour over the chocolate, stirring gently until evenly combined.

Place one of the sponge discs on a rack, and brush with raspberry syrup. Spread with 1/3 of the chocolate mousse, and arrange 1/3 of the raspberries on the mousse. Place the second disk on the rack, brush with the raspberry syrup then place it on top of the first layer. Spread it with another 1/3 of the chocolate mousse, and arrange another 1/3 of the raspberries on the mousse. Place the remaining sponge disk on top. Cover the entire surface of the cake with the rest of the chocolate mousse and refrigerate for 20 minutes. Reheat the chocolate glaze and pour it over the cake; use a palette knife to spread it evenly over the top and around the side. Refrigerate for 50 minutes to set the glaze. Before serving, decorate with the remaining raspberries.

Chocolate and Hazelnut Cake

SERVES 6–8

DIFFICULTY ★ ★ ★

PREPARE: 20 minutes

COOK: 35 minutes

- 130 ml milk
- 100 g caster sugar
- 1 vanilla pod, split
- 100 g dark (55–70%) chocolate
- 35 g chocolate-hazelnut spread
- 30 g soft unsalted butter
- 2 eggs
- 100 g flour, sifted
- 1 tsp baking powder, sifted
- 25 g ground hazelnuts

Preheat the oven to 180°C (350°F). Butter a 20 cm round cake tin.

Place the milk and 20 g sugar in a saucepan. Using the point of a knife, scrape the seeds from the vanilla pod into the milk, add the pod and bring to the boil. Set aside to infuse.

Coarsely chop the chocolate and combine with the chocolate hazelnut spread; melt over a bain-marie.

Cream the butter and the remaining 80 g sugar. Add the eggs, one at a time, beating well after each addition. Blend in the melted chocolate and chocolate-hazelnut spread; add $1/3$ of the sifted flour and baking powder.

Remove the vanilla pod from the milk. Add the milk and the remaining sifted flour and baking powder in 2 batches to the chocolate mixture; fold in the hazelnuts.

Pour the batter into the prepared cake tin and bake for 35 minutes. Cool completely before turning out onto a rack.

CHEF'S TIP: Instead of ground hazelnuts, whole hazelnuts could be used. Chop or crush, place on a baking tray lined with baking parchment and toast lightly in a 160°C (320°F) oven for 5 minutes.

Mum's Cake

SERVES 10–12

DIFFICULTY ★ ★ ★

PREPARE: 20 minutes

COOK: 30–35 minutes

- 195 g dark chocolate
- 150 g unsalted butter
- 6 eggs
- 300 g sugar
- 95 g flour, sifted
- 1 tbsp coffee extract

Preheat the oven to 160°C (325°F). Butter a round 2.5-litre gratin or baking dish.

Coarsely chop the chocolate, combine with the butter and melt over a bain-marie. Remove from the heat and stir until smooth.

Separate the yolks and whites of 3 eggs. Place the 3 yolks and the remaining whole eggs in a bowl; add 250 g of the sugar and beat until pale yellow and creamy. In a separate bowl, whisk the 3 egg whites, gradually adding the remaining sugar, until the whites are smooth and shiny and stiff peaks form.

Stir the melted chocolate-butter mixture carefully into the egg yolk-sugar mixture. Whisk in $1/3$ of the egg whites to lighten the mixture and gently fold in the remainder. Add the sifted flour and coffee extract. Pour the batter into the gratin dish.

Prepare a roasting pan large enough to hold the gratin dish and add hot water to come halfway up the sides. Place the gratin dish in the pan, transfer to the oven and bake for 30–35 minutes, or until only the centre of the cake wobbles. Remove from the oven; cool slightly before serving.

CHEF'S TIP: To prepare your own coffee extract, infuse 80 g of ground coffee in 150 ml of hot water. If necessary, add 1 tsp of instant coffee; strain before using. This cake is also excellent served with seasonal fruits, such as apples, pears or strawberries.

Creamy Chocolate-Fig Cake

SERVES 8

DIFFICULTY ★ ★ ★

MACERATE: 12 hours (overnight)

PREPARE: 1 hour

COOK: 45 minutes

- 200 g dried figs
- 375 ml sweet dessert wine (such as Muscat)
- 120 ml milk
- 100 g caster sugar
- ½ split vanilla pod
- 100 g dark (55–70%) chocolate
- 30 g soft unsalted butter
- 2 eggs
- 100 g flour, sifted
- ½ tsp baking powder, sifted

◊ This recipe must be started a day ahead.

The day before, place the figs in a bowl, cover with the wine and macerate for at least 12 hours.

Preheat the oven to 180°C (350°F). Butter and flour a 20 cm round cake tin.

Place the milk and 20 g sugar in a saucepan. Using the point of a knife, scrape the seeds from the vanilla pod into the milk, add the pod and bring to the boil. Set aside to infuse.

Drain the figs and cut in small pieces.

Coarsely chop the chocolate and melt over a bain-marie; cool.

Cream the butter and the remaining 80 g sugar. Mix in the melted chocolate and add the eggs, one by one, beating well after each addition; fold in $1/3$ of the sifted flour and baking powder. Discard the vanilla pod and add $1/2$ of the cooled milk. Fold in another $1/3$ of the sifted flour and baking powder then add the remaining milk. Mix in the rest of the sifted flour and baking powder; add the fig pieces. Pour the batter into the cake tin to come about $3/4$ up the side. Bake for about 45 minutes, or until a knife inserted into the centre of the cake comes out clean. Cool for several minutes before turning out onto a rack.

CHEF'S TIP: You can replace the figs in this recipe with other dried fruits such as pears, peaches or apricots.

Chocolate Chip Kugelhopf

SERVES 8–10

DIFFICULTY ★ ★ ★

PREPARE: 20 minutes

PROOF: 1 hour

COOK: 45 minutes

- 25 g flaked almonds
- 17 g fresh compressed yeast
- 1 tbsp warm water
- 2 eggs
- 1 egg yolk
- 200 g plain flour
- 20 g caster sugar
- 1½ tsp salt
- 110 g unsalted butter, melted and warm
- 50 g sultanas (golden raisins)
- 25 g candied orange peel, diced
- 60 g chocolate chips

Butter an 18-cm Kugelhopf mould and sprinkle with the flaked almonds.

Dilute the yeast in a large bowl with the warm water. Add the eggs and the egg yolk, mix well. Tip in the flour, mix, then add the sugar and salt.

In a stand mixer fitted with a dough hook, knead the dough for 6 minutes. The dough is ready when it is smooth, shiny and elastic. Add the butter in three or four batches and knead again. When you press the dough with your finger, it should not feel sticky and the dough should spring back into place. Next add the sultanas, diced candied orange peel and chocolate chips.

Put the dough in the Kugelhopf mould and leave to proof in a warm place for around 1 hour until it reaches to the top of the mould.

Preheat the oven to 180°C (350°F). Bake until the Kugelhopf starts to colour, then finish baking at 170°C (335°F) (it should take around 45 minutes in total). Allow to cool before turning out.

Raspberry-Filled Chocolate Sponge

SERVES 8

DIFFICULTY ★ ★ ★

PREPARE: 30 minutes

COOK: 25 minutes

Sponge
- 20 g unsalted butter
- 4 eggs
- 125 g caster sugar
- 90 g flour, sifted
- 30 g unsweetened cocoa powder, sifted

- 120 g raspberry jam
- Icing sugar, sifted

Preheat the oven to 180°C (350°F). Butter a 20 cm round cake tin.

Sponge: Melt the butter in a saucepan over low heat; set aside. Place the eggs and sugar in a heatproof bowl; whisk to combine. Stand the bowl over a bain-marie and whisk continuously for 5–8 minutes, until the mixture becomes light and doubles in volume. Do not allow it to become too hot. Remove the bowl from the bain-marie and continue whisking quickly by hand, or with an electric beater on high speed, until cool and the batter falls in a ribbon from the whisk or beater. Gently fold in the sifted flour and cocoa powder, adding it in 2 or 3 batches. Quickly add the melted butter. Pour the batter into the prepared tin and bake for about 25 minutes, or until the surface is firm but springy to the touch. Cool for several minutes before turning it out onto a rack.

Using a long, serrated knife, cut the sponge horizontally into two layers of equal thickness. Spread one with the raspberry jam and place the other layer on top; dust with icing sugar.

CHEF'S TIP: When preparing this type of sponge, the water in the bain-marie must not be too hot. This helps the sponge retain its volume and lightness.

Marbled Chocolate Loaf

SERVES 8

DIFFICULTY ★ ★ ★

PREPARE: 30 minutes

COOK: 50 minutes

COOL: 5 minutes

- 250 g soft unsalted butter
- 260 g icing sugar
- 6 eggs
- 50 ml rum
- 300 g flour, sifted
- 2 tsp baking powder, sifted
- 40 ml milk
- 25 g unsweetened cocoa powder, sifted

Preheat the oven to 180°C (350°F). Butter and flour a 28 x 10 cm loaf pan.

Cream the butter and icing sugar. Add the eggs, one at a time, beating well after each addition. Add the rum and fold in the sifted flour and baking powder. Pour half of the batter into a separate bowl. Place the cocoa powder in a small bowl and pour over the milk; stir well to combine. Stir the chocolate mixture into one of the bowls of batter.

Fill the loaf pan with the batter. To obtain a marbled effect, alternate spoonfuls of the plain and chocolate batters. Bake for 50 minutes, or until the point of a knife inserted in the centre of the cake comes out clean. Cool for 5 minutes before turning out onto a rack.

CHEF'S TIP: You could also use 2 small loaf pans, 18 cm long, but you must reduce the baking time to 20 minutes.

Marbled Chocolate-Pistachio Loaf

SERVES 8–10

DIFFICULTY ★ ★ ★

PREPARE: 40 minutes

COOK: 1 hour

COOL: 10 minutes

Chocolate Batter
- 60 g unsalted butter
- 3 eggs
- 210 g caster sugar
- 90 ml whipping cream
- 1 pinch salt
- 135 g flour, sifted
- 30 g unsweetened cocoa powder, sifted
- 1 tsp baking powder, sifted

Pistachio Batter
- 60 g unsalted butter
- 1 tbsp water
- 200 g caster sugar
- 1 tsp mild honey
- 35 g pistachios
- 3 eggs
- 90 ml whipping cream
- 1 pinch salt
- 165 g flour, sifted
- 1 tsp baking powder, sifted

Preheat the oven to 160°C (325°F). Butter a 28 x 10 cm loaf pan.

Chocolate Batter: Melt the butter in a saucepan over low heat without letting it colour; set aside to cool. Combine the eggs and sugar and beat until the mixture is light and creamy. Stir in the cream, melted butter and salt. Then fold in the sifted flour and cocoa and baking powders.

Pistachio Batter: Melt the butter in a saucepan over low heat without letting it colour; set aside to cool. Heat the water, 20 g sugar and the honey in a small saucepan, stirring until the sugar is completely dissolved; bring to the boil. Remove the syrup from the heat. Place the pistachios in a blender and grind to a fine powder. Pour the honey syrup into the blender and mix to obtain a soft paste. Combine the eggs and the pistachio paste in a bowl, add the remaining sugar and beat until the mixture is light and creamy. Stir in the cream, melted butter and salt then fold in the sifted flour and baking powder.

To obtain a marbled effect, alternate spoonfuls of the batters when filling the prepared loaf pan. Start with the pistachio batter and then drop in the chocolate. Bake for 1 hour, or until the point of a knife inserted in the centre of the cake comes out clean. Cool for 10 minutes before turning the cake out onto a rack.

CHEF'S TIP: Wrap the cake carefully in cling film and freeze it for several weeks or keep refrigerated for 2–3 days.

The Marvel

SERVES 8–10

DIFFICULTY ★ ★ ★

PREPARE: 1½ hours

COOK: 30 minutes approx

REFRIGERATE: 25 minutes

Sponge
- 20 g unsalted butter
- 4 eggs
- 125 g caster sugar
- 90 g flour, sifted
- 30 g unsweetened cocoa powder, sifted

Caramelised Walnut Cream
- 70 ml whipping cream
- 20 g honey
- 100 g caster sugar
- 70 g chopped walnuts

Chocolate Praline Mousse
- 150 g dark chocolate
- 75 g praline paste (p.325)
- 250 ml whipping cream

Decoration
- 150 g chopped walnuts
- Chocolate shavings (p.397)

Preheat the oven to 180°C (350°F). Butter a 20 cm round cake tin.

Sponge: Melt the butter in a saucepan over low heat; set aside. In a heatproof bowl place the sugar and eggs; whisk to combine. Stand the bowl over a bain-marie and whisk continuously for 5–8 minutes, or until the mixture becomes light and doubles in volume. Do not allow it to become too hot. Remove the bowl from the bain-marie and continue whisking quickly by hand, or with an electric beater on high speed, until cool and the batter falls in a ribbon from the whisk or beater. Gently fold in the sifted flour and cocoa powder, adding it in 2 or 3 batches. Quickly add the melted butter. Pour the batter into the prepared tin and bake for about 25 minutes, or until the surface is firm but springy to the touch. Cool for several minutes before turning out onto a rack.

Caramelised Walnut Cream: Heat the cream and honey until simmering; set aside. Place the sugar in a separate saucepan, and cook slowly until it melts and becomes a golden caramel. Do not stir during the cooking process but gently shake the saucepan occasionally to move the melted sugar off the bottom. Carefully stir in the cream-honey mixture (it will spit violently when the liquid is added); stir until smooth then remove from the heat and immediately add the chopped walnuts. Pour the caramelised walnut cream into a bowl; leave to cool to room temperature.

Chocolate Praline Mousse: Roughly chop the chocolate and place it and praline paste in a bowl and melt over a slowly simmering bain-marie until the temperature reaches approximately 45°C on a digital thermometer. Beat the cream until firm peaks cling to the whisk. Whisking quickly, add about 1/3 of the whipped cream to the melted chocolate. Pour the mixture over the remaining cream and fold in gently with the whisk or a spatula to evenly blend the ingredients.

Using a long, serrated knife, cut the cooled sponge horizontally into two layers of equal thickness. Spread one with the caramelised walnut cream then add a layer of the chocolate praline mousse. Top with the other sponge layer; refrigerate 15 minutes. Coat the entire surface with the remaining mousse and press the chopped walnuts onto the side of the cake; decorate with chocolate shavings.

Molten Chocolate Cakes with Pistachio Cream

SERVES 4

DIFFICULTY ★ ★ ★

PREPARE: 20 minutes

COOK: 12 minutes

Pistachio Cream
- 20 g chopped pistachios
- 250 ml milk
- 3 egg yolks
- 60 g caster sugar
- 1 or 2 drops vanilla extract

Cake
- 125 g dark (55–70%) chocolate
- 125 g unsalted butter
- 3 eggs
- 125 g caster sugar
- 40 g flour, sifted

Pistachio Cream: Preheat the oven to 180°C (350°F). Put the chopped pistachios on a baking tray and toast in the oven for 2 minutes; stir to avoid burning. Place in a food processor and grind to a powder. Bring the milk slowly to the boil. Beat the egg yolks and sugar until pale yellow and creamy. Stir in $1/3$ of the hot milk and mix well to combine; pour the mixture into the remaining hot milk. Stirring constantly with a wooden spoon, cook over low heat until the cream is thickened and coats the back of a spoon. (Do not allow to boil!) Remove from the heat immediately and strain into a bowl. Add the vanilla extract and the powdered pistachios. Cool the pistachio cream; refrigerate until required.

Cake: Melt the chocolate and the butter over a bain-marie; stir until smooth. Beat the eggs and sugar until pale yellow and creamy. Stir in the melted chocolate-butter mixture then fold in the sifted flour. Divide the batter equally between four small baking dishes; set aside to cool then bake for 12 minutes.

Serve while still warm accompanied by the pistachio cream.

CHEF'S TIP: If you prefer a more elegant presentation, bake the cakes in 7.5 cm pastry rings then turn out onto individual dessert plates before removing the pastry ring. Cover a baking tray with baking parchment. Butter the 4 pastry rings and place on the tray then bake as above. To serve, spoon the pistachio cream around each one. This dessert is also delicious served with thinly sliced fresh, or tinned, pears.

Molten Chocolate Cakes

SERVES 6

DIFFICULTY ★ ★ ★

PREPARE: 15 minutes

COOK: 5-6 minutes

- 150 g dark chocolate
- 4 eggs
- 135 g caster sugar
- 135 g soft unsalted butter
- 40 g flour
- 20 g potato starch
- 6 squares dark chocolate

Preheat the oven to 210°C (410°F).

Butter and flour six individual foil cupcake cases (5 x 4 cm).

Chop the chocolate and melt over a bain-marie.

Put the eggs and sugar in a bowl over a bain-marie, whisk until the mixture is pale and leaves a thick ribbon trail: it should flow from the whisk without the ribbon breaking. Remove from the bain-marie and whisk the mixture with an electric whisk on high speed until it cools.

Mix the butter with the melted chocolate and add to the mixture. Gently fold in the flour and potato starch.

Fill the cupcake cases halfway, place a square of dark chocolate in the middle, then finish filling the cases.

Bake for 5 or 6 minutes. Leave to cool for 5 minutes before removing from the cupcake cases.

Serve immediately.

King's Cake

SERVES 6

DIFFICULTY ★ ★ ★

PREPARE: 35 minutes

COOK: 12 minutes

REFRIGERATE: 30 minutes

Sponge
- 120 g ground almonds
- 150 g icing sugar
- 2 eggs
- 4 egg yolks
- 25 g flour, sifted
- 25 g unsweetened cocoa
  powder, sifted
- 5 egg whites
- 60 g caster sugar

Ganache
- 300 g dark chocolate
- 300 ml whipping cream

Rum Syrup
- 100 ml water
- 100 g caster sugar
- 2 tsp rum

◊ See page 12: Making
a basic ganache.

Preheat the oven to 180°C (350°F). Line a 30 x 38 cm baking tray or Swiss roll tin with baking parchment.

Sponge: Combine the ground almonds, icing sugar, whole eggs and egg yolks in a bowl and beat for about 5 minutes until light and creamy. Fold in the sifted flour and cocoa powder. Whisk the egg whites in a large bowl, gradually adding the sugar, until the egg whites are smooth and shiny and stiff peaks form. Whisk $1/3$ of the egg whites into the chocolate mixture. Carefully fold in the remainder in 2 or 3 batches. Pour the batter into the prepared tin and bake for 12 minutes.

Ganache: Finely chop the chocolate and place in a bowl. Heat the cream in a saucepan until simmering and pour it over the chocolate; stir until smooth. Set aside until the ganache can be easily spread.

Rum Syrup: Place the water and sugar in a saucepan over low heat, stirring until the sugar dissolves then bring to the boil; remove the pan from the heat and cool. When the syrup is cold, add the rum.

Cut the sponge into 3 equal 10 x 38 cm rectangles. Brush or sprinkle the first piece with rum syrup and spread with a thin layer of ganache; place the second sponge piece on top and add some syrup and ganache. Top with the remaining sponge and add some syrup and ganache, setting some ganache aside for the final decoration; refrigerate 30 minutes.

Spread all the remaining ganache over the top of the cake. Dip a serrated knife (or a fork) in hot water; use to make wavy lines to decorate the top of the cake.

CHEF'S TIP: If you remove the cake from the refrigerator 30 minutes before serving it will be soft and moist.

Florentine-topped Chocolate Mousse-Meringue Towers

FOR 16 PIECES

DIFFICULTY ★ ★ ★

PREPARE: 1½ hours

COOK: 30 minutes approx

REFRIGERATE: 15 minutes

Almond Meringue
- 4 egg whites
- 50 g caster sugar
- 150 g icing sugar, sifted
- 150 g ground almonds, sifted

Florentines
- 50 g glacé cherries
- 50 g candied oranges
- 125 g flaked almonds
- 20 g flour
- 100 ml whipping cream
- 50 g unsalted butter
- 50 g mild honey
- 75 g caster sugar

Milk Chocolate Mousse
- 200 g milk chocolate
- 300 ml whipping cream

◇ See p.210: Shaping quenelles.

Preheat the oven to 200°C (400°F). Line 2 baking trays with baking parchment. Place 16 6 x 6 cm and 3 cm high pastry frames on the baking trays.

Almond Meringue: Sift the icing sugar and ground almonds. Whisk the egg whites in a bowl, gradually adding the sugar, until the whites are smooth and shiny and stiff peaks form. Carefully fold in the sifted icing sugar and ground almonds. Fit a piping bag with a medium-sized round nozzle and fill with the meringue. Pipe a layer 2 cm thick in each of the frames. Bake for 12 minutes. Remove the 16 meringues from the frames with a small knife and place them on a clean sheet of baking parchment.

Florentines: Lower the oven temperature to 180°C (350°F). Cut the cherries in half and the oranges into cubes, put them in a bowl with the flaked almonds and the flour, stir to combine. Put the cream, butter, honey and sugar in a small saucepan over low heat and cook until the mixture registers 110°C on a sugar thermometer. Pour the cooked cream mixture over, stirring carefully to avoid breaking the almonds. Pour a 3 cm layer of the mixture onto the prepared baking tray. Bake for 15 minutes, or until the Florentine is lightly golden. Remove from the oven and cool for a few minutes before cutting into small squares with one of the 6 x 6 cm frames.

Milk Chocolate Mousse: Roughly chop the chocolate and place it in a bowl; melt over a bain-marie. In a bowl whip the cream. Pour over the warm chocolate, whisking briskly.

With two tablespoons form quenelles of milk chocolate mousse and put one on each square of meringue. Refrigerate for 15 minutes. Before serving place a Florentine on top of each.

Chocolate Pound Cake

SERVES 12

DIFFICULTY ★ ★ ★

PREPARE: 15 minutes

COOK: 45 minutes

- 250 g soft unsalted butter
- 250 g caster sugar
- 5 eggs
- 200 g flour, sifted
- 1 tsp baking powder, sifted
- 50 g unsweetened cocoa powder, sifted

Preheat the oven to 180°C (350°F). Butter and flour a 25 x 8 cm loaf pan.

Beat the butter until creamy. Add the sugar and continue beating until the mixture is light and fluffy. Add the eggs, one at a time, beating well after each addition. Fold in the sifted flour and baking and cocoa powders; stir to combine.

Pour the batter into the prepared loaf pan to come about 3/4 of the way up the sides. Bake for 45 minutes, or until the point of a knife inserted into the centre of the cake comes out clean. Turn out onto a rack. Serve warm or cold.

CHEF'S TIP: Creaming the butter instead of melting it makes the cake much lighter.

Chocolate Chip Pound Cake

SERVES 12

DIFFICULTY ★ ★ ★

PREPARE: 15 minutes

COOK: 45 minutes

- 250 g soft unsalted butter
- 250 g caster sugar
- 5 eggs
- 200 g flour, sifted
- 50 g chocolate chips
- 50 ml rum

Preheat the oven to 180°C (350°F). Butter and flour a 25 x 8 cm loaf pan.

Beat the butter until creamy. Add the sugar and continue beating until the mixture is light and fluffy. Add the eggs, one at a time, beating well after each addition. Fold in the sifted flour and chocolate chips; stir well to combine.

Pour the batter into the prepared loaf pan to come about 3/4 up the sides. Bake for 45 minutes, or until the point of a knife inserted into the centre of the cake comes out clean. Turn out onto a rack and, while the chocolate chip pound cake is still warm, sprinkle or brush with the rum. Serve warm or cold.

CHEF'S TIP: If you like, add the rum to the cake batter before baking.

Queen of Sheba Cake

SERVES 6–8

DIFFICULTY ★ ★ ★

PREPARE: 20 minutes

COOK: 20 minutes

COOL: 15 minutes

- 100 g almond paste
- 4 egg yolks
- 50 g icing sugar
- 3 egg whites
- 35 g caster sugar
- 55 g flour, sifted
- 15 g unsweetened cocoa powder, sifted
- 25 g unsalted butter

Preheat the oven to 160°C (325°F). Butter and flour a 20 cm round cake tin.

Place the almond paste and egg yolks in a bowl and beat to combine. Add the icing sugar and continue beating until the mixture is smooth and light. Whisk the egg whites in a separate bowl, gradually adding the sugar, until the whites are smooth and shiny and stiff peaks form. Then blend in the almond paste mixture. Carefully, fold in the sifted flour and cocoa powder. Melt the butter over low heat without letting it colour and mix it into the batter.

Pour the batter into the prepared cake tin and bake for 20 minutes. Cool for 15 minutes before turning the cake out onto a rack.

CHEF'S TIP: Accompany this moist cake with assorted fresh berries such as blueberries, blackberries, raspberries or strawberries.

Chocolate-Cointreau Roulade

SERVES 12

DIFFICULTY ★ ★ ★

PREPARE: 1½ hours

COOK: 8 minutes

REFRIGERATE: 20 minutes

Sponge
- 3 egg yolks
- 75 g caster sugar
- 3 egg whites
- 70 g flour, sifted
- 15 g unsweetened cocoa
  powder, sifted

Cointreau Cream
- 1 leaf gelatine (2 g)
- 330 ml milk
- 3 egg yolks
- 70 g caster sugar
- 20 g flour, sifted
- 20 g cornflour
- 20 ml Cointreau
- 150 ml whipping cream

Cointreau Syrup
- 150 ml water
- 70 g caster sugar
- 20 ml Cointreau

Chocolate Whipped Cream
- 80 g dark chocolate
- 300 ml whipping cream

- Raspberry Jam

◇ See p.13: Rolling a sponge.

Preheat the oven to 200°C (400°F). Line a 30 x 38 cm baking tray with baking parchment.

Sponge: Whisk the egg yolks and 25 g of the sugar until pale yellow and creamy. Whisk the egg whites in a separate bowl, gradually adding the remaining sugar until the whites are smooth and shiny and stiff peaks form. Gently fold in the egg yolk-sugar mixture and the sifted flour and cocoa powder. Pour the batter onto the prepared baking tray and smooth with a palette knife. Bake approximately 8 minutes, or until firm but springy to the touch. Cool on a rack.

Cointreau Cream: Soften the leaf gelatine in cold water. Bring the milk to the boil and remove from the heat. Whisk the egg yolks and sugar until pale yellow and creamy. Add the sifted flour and cornflour and gradually whisk in some of the hot milk. Return the mixture to the saucepan; stir continuously over low heat until thickened. Stirring continuously, boil for 1 minute, remove from heat, then add the softened leaf gelatine; remove from the heat. Pour the mixture into a bowl and cover the surface with cling film; cool. Add the Cointreau. Beat the cream until firm and clinging to the whisk; gently fold into the cooled Cointreau cream.

Cointreau Syrup: Place the water and sugar in a saucepan over low heat, stirring until the sugar is completely dissolved then bring to the boil; cool. Add the Cointreau to the cold syrup.

Chocolate Whipped Cream: Chop the chocolate and melt over a bain-marie. Beat the cream until firm peaks cling to the whisk. Whisking quickly, blend in the warm melted chocolate.

Brush or sprinkle the sponge with the Cointreau syrup and spread with a layer of raspberry jam and the Cointreau cream. Start rolling on one of the long sides and fold 2 cm of the sponge over tightly. Using the baking parchment as a guide, slowly pull up the edge to form the sponge into a roll. Finish with the seam underneath and cut a small piece off each end to even it; refrigerate for 20 minutes. Fit a piping bag with a plain nozzle, fill with the chocolate whipped cream and pipe the surface of the roll with it.

Chocolate-Raspberry Roll

SERVES 8–10

DIFFICULTY ★ ★ ★

PREPARE: 25 minutes

COOK: 8 minutes

REFRIGERATE: 20 minutes

Sponge
- 20 g unsalted butter
- 4 eggs
- 125 g caster sugar
- 90 g flour, sifted
- 30 g unsweetened cocoa powder, sifted

Filling
- 150 ml whipping cream
- 50 g icing sugar
- 200 g raspberries

Decoration
- Unsweetened cocoa powder and/or icing sugar, sifted

◊ See p.13: Rolling a sponge

Preheat the oven to 200°C (400°F). Line a 30 x 38 cm baking tray with baking parchment.

Sponge: Melt the butter in a saucepan over low heat; set aside. In a heatproof bowl place the sugar and the eggs; whisk to combine. Stand the bowl over a bain-marie and whisk continuously for 5–8 minutes, or until the mixture becomes light and doubles in volume. Do not allow it to become too hot. Remove the bowl from the bain-marie and continue whisking quickly by hand, or with an electric beater on high speed, until cool and the batter falls in a ribbon from the whisk or beater. Gently fold in the sifted flour and cocoa powder, adding it in 2 or 3 batches. Quickly add the melted butter.

Pour the batter onto the prepared baking tray and smooth with a palette knife. Bake about 8 minutes, or until the surface is firm but springy to the touch. Cool on a rack. Slide the cooked sponge, with the parchment attached, onto a rack. Place a sheet of baking parchment and another rack on top of the cooked sponge and turn everything over. Remove the top rack; peel off the parchment used during cooking. Set aside to cool.

Filling: Whisk the cream and the icing sugar until firm and clinging to the whisk. Spread the sponge with the whipped cream and scatter the raspberries over the surface. Start rolling on one of the long sides and fold 2 cm of the sponge over tightly. Using the baking parchment as a guide, slowly pull up the edge to form a roll. Finish with the seam underneath and cut a small piece off each end to even it; refrigerate for 20 minutes. Before serving, dust with sifted cocoa powder and/or icing sugar.

Sachertorte

SERVES 8–10

DIFFICULTY ★ ★ ★

PREPARE: 35 minutes

COOK: 40 minutes

REFRIGERATE : 40 minutes

Sponge
- 180 g dark chocolate
- 30 g unsalted butter
- 7 egg whites
- 80 g caster sugar
- 3 egg yolks
- 40 g flour, sifted
- 20 g ground almonds, sifted

Kirsch Syrup
- 150 ml water
- 100 g caster sugar
- 1 tbsp Kirsch

Ganache
- 150 g dark chocolate
- 150 ml whipping cream

Filling
- 200 g apricot jam

Decoration
- 100 g milk chocolate

◊ See p. 329: Making a paper piping bag.

◊ See p.14: Glazing a cake or entremets.

Preheat the oven to 180°C (350°F). Butter a 22 cm round cake tin.

Sponge: Melt the chocolate and the butter over a bain-marie; stir until smooth. In a separate bowl, whisk the egg whites until frothy. Add 25 g of the sugar, a little at a time, and continue whisking until the egg whites are smooth and shiny. Gradually add the remaining sugar, whisking until stiff peaks form. Incorporate the egg yolks, sifted flour and ground almonds. Add the melted chocolate-butter mixture to the batter. Pour the batter into the prepared cake tin and bake for 40 minutes, or until the top of the sponge is springy to the touch. Cool before turning out.

Kirsch Syrup: Place the water and sugar in a saucepan over low heat, stirring until the sugar is completely dissolved then bring to the boil; cool. Add the Kirsch to the cold syrup.

Ganache: Coarsely chop the chocolate and place in a bowl. Heat the cream until simmering and pour it over the chocolate; stir until smooth. Set the ganache aside until it can be spread easily.

Using a long, serrated knife, cut the cooled sponge horizontally into two layers of equal thickness. Sprinkle or brush one with Kirsch syrup and spread it with a 1 cm layer of apricot jam. Top with the other layer and sprinkle with syrup. Refrigerate for 30 minutes.

Cover the entire surface of the sponge with ganache using a palette knife. Refrigerate for about 10 minutes, or until the ganache is firm and cool. Heat the remaining ganache in a saucepan. Place the Sachertorte on a rack and pour the warm ganache over until the entire cake is covered. Smooth the glaze immediately with a warm palette knife.

Decoration: Make a small paper piping bag (p.329). Melt the milk chocolate, cool and pour it into the piping bag; snip off the tip. Pipe the word 'Sacher' on the surface of the cake.

Chocolate Truffle Cake

SERVES 8

DIFFICULTY ★ ★ ★

PREPARE: 2 hours

COOK: 25 minutes

REFRIGERATE: 25 minutes

Sponge
- 20 g unsalted butter
- 4 eggs
- 125 g caster sugar
- 90 g flour, sifted
- 30 g unsweetened cocoa powder, sifted

Cointreau Syrup
- 150 ml water
- 200 g caster sugar
- 50 ml Cointreau

Ganache
- 250 g chocolate
- 250 ml whipping cream
- 50 ml Cointreau

Decoration
- Unsweetened cocoa powder, sifted

◇ See p.12: Preparing a basic ganache.

Preheat the oven to 180°C (350°F). Butter and flour a 22 cm round cake tin.

Sponge: Melt the butter in a saucepan over low heat; set aside. Place the eggs and the sugar in a heatproof bowl; whisk to combine. Stand the bowl over a bain-marie and whisk continuously for 5–8 minutes, or until the mixture becomes light and doubles in volume. Do not allow it to become too hot. Remove the bowl from the bain-marie and continue whisking quickly by hand, or with an electric beater on high speed, until cool and the batter falls in a ribbon from the whisk or beater. Gently fold in the sifted flour and cocoa powder, adding it in 2 or 3 batches. Quickly add the melted butter and pour the batter into the prepared tin. Bake for about 25 minutes, or until the surface of the sponge is firm but springy to the touch. Cool for several minutes before turning out onto a rack.

Cointreau Syrup: Place the water and sugar in a saucepan over low heat, stirring until the sugar is completely dissolved, then bring to the boil; cool. Add the Cointreau to the cold syrup.

Ganache: Coarsely chop the chocolate and place in a bowl. Heat the cream until simmering and pour it over the chocolate. Stir until smooth and add the Cointreau. Set the ganache aside until it can be easily spread.

Using a long, serrated knife, cut the cooled sponge horizontally into 3 layers of equal thickness. Sprinkle or brush the first layer with Cointreau syrup and spread it with a 2 cm layer of ganache. Place the second layer on top and repeat with the syrup and ganache. Top with the remaining layer and brush with syrup. Refrigerate for 15 minutes, or until the ganache is firm.

Coat the entire surface of the cake with the remaining ganache. To obtain a spiked effect, tap the ganache lightly with a spatula and carefully pull away. Refrigerate for another 10 minutes, or until firm. Lightly dust with cocoa powder.

Chocolate Saint-Honoré

Sweet Shortcrust Pastry
- 75 g unsalted butter
- 50 g icing sugar
- 1 pinch salt
- 1 egg yolk
- 125 g flour, sifted

Choux Pastry Dough
- 100 g unsalted butter
- 125 ml water
- 125 ml milk
- 1 tsp salt
- 15 g caster sugar
- 150 g flour, sifted
- 4 eggs + 1 beaten egg for glazing

Caramel
- 35 ml water
- 120 g caster sugar

Chocolate Cream
- 120 g dark (70%) chocolate
- 200 ml milk
- 5 egg yolks
- 40 g caster sugar
- 20 g cornflour
- 2½ leaves gelatine

Italian Meringue
- 4 egg whites
- 35 ml water
- 120 g caster sugar

Decoration
- 100 g dark chocolate shavings (see page 397)

Sweet Shortcrust Pastry: Combine the butter, icing sugar and salt in a bowl. Add the egg yolk, then the sifted flour. Form a ball with the dough and lightly flatten. Wrap in cling film and refrigerate for 30 minutes.

Choux Pastry Dough: See page 209. Transfer the dough to a piping bag fitted with a plain 12 mm nozzle.

Preheat the oven to 180°C (350°F). Line a 30 x 38 cm baking tray with baking parchment. Roll out the sweet shortcrust pastry dough to make a 20 cm diameter circle with a thickness of about 3 mm and place on the baking tray. Pipe a spiral of choux pastry dough starting from the outside and moving to the centre with a spacing of about 2 cm and gradually make finer towards the centre.

Pipe 17 small choux balls around 1.5 cm in diameter onto the same baking tray. Brush with the egg glaze. Bake for 20 minutes. Leave to cool on a rack.

Caramel: Heat the water and sugar in a saucepan until the sugar dissolves completely. Increase the heat and cook for around 10 minutes (until a digital thermometer reads 165°C). Gently dip the base of the choux puffs into the caramel and attach around the edge of the spiral with a drop of caramel, caramel-coated side facing up.

Chocolate Cream: Using the ingredients listed, follow the method on page 276, but do not refrigerate, and add softened gelatine.

Italian Meringue: Whisk the 4 egg whites until frothy. Combine the water and sugar, then heat until a digital thermometer reads 121°C. Pour the sugar syrup over the egg whites and whisk until cool.

Whisk $1/3$ of the meringue into the hot cream, then fold in the remaining $2/3$ with a flexible spatula. Pour into a piping bag fitted with a plain nozzle and refrigerate.

Pipe a layer of chocolate cream in a wave pattern onto the choux spiral. Refrigerate the Saint-Honoré for at least 4 hours. Decorate with chocolate shavings.

Tarts to
die for

The best way to prepare pastry dough

Adapt this version of pastry using the ingredients indicated in the recipe of your choice (for example, p.112). You could also add sifted ground almonds or cocoa powder at the same time as the flour.

(1) Put 150 g soft unsalted butter, 250 g sifted plain flour, 1 pinch salt, 100 g icing sugar and ¼ tsp natural vanilla essence into a bowl. Rub the butter into the dry ingredients with your fingertips until the mixture resembles fine breadcrumbs.

(2) Using a wooden spoon, incorporate an egg; form the dough into a ball.

(3) Dust the work surface with flour and place the dough on it. Use the heel of your hand to push pieces of the dough away from you, smearing them across the work surface until smoothly blended. Work quickly; if you overwork the dough, it will become too fragile. Scrape into a ball, flatten slightly and wrap in cling film; refrigerate for 30 minutes to rest before using.

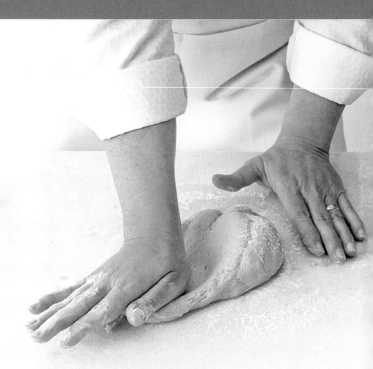

The best way to roll out pastry dough

Prepare a shortcrust, shortbread or sweet pastry for the tart or tartlet recipe of your choice.

(1) Dust a cool work surface with flour; flatten the chilled ball of dough between your hands.

(2) Using a rolling pin, place it on the centre of the dough. Roll, in a backwards and forwards motion, to the edge of the dough. To form a disc of even thickness, give the dough quarter-turns; work quickly so that it remains cool.

If the dough starts to stick, add more flour to the work surface.

(3) If the dough is too fragile to turn by hand, but not yet large enough to line the tart tin, carefully roll it around the rolling pin and lift to make the quarter-turns.

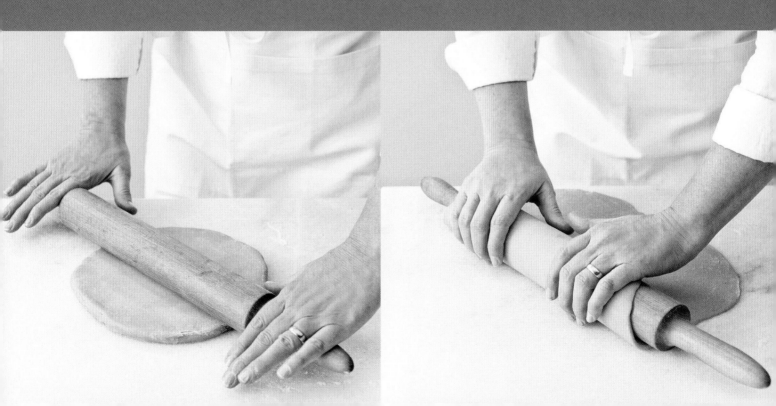

The best way to line a tart tin with pastry dough

Prepare the pastry dough for the tart of your choice. Roll the dough out to a thickness of 3 mm. The finished circle should be approximately 5 cm larger than the diameter of the tin.

① Gently roll the dough around the rolling pin, place it over the tin and unroll loosely, allowing the excess to hang over the rim.

② Press the dough gently into the tin to cover the base, inside seam and side.

③ Roll the rolling pin over the rim of the tin, pressing down firmly with your hand to remove excess dough. If indicated in the recipe, prick the base of the dough-lined tin with a fork and bake as described.

The best way to line a tartlet tin with pastry dough

Prepare the pastry dough for the tartlet recipe of your choice. Roll the dough out to a thickness of 3 mm.

① Use an upturned bowl or pastry cutter of the required size or shape to cut out the dough.

② Place a circle of cut-out dough in each tartlet tin.

③ Press the dough gently into each tin to cover the base, seam and side. If indicated in the recipe, prick the base of the dough-lined tartlet tin with a fork and bake as described.

Milk Chocolate Mousse Boats

MAKES 12–14

DIFFICULTY ★ ★ ★

PREPARE: 45 minutes

COOK: 10–15 minutes

REFRIGERATE: 45 minutes

Sweet Pastry
- 120 g soft unsalted butter
- 100 g icing sugar
- 1 pinch salt
- 1 egg
- 200 g flour, sifted

Milk Chocolate Mousse
- 150 g milk chocolate
- 250 ml whipping cream

Decoration
- Unsweetened cocoa powder and/or icing sugar

◇ See p.88: Preparing pastry dough.

◇ See p.210: Forming quenelles.

Sweet Pastry: Beat the butter with the icing sugar and salt; combine well. Blend in the egg then the sifted flour; mix roughly to combine. Press the crumbs into a ball then, on a lightly floured work surface, use the heel of the hand to push bits of dough away from you, smearing them across the work surface to blend the butter and flour. Work quickly; repeat if necessary. Then form into a ball, flatten slightly and wrap in cling film. Refrigerate for 30 minutes.

Preheat the oven to 180°C (350°F). Butter 12–14 small (8.5 x 3.5 cm) fluted oval moulds. Dust the work surface with flour. Roll out the dough to a thickness of 3 mm. Cut out 12–14 ovals about 1.5 cm larger than the moulds. Use the dough to line the moulds and prick the bases using a fork. Refrigerate for 15 minutes.

Bake the dough-lined moulds for 10–15 minutes, or until lightly golden. Set aside to cool on a rack.

Milk Chocolate Mousse: Coarsely chop the chocolate and place in a bowl; melt over a slowly simmering bain-marie until the temperature reaches approximately 45°C on a digital thermometer. Beat the cream until firm peaks cling to the whisk. Whisking quickly, add about 1/3 of the whipped cream to the hot chocolate. Pour the mixture over the remaining cream and fold in gently with the whisk or a spatula to evenly blend the ingredients.

Shape the mousse into quenelles using 2 tablespoons and place one in each pastry boat. Using a fine-meshed sieve, dust the mousse boats with cocoa powder and/or icing sugar.

Chocolate Flan with a Crumble and Cream Topping

SERVES 6

DIFFICULTY ★ ★ ★

PREPARE: 55 minutes

COOK: 1¼ hours approx

REST: 20 minutes

REFRIGERATE: 2 hours

Chocolate Flan
- 75 g Cuzco or dark (70%) chocolate, chopped
- 200 ml water
- 600 ml milk
- 150 ml whipping cream
- 1 clove
- 1 stick cinnamon
- 5 eggs
- 125 g caster sugar

Crumble
- 25 g quinoa grains
- 50 g unrefined cane sugar
- 50 g unsalted butter
- 50 g flour
- Cinnamon powder

Chantilly Cream
- 150 ml whipping cream
- Vanilla extract
- 15 g icing sugar

Chocolate Flan: Place the chocolate in a saucepan with the water; melt gently over very low heat. Bring to the boil, lower the heat and cook for about 5 minutes. Add the milk, cream, clove and cinnamon stick; heat until simmering. Combine the eggs and sugar; beat until pale yellow and creamy. Stir in the cooked chocolate mixture and set aside to rest for 20 minutes.

Preheat the oven to 80°C (175°F). Strain the chocolate flan mixture and divide it evenly between six 8 cm ramekins (to come 3/4 up the sides); bake for 40 minutes, or until firm. Remove from the oven and cool; refrigerate for 2 hours.

Crumble: Wash and drain the quinoa. Fill a large saucepan with water and add the quinoa. Bring to the boil, cover and simmer for 20 minutes, or until the grains open; drain in a colander and set aside until dry. Increase the oven temperature to 180°C (350°F); cover a baking tray with baking parchment. Put all the crumble ingredients into a bowl; mix until it resembles coarse breadcrumbs. Spread a 1 cm layer of the crumble mixture on the baking tray and bake for 10–15 minutes. Break or crush the cooked crumble into small pieces; set aside to cool.

Chantilly Cream: Combine the cream and a few drops of vanilla, whisk until firm peaks form and cling to the whisk; add the icing sugar.

Decorate each flan with a spoonful of the quinoa crumble and Chantilly cream.

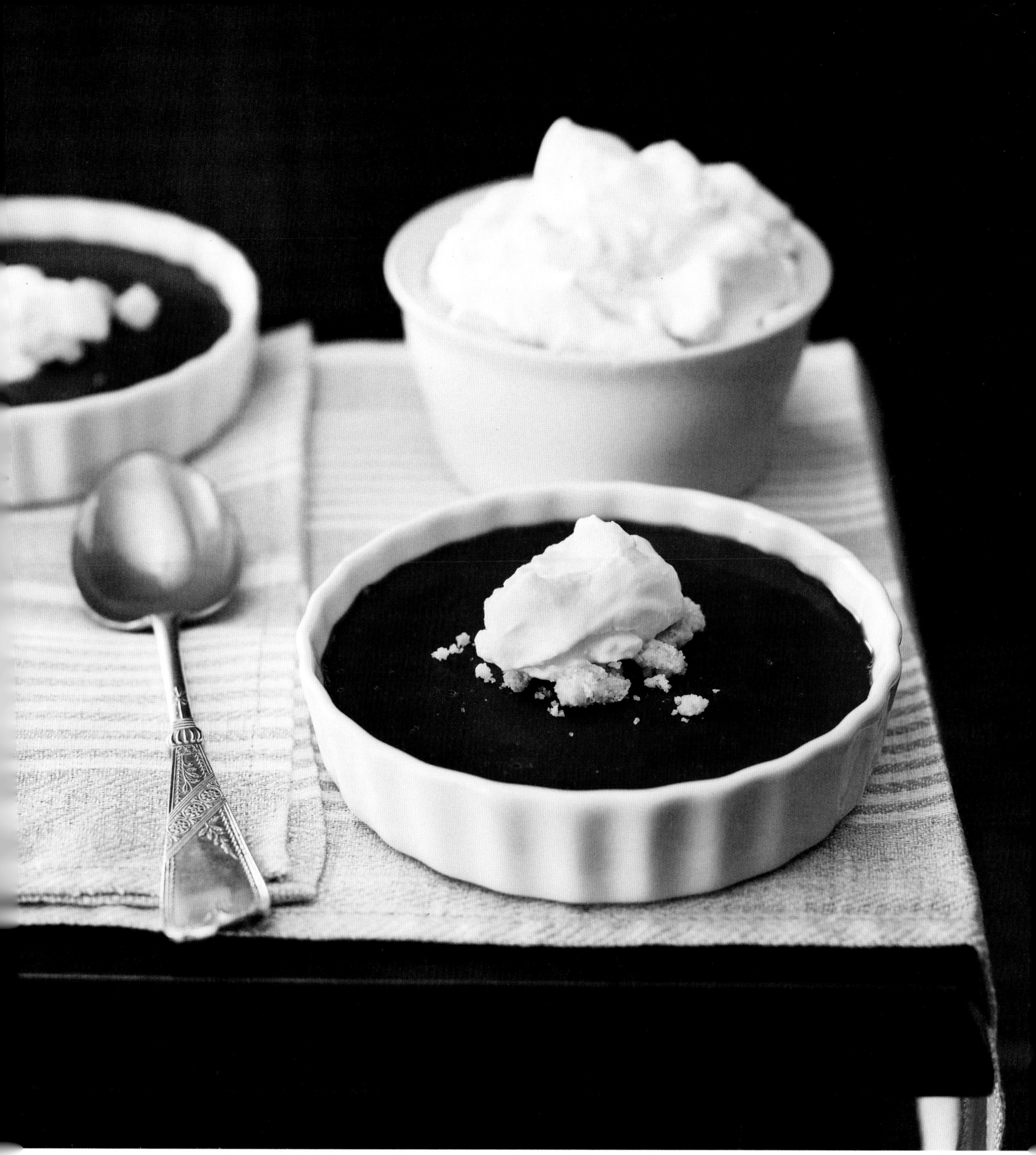

Peruvian-Style Chocolate Cheesecake

SERVES 6

DIFFICULTY ★ ★ ★

DRAIN: Overnight

PREPARE: 45 minutes

COOK: 1¼ hours approx

REFRIGERATION: 4½ hours

- 115 g fromage frais or fresh curd cheese (40% butterfat)

Sweetened Potato Purée
- 200 g floury potatoes
- 200 ml milk
- 20 g caster sugar
- Grated zest of ½ orange

Cocoa Paste
- 1½ tbsp unsweetened cocoa powder
- 30 ml water (2 tbsp)

Chocolate Biscuit Crust
- 30 g unsalted butter
- 30 g chocolate-coated digestive biscuits
- 30 g plain digestive biscuits
- 15 g chopped walnuts

Cheesecake Filling
- 110 ml whipping cream
- 1 egg + 1 egg yolk
- 55 g caster sugar
- 1 tbsp mild honey

Honey Glaze
- ½ leaf gelatine
- 35 g mild honey
- 30 ml water

This recipe must be started the day before. Drain the cheese (fromage frais) overnight and refrigerate.

Sweetened Potato Purée: Peel, wash and dice the potatoes. Bring the milk, sugar and orange zest to the boil. Add the potatoes and cook for about 30 minutes, or until they crush easily; drain. Purée the potatoes using a drum sieve or a Mouli set over a bowl; cool.

Cocoa Paste: Put the cocoa powder and water in a saucepan, stir to combine and bring to the boil. Set aside.

Preheat the oven to 180°C (350°F). Cover a baking tray with baking parchment. Butter an 18 cm springform pan ring and place it on the baking tray.

Chocolate Biscuit Crust: Melt the butter. Crush the biscuits or pulverise to evenly sized crumbs in a food processor. Stir the butter and chopped walnuts into the biscuit crumbs; mix thoroughly. Pack the crust mixture firmly in an even layer onto the bottom of the ring.

Cheesecake Filling: Combine the drained cheese with the potato purée. Mix together the cream, egg and yolk, sugar, honey and the cocoa paste until well combined; stir into the cheese-potato mixture. Pour the filling into the prepared ring and bake for 45 minutes. Cool the cheesecake without removing the ring, then refrigerate for 4 hours.

Honey Glaze: Soften the gelatine in a small bowl of cold water. Put the honey and water into a saucepan and stir over low heat until the sugar dissolves completely; boil the syrup for 2 minutes. Squeeze the water out of the gelatine leaf and add to the honey syrup, stir to dissolve; cool. Spread the honey glaze over the surface of the cold cheesecake and refrigerate for 15–20 minutes. Slide the point of a knife around the ring to release the cheesecake; serve.

Crunchy Chocolate-Almond Tart

SERVES 8–10

DIFFICULTY ★ ★ ★

PREPARE: 2 hours

COOK: 1 hour approx

REFRIGERATE: 1 hour

Pastry
- 120 g soft unsalted butter
- 100 g icing sugar
- 1 pinch salt
- 1 egg
- 200 g flour, sifted

Almond Cream
- 100 g soft unsalted butter
- 100 g caster sugar
- 1 pinch vanilla powder
- 2 eggs
- 100 g ground almonds

Ganache
- 125 g dark chocolate
- 125 ml whipping cream
- 25 g caster sugar
- 25 g soft unsalted butter

Cocoa Syrup
- 50 ml water
- 40 g caster sugar
- 15 g unsweetened cocoa powder

Crunchy Chocolate
- 25 g milk chocolate
- 30 g soft unsalted butter
- 125 g praline paste (p.325)
- 15 crêpe dentelle biscuits (60 g), lightly crushed
- 5 crêpe dentelle biscuits, broken in pieces

Pastry: Beat the butter with the icing sugar and salt; combine well. Blend in the egg then add the sifted flour; roughly mix to combine. Press the crumbs into a ball then, on a lightly floured work surface, use the heel of the hand to push bits of dough away from you, smearing them across the work surface to blend the butter and flour. Work quickly; repeat if necessary. Form into a ball, flatten slightly and wrap in cling film. Refrigerate for 30 minutes.

Preheat the oven to 180°C (350°F). Butter a 24 cm round tart tin. Dust the work surface with flour. Roll out the dough to a thickness of 3 mm, to form a circle about 30 cm in diameter. Line the tin with the dough. Refrigerate for 10 minutes. Cut out a 35 cm round of baking parchment and place it in the dough-lined tin; fill with baking beans. Bake for about 10 minutes, or until lightly coloured; remove the parchment and beans. Lower the oven temperature to 160°C (325°F) and bake for another 8 minutes. Remove from the oven and set aside on a rack.

Almond Cream: Cream the butter and sugar; add the vanilla. Incorporate the eggs one at a time then fold in the almonds. Pour the almond cream into the pastry shell and bake for about 30–40 minutes, or until firm.

Ganache: Coarsely chop the chocolate and place in a bowl. Heat the cream and sugar until simmering, stir until the sugar dissolves. Pour the mixture over the chocolate, stirring until smooth; add the butter. Set the ganache aside at room temperature until it can be easily spread.

Cocoa Syrup: Put the water and sugar into a saucepan and stir over low heat until the sugar completely dissolves; boil for 2 minutes. Add the cocoa powder, whisking to combine and bring to the boil again. Set aside to cool.

Crunchy Chocolate: Finely chop the milk chocolate and melt over a bain-marie. Blend in the butter, praline paste and 60 g of the biscuits. Trace a 20 cm circle on baking parchment and spread the chocolate mixture inside the circle to form a disc; refrigerate for 20 minutes. Remove the tart from its tin, sprinkle or brush the almond cream with cocoa syrup and spread it with a thin layer of ganache. Place the crunchy chocolate disc on top and spread with the remaining ganache. Scatter the rest of the biscuits over the surface of the tart.

Chocolate Crumble with Sweet Mango Slices

SERVES 6

DIFFICULTY ★ ★ ★

PREPARE: 30 minutes

COOK: 20–25 minutes

Chocolate Crumble
- 75 g unsalted butter
- 50 g flour
- 25 g unsweetened cocoa powder
- 75 g unrefined cane sugar
- 75 g ground hazelnuts

Mangoes
- 3 mangoes
- 60 g unsalted butter
- 150 g unrefined cane sugar

Preheat the oven to 180°C (350°F). Cover a baking tray with baking parchment.

Chocolate Crumble: Put all the crumble ingredients into a bowl; mix until they resemble breadcrumbs. Spread a 1 cm layer of crumble mixture on the baking tray and bake for 10–15 minutes. Break or crush the cooked crumble into small pieces; set aside to cool.

Mangoes: Peel and thinly slice the mangoes. Melt the butter in a frying pan, add the sliced mangoes and sprinkle with sugar. Cook over low heat for 10 minutes, or until tender.

Prepare 6 plates and put several mango slices on each one. Divide the chocolate crumble equally between each plate and top with the remaining sliced mango; serve hot.

Bitter Chocolate Tart

SERVES 10

DIFFICULTY ★ ★ ★

PREPARE: 35 minutes

COOK: 50 minutes approx

REFRIGERATE: 40 minutes

Pastry
- 200 g flour, sifted
- 30 g caster sugar
- 1 pinch salt
- 100 g unsalted butter, cut in pieces
- 1 egg, beaten
- 1 tbsp water

Bitter Chocolate Cream
- 150 g dark (55–70%) chocolate
- 150 g unsalted butter
- 13 eggs
- 200 g caster sugar
- 160 g flour
- 150 ml whipping cream

Crème Anglaise (Optional)
- 6 egg yolks
- 180 g caster sugar
- 1 vanilla pod, split
- 500 ml milk

Decoration
- Icing sugar, sifted

◇ See p.208: Making crème Anglaise.

Pastry: Combine the sifted flour, sugar and salt in a bowl. Rub in the butter until the mixture resembles coarse breadcrumbs. Make a well in the centre of the mixture and place the egg and water in it; roughly mix to combine. Press the crumbs into a ball then, on a lightly floured work surface, use the heel of the hand to push bits of dough away from you, smearing them across the work surface to blend the butter and flour. Work quickly; repeat if necessary. Form into a ball, flatten slightly and wrap in cling film. Refrigerate for 30 minutes.

Preheat the oven to 180°C (350°F). Butter a 26 cm round tart tin. Dust the work surface with flour. Roll out the dough to a thickness of 3 mm, to form a circle about 30 cm in diameter. Line the tin with the dough. Refrigerate for 10 minutes.

Cut out a 35 cm round of baking parchment and place it in the dough-lined tin; fill with baking beans. Bake for about 10 minutes, or until coloured then remove the parchment and beans. Lower the oven temperature to 160°C (325°F); bake for another 8 minutes. Remove from the oven and set aside on a rack. Lower the oven temperature to 120°C (250°F).

Bitter Chocolate Cream: Coarsely chop the chocolate and melt with the butter over a bain-marie. Remove from the heat and quickly blend in the eggs. Add the sugar, flour and cream. Pour the chocolate cream into the pastry shell and bake for 30 minutes, or until firm.

Crème Anglaise (Optional): Put the egg yolks and sugar into a bowl and beat until pale yellow and creamy. Using the point of a knife, scrape the seeds from the vanilla pod into the milk, add the pod; bring slowly to the boil. Stir $1/3$ of the hot milk quickly into the egg-sugar mixture and mix well to combine; pour the mixture into the remaining hot milk. Cook over low heat, stirring continuously with a wooden spoon, until thickened and the sauce coats the back of the spoon. (Do not allow to boil!) Remove from the heat immediately and strain into a bowl.

Dust the tart with sifted icing sugar and serve warm. If desired, accompany with the crème Anglaise.

CHEF'S TIP: If you want to create a lattice effect, cut strips of cardboard and lay them on the surface of the tart. Sift the icing sugar over the top then carefully remove the strips.

Chocolate Tart with a Hint of Lime

SERVES 8

DIFFICULTY ★ ★ ★

PREPARE: 1¾ hours; lime slices need to be prepared 24 hours ahead

COOK: 1½ hours approx

REFRIGERATE: 1 hour 10 minutes

Glazed Lime Slices
• 2 limes, finely sliced
• 100 g caster sugar
• 100 ml water

Pastry
• 120 g soft unsalted butter
• 100 g icing sugar
• 1 pinch salt
• 1 egg
• 200 g flour, sifted

Chocolate-Lime Ganache
• 2 limes
• 300 g dark chocolate
• 250 ml whipping cream
• 125 g unsalted butter

Decoration
• Unsweetened cocoa powder, sifted

◊ See p.90: Lining a tart tin with pastry dough.

◊ This recipe must be started a day ahead.

Glazed Lime Slices: Prepare at least 12 hours before cooking the tart. Preheat the oven to 80– 100°C (175– 210°F). Cover a baking tray with baking parchment. Place the sugar and water in a saucepan over low heat and stir until the sugar dissolves completely. Raise the heat and boil for 2 minutes; then remove pan from the heat. Place the lime slices in the syrup and macerate for 1 hour; drain. Place on the baking tray and transfer to the oven to cook for 1 hour. Set aside overnight.

Pastry: The next day, beat the butter with the icing sugar and salt; combine well. Add the egg then the sifted flour; mix roughly to combine. Press the crumbs into a ball then, on a lightly floured work surface, use the heel of the hand to push bits of dough away from you, smearing them across the work surface to blend the butter and flour. Work quickly; repeat if necessary. Form into a ball, flatten slightly and wrap in cling film. Refrigerate for 30 minutes.

Preheat the oven to 180°C (350°F). Butter a 22 cm round tart tin. Dust the work surface with flour. Roll out the dough to a thickness of 3 mm, to form a circle about 27 cm in diameter. Line the tin with the dough. Refrigerate for 10 minutes.

Cut out a 35 cm round of baking parchment and place it in the dough-lined tin; fill with baking beans. Bake for about 10 minutes, or until lightly coloured then remove the parchment and beans. Lower the oven temperature to 160°C (325°F); bake the pastry for another 10– 15 minutes, or until golden. Remove from the oven and set aside on a rack.

Chocolate-Lime Ganache: Cut long, thin strips of lime zest using a canelle knife or vegetable peeler being careful to remove the pith. Coarsely chop the chocolate and place in a bowl. Bring the cream and lime zest to the boil in a small saucepan then pour the mixture over the chocolate. Stir until well combined and add the butter. Pour the ganache into the cooked pastry shell, saving some for decoration; refrigerate for 30 minutes.

Before serving, sprinkle the tart with the cocoa powder. Fit a piping bag with a star nozzle, fill it with the reserved ganache and pipe rosettes on the top of the tart. Add the lime slices.

Chocolate-Fig Tart

SERVES 8

DIFFICULTY ★ ★ ★

PREPARE: 45 minutes

COOK: 1¼ hours approx

REFRIGERATE: 1¼ hours approx

Pastry
- 150 g soft unsalted butter
- 250 g flour, sifted
- 15 g unsweetened cocoa powder, sifted
- 1 pinch salt
- 95 g icing sugar
- 1 egg

Fig Compote
- 400 g dried figs
- 85 g caster sugar
- 200 ml red wine
- 125 g raspberry purée

Ganache
- 300 g dark chocolate
- 375 ml whipping cream
- 100 g soft unsalted butter

◊ See p.12: Making a basic ganache.

Pastry: Rub the butter into the sifted flour and cocoa powder, salt and icing sugar with the fingertips until the mixture resembles fine breadcrumbs. Add the egg and roughly mix to combine. Press the crumbs into a ball then, on a lightly floured work surface, use the heel of the hand to push bits of dough away from you, smearing them across the work surface to blend the butter and flour. Work quickly; repeat if necessary. Form into a ball, flatten slightly and wrap in cling film. Refrigerate for 30 minutes.

Preheat the oven to 180°C (350°F). Butter a 22 cm round tart tin. Dust the work surface with flour. Roll the dough out to a thickness of 3 mm, to form a circle approximately 27 cm in diameter. Line the tin with the dough. Refrigerate for 10 minutes.

Cut out a 35 cm round of baking parchment and place it in the dough-lined tin; fill with baking beans. Bake for about 10 minutes, or until coloured then remove the parchment and beans. Lower the oven temperature to 160°C (325°F); bake the pastry for another 10– 15 minutes. Remove from the oven and set aside on a rack.

Fig Compote: Soften the figs in boiling water for 3 minutes; drain. Put the softened figs, sugar, wine and raspberry purée into a saucepan and simmer very slowly for 40 minutes, or until the figs are tender and the mixture thickens. After 5 minutes cooking, remove two figs, cut into slices and set aside for decoration. Let cool. Pour the fig compote into the cooked pastry shell, to come $^2/_3$ up the side; smooth the surface with a spatula.

Ganache: Coarsely chop the chocolate and place in a bowl. Heat the cream to simmering and pour it over the chocolate, stir until smooth; add the butter. Pour the ganache into the pastry shell over the fig compote, decorate with reserved fig slices and refrigerate for 30 minutes.

CHEF'S TIP: If you prefer a smoother fig compote, work the cooked mixture in a food processor to the desired consistency before placing in the pastry shell.

'Grand Cru' Chocolate Tart

SERVES 8–10

DIFFICULTY ★ ★ ☆

PREPARE: 45 minutes

COOK: 20–25 minutes

REFRIGERATE: 40 minutes

Sweet Pastry

- 120 g soft unsalted butter
- 100 g icing sugar
- 1 pinch salt
- 1 egg
- 200 g flour, sifted

'Grand Cru' Chocolate Cream

- 2 egg yolks
- 40 g caster sugar
- 130 ml milk
- 120 ml whipping cream
- 190 g 'grand cru' or dark (70%) chocolate, chopped

◊ See p.90: Lining a tart tin with pastry dough.

Sweet Pastry: Beat the butter with the icing sugar and salt; combine well. Add the egg then the sifted flour; mix roughly to combine. Press the crumbs into a ball then, on a lightly floured work surface, use the heel of the hand to push bits of dough away from you, smearing them across the work surface to blend the butter and flour. Work quickly; repeat if necessary. Form into a ball, flatten slightly and wrap in cling film. Refrigerate for 30 minutes.

Preheat the oven to 180°C (350°F). Butter a 24 cm round tart tin. Dust the work surface with flour. Roll out the dough to a thickness of 3 mm, to form a circle about 30 cm in diameter. Line the tin with the dough. Refrigerate for 10 minutes.

Cut out a 35 cm round of baking parchment and place it in the dough-lined tin; fill with baking beans. Bake for about 10 minutes, or until lightly coloured then remove the parchment and beans. Lower the oven temperature to 160°C (325°F); bake the pastry for another 10–15 minutes, or until golden. Remove from the oven and set aside on a rack.

'Grand Cru' Chocolate Cream: Put the egg yolks and sugar into a bowl and beat until pale yellow and creamy. Heat the milk and cream until simmering. Stir a third of the hot milk-cream mixture quickly into the eggs and sugar and mix well to combine; return the mixture to the remaining hot milk. Cook over low heat, stirring continuously, until thickened and the mixture coats the back of a spoon. (Do not allow to boil!) Remove from the heat immediately and strain over the chopped chocolate, stirring carefully until smooth. Pour the chocolate cream into the pastry shell. Refrigerate the tart until serving.

CHEF'S TIP: The term 'grand cru', in this case, designates a specific type of chocolate coming from Cuba, Sao Tomé or Venezuela containing 66% cocoa solids. You can replace it by using a dark (70%) chocolate. If you want to give the tart a fruity taste, scatter fresh raspberries over the base of the cooked pastry shell before filling it with the chocolate cream.

Chocolate-Coconut Tart

SERVES 8

DIFFICULTY ★ ★ ★

PREPARE: 1 hour

COOK: 40 minutes approx

REFRIGERATE: 40 minutes

Coconut Pastry
- 165 g soft unsalted butter
- 75 g icing sugar
- 30 g ground almonds
- 30 g desiccated coconut
- 1 pinch salt
- 1 egg
- 175 g flour, sifted

Coconut Filling
- 190 g desiccated coconut
- 170 g caster sugar
- 40 g apple sauce
- 3 egg whites

Crumble Topping
- 50 g unsalted butter
- 35 g flour
- 15 g unsweetened cocoa powder
- 50 g unrefined cane sugar
- 50 g desiccated coconut
- ½ tsp baking powder

◇ See p.90: Lining a tart tin with pastry dough.

Coconut Pastry: Beat the butter with the icing sugar, almonds, coconut and salt; blend well. Add the egg then the sifted flour; mix roughly to combine. Press the crumbs into a ball then, on a lightly floured work surface, use the heel of the hand to push bits of dough away from you, smearing them across the work surface to blend the butter and flour. Work quickly; repeat if necessary. Form into a ball, flatten slightly and wrap in cling film. Refrigerate for 30 minutes.

Preheat the oven to 180°C (350°F). Butter a 22 cm tart ring and place on a baking sheet. Dust the work surface with flour. Roll out the dough to a thickness of 3 mm, to form a circle about 27 cm in diameter. Line the ring with the dough. Refrigerate for 10 minutes.

Cut out a 30 cm round of baking parchment and place it in the dough-lined ring; fill with baking beans. Bake for about 10 minutes, or until lightly coloured then remove the parchment and beans. Lower the oven temperature to 160°C (325°F); bake for another 8 minutes. Remove from the oven and set aside on a rack (leave the oven on).

Coconut Filling: Combine the coconut, sugar and apple sauce. Beat the egg whites until stiff peaks form. Stir $^1/_3$ of the beaten egg whites into the coconut mixture; gently fold in the remainder of the egg whites. Pour the coconut filling into the pastry shell.

Crumble Topping: Put all the crumble ingredients into a bowl; mix with the fingertips to obtain a breadcrumb-like consistency. Scatter the crumble mixture over the coconut filling.

Bake the tart for 20 minutes, or until the pastry is golden. Cool and cut in 8 servings; serve warm or cold.

Chocolate-Orange Tart with a Hint of Coriander

SERVES 8–10

DIFFICULTY ★ ★ ☆

PREPARE: 1¾ hours

COOK: 20–25 minutes

REFRIGERATE: 40 minutes

Coriander-Orange Slices
- 150 ml water
- 150 g caster sugar
- 25 g coriander seeds
- 1 orange, finely sliced

Pastry
- 150 g soft unsalted butter
- 250 g flour, sifted
- 1 pinch salt
- 95 g icing sugar
- ¼ tsp natural vanilla essence
- 1 egg

Chocolate Cream
- 3 egg yolks
- 50 g caster sugar
- 250 ml milk
- 1 vanilla pod, split
- 275 g dark chocolate, chopped

Decoration
- Coriander sprig

Coriander-Orange Slices: Place the sugar and water in a saucepan over low heat, stir until the sugar is dissolved then raise the heat and boil for 2 minutes; remove the pan from the heat. Add the coriander seeds to the syrup and infuse for 5–10 minutes. Strain the syrup into a bowl then add the orange slices; macerate for 1 hour.

Pastry: Rub the butter into the sifted flour, salt, icing and vanilla sugar with your fingertips until the mixture resembles fine breadcrumbs. Blend in the egg and roughly mix to combine. Press the crumbs into a ball then, on a lightly floured work surface, use the heel of the hand to push bits of dough away from you, smearing them across the work surface to blend the butter and flour. Work quickly; repeat if necessary. Form into a ball, flatten slightly and wrap in cling film. Refrigerate for 30 minutes.

Preheat the oven to 180°C (350°F). Butter a 24 cm tart tin. Dust the work surface with flour. Roll out the dough to a thickness of 3 mm, to form a circle about 30 cm in diameter. Line the tin with the dough. Refrigerate for 10 minutes.

Cut out a 35 cm round of baking parchment and place it in the dough-lined tin; fill with baking beans. Bake for about 10 minutes, or until lightly coloured then remove the parchment and beans. Lower the oven temperature to 160°C (325°F); bake the pastry for another 10–15 minutes, or until golden. Remove from the oven and set aside on a rack.

Chocolate Cream: Put the egg yolks and sugar into a bowl and beat until pale and creamy. Using the point of a knife, scrape the seeds from the vanilla pod into the milk, add the pod; bring slowly to the boil. Stir $1/3$ of the hot milk quickly into the egg yolks and sugar and mix well to combine; pour the mixture into the remaining hot milk. Cook over low heat, stirring continuously with a wooden spoon, until thickened and the mixture coats the back of the spoon. (Do not allow to boil!) Remove from the heat and strain over the chopped chocolate, stirring carefully until smooth. Pour the chocolate cream into the pastry shell and refrigerate.

Just before serving, drain and dry the orange slices on kitchen paper; arrange on the surface of the tart with a sprig of coriander.

Chocolate and Caramelised Pear Tart

SERVES 8

DIFFICULTY ★ ★ ★

PREPARATION: 1 hour

COOK: 40 minutes

REFRIGERATE: 40 minutes

Chocolate Pastry
- 175 g soft unsalted butter
- 125 g icing sugar
- 1 egg
- 250 g flour, sifted
- 20 g unsweetened cocoa powder, sifted

Chocolate Filling
- 100 g dark chocolate
- 200 ml whipping cream
- 50 g mild honey
- 5 egg yolks

Caramelised Pears
- 850 g tinned pear halves
- 50 g mild honey
- 20 g unsalted butter

◇ See p.90: Lining a tart tin with pastry dough.

Chocolate Pastry: Beat the butter with the icing sugar; blend well. Add the egg then the sifted flour and cocoa powder; roughly mix to combine. Press the crumbs into a ball then, on a lightly floured work surface, use the heel of the hand to push bits of dough away from you, smearing them across the work surface to blend the butter and flour. Work quickly; repeat if necessary. Form into a ball, flatten slightly and wrap in cling film. Refrigerate for 30 minutes.

Preheat the oven to 180°C (350°F). Butter a 22 cm round tart tin. Dust the work surface with flour. Roll out the dough to a thickness of 3 mm, to form a circle about 27 cm in diameter. Line the tin with the dough. Refrigerate for 10 minutes.

Cut out a 30 cm round of baking parchment and place it in the dough-lined tin; fill with baking beans or rice. Bake for about 10 minutes, or until coloured then remove the parchment and beans. Lower the oven temperature to 160°C (325°F); bake the pastry for another 8 minutes. Remove from the oven and set aside on a rack.

Lower the oven temperature to 140°C (285°F).

Chocolate Filling: Coarsely chop the chocolate and place in a bowl. Heat the cream and honey until simmering. Whisk the eggs and quickly stir in the hot honey cream. Strain the mixture over the chocolate and stir carefully until smooth; set aside.

Caramelised Pears: Strain the pear halves. Heat the honey and butter in a non-stick pan, add the pears and cook over high heat until the pears turn golden. Transfer cut-side down to a cutting board, cool and slice crosswise into half-moons.

Pour the chocolate filling into the cooked pastry shell. Transfer the pear slices to the tart using a flat spatula. Bake for 20 minutes; serve.

Chocolate Praline Tart

SERVES 10–12

DIFFICULTY ★ ★ ★

PPEPARE: 1 hour

COOK: 20– 25 minutes

REFRIGERATE: 1 hour

Almond Pastry
- 100 g soft unsalted butter
- 20 g ground almonds
- 175 g flour, sifted
- 1 pinch salt
- 65 g icing sugar
- ¼ tsp natural vanilla essence
- 1 egg

Chocolate Praline Cream
- 400 g dark chocolate
- 400 ml whipping cream
- 60 g praline paste (p.325)
- 1 or 2 drops vanilla extract
- 90 g unsalted butter

Caramelised Nuts
- 50 ml water
- 100 g caster sugar
- 50 g blanched almonds
- 50 g blanched hazelnuts
- 10 g unsalted butter

◊ See p.88: Making pastry dough.

Almond Pastry: Rub the butter into the almonds, sifted flour, salt, icing and vanilla sugar with the tips of the fingers until the mixture resembles breadcrumbs. Blend in the egg and roughly mix to combine. Press the crumbs into a ball then, on a lightly floured work surface, use the heel of the hand to push bits of dough away from you, smearing them across the work surface to blend the butter and flour. Work quickly; repeat if necessary. Then form into a ball, flatten slightly and wrap in cling film. Refrigerate for 30 minutes.

Preheat the oven to 180°C (350°F). Butter a 25 x 10 cm rectangular tart tin. Dust the work surface with flour. Roll out the dough to a thickness of 3 mm, and cut out a rectangle, 30 x 15 cm. Line the tin with the dough. Refrigerate for 10 minutes.

Cut out a 35 x 20 cm rectangle of baking parchment and place it in the dough-lined tin; fill with baking beans. Bake for about 10 minutes, or until coloured then remove the parchment and beans. Lower the oven temperature to 160°C (325°F); bake for another 10– 15 minutes, or until golden. Remove from the oven and set aside on a rack.

Chocolate Praline Cream: Coarsely chop the chocolate and place in a bowl. Heat the cream until simmering, pour it over the chocolate; stir carefully until smooth. Blend in the praline paste, vanilla and butter. Pour the chocolate praline cream into the pastry shell; refrigerate 20 minutes.

Caramelised Nuts: Put the sugar and water into a saucepan over low heat; stir until the sugar is completely dissolved. Increase the heat and boil the syrup without stirring for about 5 minutes (or 117°C on a digital thermometer). Remove from the heat, add the nuts and stir with a wooden spoon until the syrup crystallises, covering them with a white powder. Cook the crystallised sugar and nuts over low heat until the nuts turn golden brown then incorporate the butter. Remove from the heat immediately and spread on baking parchment; stir until cool. When cold, rub between the hands to separate the nuts and arrange on the tart just before serving.

CHEF'S TIP: If a rectangular tin is not available, use a 26 cm round flan or tart tin. Simply roll the dough into a disc and line the tin with it.

Chocolate-Passion Fruit Tart

SERVES 8

DIFFICULTY ★ ★ ☆

PREPARE: 1 hour

COOK: 35 minutes

REFRIGERATE: 2¾ hours

Almond Pastry
- 120 g soft unsalted butter
- 65 g icing sugar
- 1 small egg
- 200 g flour, sifted
- 20 g ground almonds

Chocolate "Mi-Cuit" Filling
- 50 g milk chocolate
- 30 g dark (70%) chocolate
- 60 g soft unsalted butter
- 2 eggs
- 50 g caster sugar
- 2 tsp Malibu® liqueur

Passion Fruit Cream
- 2 leaves gelatine
- 80 g passion fruit purée
- 85 g caster sugar
- 2 eggs
- 140 g unsalted butter

Glaze
- 100 g neutral glaze
- 1 passion fruit

Decoration
- 100 g raspberries

◊ See p.90: Lining a tart tin with pastry dough.

Almond Pastry: Combine the butter with the icing sugar in a large bowl. Add the egg, then the sifted flour and ground almonds. Form a ball with the dough and lightly flatten. Wrap in cling film and refrigerate for 30 minutes.

Preheat the oven to 170°C (335°F). Butter a 22 cm tart tin. Dust a work surface with flour. Roll out the dough to a thickness of 3 mm, to form a circle 27 cm in diameter. Line the tart tin with the dough. Refrigerate for 10 minutes.

Place a sheet of baking parchment slightly bigger than the tin on the tart base and fill with baking beans. Bake for about 10 minutes, or until the pastry is lightly coloured; then remove the parchment and beans. Lower the oven temperature to 160°C (325°F), bake for another 10–15 minutes, or until golden brown. Remove from the oven and set aside on a rack.

Chocolate "Mi-Cuit" Filling: Increase the oven temperature to 190°C (375°F). Melt the two chocolates over a bain-marie. Remove from the heat and mix in the butter. Beat the eggs, sugar and Malibu® liqueur together in a bowl. Next, add the melted chocolate. Mix thoroughly. Pour the filling into the tart tin until ¾ full and bake for 7 minutes. Set aside.

Passion Fruit Cream: Soften the gelatine leaves in a bowl of cold water. Heat the passion fruit purée in a saucepan. Whisk the sugar and eggs in a bowl until the mixture turns pale and thickens, fold into the hot purée and bring to the boil.

Squeeze the excess water from the leaves of gelatine and, off the heat, stir into the mixture, then add the butter. Let the passion fruit cream cool and pour over the tart. Gently tilt the tart from left to right to evenly distribute the cream. Refrigerate for 2 hours.

Glaze: Combine the neutral glaze with the passion fruit pulp. Brush the glaze over the tart. Decorate with fresh raspberries. Serve immediately.

Chocolate Tart topped with Caramelised Apple

SERVES 8

DIFFICULTY ★ ★ ★

PREPARE: 1 hour

COOK: 40 minutes approx

REFRIGERATE: 1 hour
40 minutes

Chocolate Pastry
- 125 g flour, sifted
- 10 g unsweetened cocoa powder, sifted
- 50 g caster sugar
- 1 pinch salt
- 75 g unsalted butter, cut in pieces
- 1 egg yolk
- 45 ml water
- 15 g chocolate sprinkles

Chocolate Nib Ganache
- 200 g dark chocolate with nibs
- 200 ml whipping cream
- 2 pinches ground nutmeg
- 1 tsp vanilla extract

Caramelised Apples
- 2 Granny Smith apples
- 30 g unsalted butter
- 30 g caster sugar

Decoration (Optional)
- 20 g Chocolate nibs or chocolate sprinkles

Chocolate Pastry: Combine the sifted flour and cocoa powder, sugar and salt in a bowl. Rub in the butter until the mixture resembles coarse breadcrumbs. Make a well in the centre of the mixture, place the egg and water in it and roughly mix to combine; add the chocolate sprinkles. Press the crumbs into a ball then, on a lightly floured work surface, use the heel of the hand to push bits of dough away from you, smearing them across the work surface to blend the butter and flour. Work quickly; repeat if necessary. Form into a ball, flatten slightly and wrap in cling film. Refrigerate for 30 minutes.

Preheat the oven to 180°C (350°F). Butter a 22 cm round tart tin. Dust the work surface with flour. Roll out the dough to a thickness of 3 mm, to form a circle about 27 cm in diameter. Line the tin with the dough. Refrigerate for 30 minutes.

Cut out a 30 cm round of baking parchment and place it in the dough-lined tin; fill with baking beans. Bake for about 10 minutes then remove the parchment and beans. Lower the oven temperature to 160°C (325°F); bake the pastry for a further 10–15 minutes. Remove from the oven and set aside on a rack.

Chocolate Nib Ganache: Coarsely chop the chocolate and place in a bowl. Bring the cream and nutmeg to the boil, pour over the chocolate and stir until smooth; incorporate the vanilla. Pour the ganache into the pastry shell; set aside.

Caramelised Apples: Peel and cut the apples in quarters. Heat the butter and sugar in a non-stick pan. Add the apples and cook over low heat for about 10 minutes, or until tender then increase the heat until the apples turn golden; let cool.

Use a flat spatula to place the caramelised apples on the still soft ganache; refrigerate. Remove from the refrigerator 30 minutes before serving; scatter the surface with chocolate nibs or sprinkles.

CHEF'S TIP: Chocolate or cocoa nibs are roasted cocoa beans separated from their husks and broken into small bits. If unavailable, they could be replaced with chocolate sprinkles.

Chocolate Cream Tart with Caramelised Nuts

SERVES **8**

DIFFICULTY ★ ★ ★

PREPARE: 1 hour

COOK: 1 hour 10 minutes

REFRIGERATE: 40 minutes

Almond Pastry
- 120 g soft unsalted butter
- 75 g icing sugar
- 1 pinch salt
- 25 g ground almonds
- 1 egg
- 200 g flour, sifted

Chocolate Cream
- 200 ml milk
- 30 g unsweetened cocoa powder
- 20 g chocolate
- 200 ml crème fraîche
- 4 egg yolks
- 120 g caster sugar

Chocolate Glaze
- 60 g crème fraîche
- 10 g caster sugar
- 10 g mild honey
- 60 g grated chocolate
- 10 g unsalted butter

Caramelised Nuts
- 10 ml water
- 35 g caster sugar
- 35 g blanched hazelnuts
- 35 g blanched almonds
- 5 g unsalted butter

Almond Pastry: Beat the butter with the salt, almonds and icing sugar; combine well. Blend in the egg then the sifted flour; mix roughly to combine. Press the crumbs into a ball then, on a lightly floured work surface, use the heel of the hand to push bits of dough away from you, smearing them across the work surface to blend the butter and flour. Work quickly; repeat if necessary. Form into a ball, flatten slightly and wrap in cling film. Refrigerate for 30 minutes.

Preheat the oven to 180°C (350°F). Butter a 22 cm flan or tart tin and dust the work surface with flour. Roll the dough out to a thickness of 3 mm, to form a circle about 27 cm in diameter. Line the tin with the dough. Refrigerate for 10 minutes.

Cut out a 30 cm round of baking parchment and place it in the dough-lined tin; fill with baking beans. Bake for about 10 minutes, or until coloured, then remove the parchment and beans. Lower the oven temperature to 160°C (325°F); bake the pastry for another 8 minutes. Remove from the oven and set aside on a rack.

Chocolate Cream: Bring the milk, cocoa powder and chocolate to the boil, add the crème fraîche and remove the saucepan from the heat. Place the egg yolks and sugar in a bowl, beat until pale yellow and creamy; add the milk and chocolate. Pour the chocolate cream into the pastry shell and bake for 45 minutes; set aside to cool.

Chocolate Glaze: Heat the crème fraîche, sugar and honey; pour over the grated chocolate and stir until smooth. Blend in the butter.

Caramelised Nuts: Put the sugar and water into a small saucepan over low heat and stir until the sugar is completely dissolved. Increase the heat and boil the syrup for about 2 minutes without stirring. Remove from the heat, add the nuts and stir with a wooden spoon until the syrup crystallises, covering them with a white powder. Cook the crystallised sugar and nuts over low heat until the nuts turn golden brown then incorporate the unsalted butter. Remove from the heat immediately and spread on baking parchment; stir until cool. When cold, pour the chocolate glaze over the surface of the tart, scatter the caramelised nuts on top; serve.

Smarties® Tart

SERVES 8

DIFFICULTY ★ ★ ★

PREPARE: 40 minutes

COOK: 20– 25 minutes

REFRIGERATE: 1 hour
10 minutes

Sweet Pastry
- 120 g soft unsalted butter
- 100 g icing sugar
- 1 pinch salt
- 1 egg
- 200 g flour, sifted

Ganache
- 100 g dark (55– 70%) chocolate
- 100 ml whipping cream
- 110 g Smarties®

◊ See p.12: Making a basic ganache.

Sweet Pastry: Beat the butter with the icing sugar and salt; blend well. Add the egg, then add the sifted flour; mix roughly to combine. Press the crumbs into a ball then, on a lightly floured work surface, use the heel of the hand to push bits of dough away from you, smearing them across the work surface to blend the butter and flour. Work quickly; repeat if necessary. Form into a ball, flatten slightly and wrap in cling film. Refrigerate for 30 minutes.

Preheat the oven to 180°C (350°F). Butter a 22 cm round tart tin. Dust the work surface with flour. Roll the dough out to a thickness of 3 mm, to form a circle about 27 cm in diameter. Line the tin with the dough. Refrigerate for 10 minutes.

Cut out a 30 cm round of baking parchment and place it in the dough-lined tin; fill with baking beans. Bake for about 10 minutes, or until lightly coloured then remove the parchment and beans. Lower the oven temperature to 160°C (325°F); bake the pastry for a further 10– 15 minutes, or until golden. Remove from the oven and set aside on a rack.

Ganache: Coarsely chop the chocolate and place in a bowl. Heat the cream until simmering and pour over the chocolate; stir until smooth. Pour the ganache evenly into the pastry shell, arrange the Smarties® on the surface; refrigerate for 30 minutes before serving.

Chocolate-Walnut Tartlets

SERVES 8

DIFFICULTY ★ ★ ★

PREPARE: 1¼ hours

COOK: 25–30 minutes

REFRIGERATE: 1¾ hours

Chocolate Pastry
- 175 g soft unsalted butter
- 125 g icing sugar
- 1 pinch salt
- 1 egg
- 250 g flour, sifted
- 20 g unsweetened cocoa powder, sifted

Walnut Caramel
- 200 g walnut halves
- 200 g caster sugar
- 50 g mild honey
- 30 g unsalted butter
- 170 ml whipping cream

Decoration
- 200 g walnut halves

◊ See p.91: Lining tartlet tins with pastry dough.

Chocolate Pastry: Beat the butter with the icing sugar and salt; blend well. Add the egg then the sifted flour and cocoa powder; mix roughly to combine. Press the crumbs into a ball then, on a lightly floured work surface, use the heel of the hand to push bits of dough away from you, smearing them across the work surface to blend the butter and flour. Work quickly; repeat if necessary. Form into a ball, flatten slightly and wrap in cling film. Refrigerate for 30 minutes.

Preheat the oven to 180°C (350°F). Butter eight 8 cm fluted tartlet moulds. Dust the work surface with flour. Roll out the dough to a thickness of 3 mm. Use a 10 cm pastry cutter to stamp out 8 rounds of dough, line the moulds and prick the bases using a fork. Refrigerate for 10 minutes.

Bake the dough-lined moulds for 20 minutes. Set aside to cool on a rack.

Walnut Caramel: Maintain the oven at the 180°C (350°F). Coarsely chop the walnuts, place on a baking sheet and toast for 5–10 minutes in the oven. Place the sugar and honey in a saucepan over low heat and stir until the sugar dissolves completely. Increase the heat and boil (do not stir) for about 10 minutes until the syrup becomes a golden caramel colour. Remove from the heat and add the butter. Return the saucepan to the heat and pour the cream very slowly into the caramel to stop the cooking. (Be careful as it will spit violently when the liquid is added.) Reduce the heat and stir with a wooden spoon until the mixture is smooth. Strain it into a bowl to cool then add the toasted walnuts; set aside.

Spoon the cooled walnut caramel into the tartlet shells, refrigerate for 1 hour before serving; decorate each tartlet with a walnut half.

CHEF'S TIP: If you want the tartlets to have a more nutty flavour, you could combine fresh pistachios with the walnuts.

Chocolate Nougatine Tartlets

SERVES 12–14

DIFFICULTY ★ ★ ★

PREPARE: 1½ hours

COOK: 20 minutes

REFRIGERATE: 1 hour

Almond Pastry
- 120 g soft unsalted butter
- 75 g icing sugar
- 1 pinch salt
- 25 g ground almonds
- 1 egg
- 200 g flour, sifted

Nougatine
- 40 g flaked almonds
- 75 g caster sugar
- 30 g mild honey

Chocolate Cream
- 300 ml whipping cream
- 3 eggs
- 60 g caster sugar
- 120 g dark (70%) chocolate, chopped

◊ See p.91: Lining tartlet tins with pastry dough.

Almond Pastry: Beat the butter with the icing sugar, salt and almonds; blend well. Add the egg then the sifted flour; roughly mix to combine. Press the crumbs into a ball then, on a lightly floured work surface, use the heel of the hand to push bits of dough away from you, smearing them across the work surface to blend the butter and flour. Work quickly; repeat if necessary. Form into a ball, flatten slightly and wrap in cling film. Refrigerate for 30 minutes.

Preheat the oven to 180°C (350°F). Butter 12–14 x 8 cm tartlet moulds. Dust the work surface with flour. Roll out the dough to a thickness of 3 mm. Using a 10 cm pastry cutter, stamp out 12–14 rounds of dough. Line the moulds with the dough and prick the pastry bases using a fork. Refrigerate for 10 minutes.

Bake the dough-lined moulds for 20 minutes. Set aside to cool on a rack. Lower the oven temperature to 150°C (300°F).

Nougatine: Cover a baking tray with baking parchment and place the almonds on it. Toast in the oven for 5 minutes, or until lightly coloured. Place the sugar and honey in a saucepan and stir over low heat until the sugar dissolves completely. Increase the heat and boil (do not stir) for about 10 minutes, or until the syrup becomes amber coloured. Remove from the heat and carefully stir in the toasted almonds. Pour the mixture onto the prepared baking tray and place another sheet of parchment on top. Using a rolling pin, spread the nougatine into a layer 2 mm thick. When cool, coarsely grind in a food processor.

Chocolate Cream: Heat the cream until simmering. Place the eggs and sugar in a bowl and beat until pale yellow and creamy. Stir $1/3$ of the cream quickly into the eggs and sugar and mix well to combine; return the mixture to the saucepan. Cook over low heat, stirring continuously with a wooden spoon, until thickened and the mixture coats the back of the spoon. (Do not allow to boil!) Remove from the heat immediately and strain over the chopped chocolate; stir carefully until smooth.

Place the nougatine in the tartlet shells to come $3/4$ up the sides and fill with the chocolate cream. Refrigerate for 30 minutes, or until the cream is firm. Sprinkle with the remaining nougatine.

Chocolate Chestnut Tartlets

SERVES 8

DIFFICULTY ★ ★ ★

PREPARE: 1 hour approx

COOK: 20 minutes

REFRIGERATE: 40 minutes

• 16 tinned chestnuts in vanilla syrup or 16 glacé chestnuts (marrons glacés)

Pastry
• 80 g soft unsalted butter
• 115 g flour, sifted
• 10 g unsweetened cocoa powder, sifted
• 1 pinch salt
• 80 g icing sugar
• 1 egg

Chestnut Ganache
• 130 g dark chocolate
• 50 ml whipping cream
• 100 g sweet chestnut cream (crème de marron)

Decoration (Optional)
• 100 g dark chocolate, tempered (p.320)
• 50 g caster sugar

◇ Start this recipe the day before.

◇ See p.91: Lining tartlet tins with pastry dough.

The day before, drain the tinned chestnuts. Then, cut the chestnuts in pieces. Reserve overnight.

Pastry: The next day, rub the butter into the sifted flour, cocoa powder, salt and icing sugar with the tips of the fingers, until the mixture resembles breadcrumbs. Incorporate the egg and roughly mix to combine. Press the crumbs into a ball then, on a lightly floured work surface, use the heel of the hand to push bits of dough away from you, smearing them across the work surface to blend the butter and flour. Work quickly; repeat if necessary. Form into a ball, flatten slightly and wrap in cling film. Refrigerate for 30 minutes.

Preheat the oven to 180°C (350°F). Butter 2 baking trays.

Dust the work surface with flour. Roll out the dough to a thickness of 3 mm. Using a 10 cm pastry cutter, stamp out 8 rounds of dough, prick with a fork and transfer to the baking trays; refrigerate for 10 minutes.

Bake for 20 minutes. Set the pastry rounds aside to cool on a rack.

Chestnut Ganache: Coarsely chop the chocolate and place in a bowl. Heat the cream and sweet chestnut cream until simmering and pour it over the chocolate; stir until smooth. Set the ganache aside until firm and it can be spread easily.

Spread each pastry round with the chestnut ganache and top with chestnut pieces. Cool before serving.

Making the decorations: If desired, the tartlets could be decorated with tempered chocolate and sugar medallions. Make a small paper piping bag (p.329) and fill with the tempered chocolate (p.320). Put a layer of sugar on a large plate and pipe a chocolate design in the sugar, for each tartlet (see photo opposite). Let the medallions harden in the sugar then place one on each tartlet.

Soft-Textured Chocolate Tartlets

SERVES 12

DIFFICULTY ★ ★ ★

PREPARATION: 1¼ hours

COOK: 30 minutes

REFRIGERATE: 40 minutes

Sweet Pastry

- 120 g soft unsalted butter
- 100 g icing sugar
- 1 pinch salt
- 1 egg
- 200 g flour, sifted

Chocolate Pastry Cream

- 20 g unsweetened cocoa powder, sifted
- 50 ml water
- 200 ml milk
- 3 egg yolks
- 40 g caster sugar
- 20 g flour

- 3 egg whites
- 20 g sugar

◊ See p.91: Lining tartlet tins with pastry dough.

Sweet Pastry: Beat the butter with the icing sugar and salt; combine well. Blend in the egg then add the sifted flour; roughly mix to combine. Press the crumbs into a ball then, on a lightly floured work surface, use the heel of the hand to push bits of dough away from you, smearing them across the work surface to blend the butter and flour. Work quickly; repeat if necessary. Form into a ball, flatten slightly and wrap in cling film. Refrigerate for 30 minutes.

Preheat the oven to 180°C (350°F). Butter 12 x 8 cm tartlet moulds. Dust the work surface with flour. Roll out the dough to a thickness of 3 mm. Using a 10 cm pastry cutter, stamp out 12 rounds of dough; line the moulds with the dough and prick the bases using a fork. Refrigerate for 10 minutes.

Bake the dough-lined moulds for 15 minutes, or until lightly golden. Turn out to cool on a rack and set aside.

Chocolate Pastry Cream: Put the cocoa powder and water into a saucepan; stir to combine. Add the milk and bring to the boil; remove from the heat. Put 2 egg yolks and the sugar into a bowl and beat until pale yellow and creamy; add the flour. Whisk half the hot chocolate milk quickly into the egg yolk-sugar mixture. Add the remaining milk and return the mixture to the saucepan. Cook over low heat, whisking continuously until the cream thickens. Boil for 1 minute while continuing to whisk. Remove from the heat and when cooled, stir in the remaining egg yolk. Pour the chocolate pastry cream into a bowl, cover the surface with cling film; cool.

Preheat the oven to 180°C (350°F). Beat the egg whites, gradually adding the sugar, until the whites are smooth, shiny and stiff peaks form. Stir 1/3 into the chocolate pastry cream and carefully fold in the remainder using a spatula. Divide the mixture evenly between the tartlet shells to come 2/3 up the sides. Bake for 15 minutes, or until the chocolate soufflé has risen in each tartlet.

CHEF'S TIP: These tartlets go well with a pistachio cream. To do this, prepare the crème Anglaise (see p.208); after pouring the preparation into the pan remove the vanilla pod and incorporate 20 g of pistachio paste.

Chocolate-Hazelnut Soufflé Tartlets

SERVES 10

DIFFICULTY ★ ★ ★

PREPARATION: 1¼ hours

COOK: 30 minutes approx

REFRIGERATE: 40 minutes

Hazelnut Pastry
- 100 g soft unsalted butter
- 45 g icing sugar
- 1 pinch salt
- 40 g ground hazelnuts, sifted
- ¼ tsp natural vanilla essence
- 1 egg
- 200 g flour, sifted

Chocolate Cream
- 25 g unsweetened cocoa powder
- 50 ml water
- 200 ml milk
- 3 egg yolks
- 15 g caster sugar
- 20 g flour
- 1 tbsp hazelnut liqueur (such as Frangelico)

- 3 egg whites
- 50 g caster sugar

Decoration
- Icing sugar, sifted

Hazelnut Pastry: Beat the butter with icing sugar, salt, hazelnuts and vanilla; combine well. Blend in the egg then the sifted flour and roughly mix to combine. Press the crumbs into a ball then, on a lightly floured work surface, use the heel of the hand to push bits of dough away from you, smearing them across the work surface to blend the butter and flour. Work quickly; repeat if necessary. Form into a ball, flatten slightly and wrap in cling film. Refrigerate for 30 minutes.

Preheat the oven to 180°C (350°F). Butter 10 x 8 cm tartlet moulds. Dust the work surface with flour. Roll out the dough to a thickness of 3 mm. Using a 10 cm pastry cutter, stamp out 10 rounds of dough; line the moulds with dough and prick the bases with a fork. Refrigerate 10 minutes.

Bake the dough-lined moulds for 15 minutes, or until lightly golden. Cool before turning out onto a rack; set aside.

Chocolate Cream: Put the cocoa powder and water into a saucepan and stir to combine. Add the milk and bring to the boil; remove from the heat. Put the egg yolks and sugar into a bowl and beat until pale yellow and creamy; add the flour. Whisk half the hot chocolate milk quickly into the eggs and sugar. Add the remaining milk and return the mixture to the saucepan. Cook over low heat, whisking continuously until the cream thickens. Boil for 1 minute while continuing to whisk. Pour the chocolate cream into a bowl; cover the surface with cling film. When cool, add the hazelnut liqueur.

Preheat the oven to 180°C (350°F). Beat the egg whites until foamy. Gradually add the sugar, beating until the egg whites are smooth, shiny and stiff peaks form. Stir $1/3$ into the chocolate cream; carefully fold in the remainder using a spatula. Divide the mixture evenly between the tartlet shells to come $2/3$ up the sides. Bake for 15 minutes, or until the chocolate soufflé has risen in each tartlet. Dust with sifted icing sugar and serve immediately.

Mouth-watering mousses & creams

The best way to prepare a chocolate meringue

You can adapt this version of chocolate meringue using the ingredients shown in the recipe of your choice (see p.172).

 1 Put 4 egg whites into a bowl and whisk until frothy. Add 1/3 of the caster sugar a little at a time, whisking until the egg whites are smooth and shiny.

2 Gradually add the remaining sugar, whisking until stiff peaks form on the whisk.

3 Use a wooden spoon to carefully fold 100 g of sifted icing sugar and 20 g of unsweetened cocoa powder into the whisked egg whites. Cut straight down to the bottom of the bowl with a wooden spoon, then lift up the contents, bringing the spoon up the side of the bowl while giving it a quarter turn. Continue until the mixture is smooth and shiny.

The best way to prepare soufflé dishes or ramekins

Prepare a soufflé using the recipe of your choice (see pp.194-202). The following technique is the same whatever the size of the ramekin or dish.

① Brush the ramekins with butter. Dust evenly with caster sugar, tipping out the excess.

② Divide the soufflé mixture evenly between the ramekins and smooth with a spatula.

③ Run your thumb around the inside rim of the ramekin to open a 5 mm channel, which will allow the soufflé mixture to rise cleanly and evenly during cooking. Cook according to the directions indicated in the recipe.

Chocolate Charlotte

SERVES 10–12

DIFFICULTY ★ ★ ★

PREPARE: 1½ hours

COOK: 8 minutes

REFRIGERATE: 1 hour

Sponge Fingers
- 4 egg yolks
- 120 g caster sugar
- 4 egg whites
- 120 g flour, sifted
- Icing sugar

Chocolate Bavarian Cream
- 200 g dark chocolate, chopped
- 3 leaves gelatine
- 170 ml milk
- 500 ml whipping cream
- 60 g caster sugar
- 6 egg yolks

Decoration (Optional)
- Chocolate shavings (p.397)

Preheat the oven to 180°C (350°F). Butter and dust a 22 cm springform pan with sugar. Trace a 22 cm circle on a sheet of baking parchment and turn the marked side over onto a baking tray.

Sponge Fingers: Combine the egg yolks and 60 g of the sugar; beat until the mixture is pale yellow and creamy. In a separate bowl, whisk the egg whites, gradually adding the remaining sugar, until the egg whites are smooth, shiny and stiff peaks form. Gently fold in the egg yolk-sugar mixture then the sifted flour. Fit a piping bag with a plain round nozzle and fill it with the batter. Start piping in the centre of the traced circle, working outwards in a spiral and finishing 1 cm from the inside edge. On the same or another baking tray, pipe touching fingers of batter to form a band at least 22 cm long; it should be the same width as the height of the pastry ring. Dust the piped fingers with icing sugar, wait 5 minutes then dust generously a second time. Bake for 8 minutes, or until golden. Set the sponge disc and band of sponge fingers aside to cool.

Chocolate Bavarian Cream: Place the chopped chocolate in a large bowl. Soften the gelatine leaves in cold water. Heat the milk, cream and 30 g of the sugar until simmering. Beat the egg yolks and remaining sugar, until pale yellow and creamy. Add $^1/3$ of the hot milk mixture and mix well to combine. Pour it into the remaining hot milk mixture, stirring constantly with a wooden spoon; cook over low heat until the cream is thickened and coats the back of the spoon. (Do not allow to boil!) Remove from the heat immediately. Squeeze the excess water from the gelatine and stir into the cream to dissolve. Strain the hot mixture over the chopped chocolate; stir until smooth. Stand the bowl in crushed ice to cool. Beat the remaining cream until firm and clinging to the whisk; gently fold into the cooled chocolate cream.

Place the sponge disc in the bottom of the springform pan. Trim the band of sponge fingers to the height of the pan and place the sugared side against the inner wall, with the rounded ends pointing upwards. Fill with the chocolate Bavarian cream and refrigerate 1 hour, or until firm. Remove the side of the pan and decorate with chocolate shavings.

Chocolate Crème Brûlée

SERVES 6

DIFFICULTY ★ ★ ★

PREPARE: 10 minutes

COOK: 25 minutes

REFRIGERATE: 1 hour

- 4 egg yolks
- 50 g caster sugar
- 125 ml milk
- 125 ml whipping cream
- 100 g dark chocolate, chopped

Decoration
- Caster sugar

Preheat the oven to 95°C (205°F). Prepare 4 small baking dishes or low-sided ramekins.

Combine the egg yolks and 40 g of the sugar in a large bowl; beat until the mixture is pale and creamy.

Heat the milk, cream and remaining caster sugar until simmering. Add the chopped chocolate and stir until well combined and smooth. Slowly stir the chocolate mixture into the egg yolk-sugar mixture. Pour the chocolate mixture into the dishes, to come 3/4 up the sides.

Bake for 25 minutes, or until firm; cool. Refrigerate for 1 hour.

Preheat the oven grill to its maximum temperature. Sprinkle the creams evenly with caster sugar and place under the grill until the sugar becomes a dark brown topping. Let cool and serve once the topping has hardened.

CHEF'S TIP: To correctly caramelise or gratinée creams, put the oven rack as close to the heat source as possible.

White Chocolate Crème Brûlée

SERVES 6

DIFFICULTY ★ ★ ★

PREPARE: 30 minutes + 5 min

INFUSE: 1 hour

REFRIGERATE: Overnight

• 400 ml crème fraîche
• 1 vanilla pod, split
• 130 g white chocolate
• 6 egg yolks
• 60 g unrefined cane sugar

◇ The white chocolate crème brulée should be prepared the day before serving.

Place the crème fraîche in a saucepan. Using the point of a knife, scrape the seeds from the vanilla pod into the cream; add the pod and heat until simmering. Remove from the heat and set aside to infuse for 1 hour.

Chop the white chocolate, and melt over a bain-marie; remove from the heat, stirring until smooth. Add the egg yolks and mix well to combine; stir in the vanilla-flavoured cream. Pour the mixture into a clean saucepan. Stirring constantly with a wooden spoon, cook over low heat until the cream is thickened and coats the back of the spoon. (Do not allow to boil!) Strain and divide the mixture equally between six 8 cm diameter ramekins and refrigerate overnight.

When ready to serve, preheat the oven grill to its maximum temperature. Sprinkle the creams evenly with the sugar and place under the grill until the sugar melts and turns golden. Serve immediately.

Chocolate Cream topped with Peppered Chantilly Cream and Caramel 'Leaves'

SERVES 12–15

DIFFICULTY: ★ ★ ★

PREPARE: 1 hour

REFRIGERATE: 30 minutes

Chocolate Cream

- 220 g dark chocolate
- 2 leaves gelatine
- 250 ml milk
- 250 ml whipping cream
- 1 vanilla pod, split
- 5 egg yolks
- 60 g caster sugar

Caramel Leaves

- 250 g caster sugar
- 150 g mild honey

Peppered Chantilly Cream

- 200 ml whipping cream
- 1 pinch freshly ground pepper
- 20 g icing sugar

Chocolate Cream: Chop the chocolate and set aside in a large bowl. Soften the gelatine in cold water. Pour the milk and cream into a saucepan. Using the point of a knife, scrape the seeds from the vanilla pod into the milk-cream mixture, add the pod and heat to simmering. Beat the egg yolks and sugar until pale yellow and creamy. Slowly whisk in $^1/_3$ of the hot cream mixture and mix well to combine; pour the egg yolk-sugar mixture into the remaining hot cream. Stirring constantly with a wooden spoon, cook the cream over low heat until thickened and it coats the back of the spoon. (Do not allow to boil!) Remove from the heat immediately and discard the vanilla pod. Squeeze the excess water from the gelatine and stir into the cream to dissolve. Pour over the chopped chocolate and stir until smooth. Divide the chocolate cream equally between 12–15 glasses and refrigerate for 30 minutes.

Caramel Leaves: Lightly brush a baking tray with oil. Heat the sugar and honey over low heat, stirring until the sugar dissolves completely. Increase the heat and boil without stirring for about 10 minutes, or until the syrup turns a dark gold. Pour a thin layer of this caramel onto the baking tray. When hard, break in large pieces.

Peppered Chantilly Cream: Combine the cream and ground pepper; whisk until the cream begins to firm. Add the icing sugar and continue whisking until stiff peaks cling to the whisk. Fit a piping bag with a plain nozzle and fill with the peppered Chantilly cream. Decorate each glass of chocolate cream with Chantilly and a caramel 'leaf'.

CHEF'S TIP: There are several types of pepper such as Sarawak, Sichuan or Cubeb that will give your Chantilly a hot spicy flavour; they also marry well with chocolate. Grind your pepper just before using to give it a stronger taste.

Irish Coffee Cream

SERVES 4

DIFFICULTY: ★ ★ ★

PREPARE: 25 minutes

REFRIGERATE: 30 minutes

Ganache
- 200 g dark (55–70%) chocolate
- 200 g crème fraîche
- 2 tbsp caster sugar
- 2 tbsp whisky

Coffee Cream
- 200 ml whipping cream
- 45 g icing sugar, sifted
- 1 tbsp coffee extract

Decoration
- Unsweetened cocoa powder, sifted

Ganache: Coarsely chop the chocolate and place in a bowl. Heat the crème fraîche and sugar until simmering and pour over the chocolate. Stir until smooth and then add the whisky. Divide the mixture evenly between four 150-ml glasses. Refrigerate for 15 minutes.

Coffee Cream: Whisk the cream until it begins to firm. Add the icing sugar and continue whisking until stiff peaks cling to the whisk; fold in the coffee extract. Fit a piping bag with a plain round nozzle and fill with the coffee cream.

Just before serving, remove the glasses from the refrigerator and pipe the coffee cream on top. Dust with sifted cocoa powder and serve.

CHEF'S TIP: If you don't have coffee extract, make your own by dissolving 1 tbsp of instant coffee in 1 tsp of hot water.

Old Fashioned Cream Soufflé

SERVES 4

DIFFICULTY ★ ★ ★

PREPARE: 15– 20 minutes

COOK: 7 or 8 minutes

- 100 g dark (55– 70%) chocolate
- 60 g unsalted butter
- 30 g unsweetened cocoa powder, sifted
- 2 egg yolks
- 3 egg whites
- 50 g caster sugar
- Icing sugar, sifted

Preheat the oven to 200°C (400°F). Brush four 14 cm low-sided 160-ml gratin or baking dishes with unsalted butter. Dust evenly with caster sugar, tipping out the excess.

Chop the chocolate, place in a large bowl and melt over a bain-marie. Add the butter, stirring until smooth then blend in the cocoa powder. Remove from the bain-marie and cool. Slowly stir the egg yolks into the cooled chocolate and butter mixture.

Put the egg whites into a bowl and whisk until frothy. Add 15 g of the sugar a little at a time, whisking until the egg whites are smooth and shiny. Gradually add the remaining sugar, whisking until stiff peaks form.

Whisk 1/3 of the egg whites into the chocolate mixture to lighten it. Using a spatula, carefully fold in the remainder, in two separate batches. Divide the soufflé mixture equally between the prepared dishes and bake for 7– 8 minutes. As soon as they come out of the oven, dust with sifted icing sugar; serve immediately.

CHEF'S TIP: Room temperature egg whites whisk more successfully than refrigerated ones.

Two-Mousse Terrine

SERVES 10–12

DIFFICULTY ★ ★ ★

PREPARE: 1½ hours

COOK: 8 minutes

REFRIGERATE: 2 hours or freeze 1 hour

Chocolate Sponge
- 20 g unsalted butter
- 125 g caster sugar
- 4 eggs
- 90 g flour, sifted
- 30 g unsweetened cocoa powder, sifted

Milk Chocolate Mousse
- 100 g milk chocolate
- 200 ml whipping cream
- 2 egg yolks
- 30 ml water
- 20 g caster sugar

Dark Chocolate Mousse
- 150 g dark chocolate
- 300 ml whipping cream
- 2 egg yolks
- 40 ml water
- 30 g caster sugar

Preheat the oven to 200°C (400°F). Line an oven tray with baking parchment. Set a 25 x 10 cm terrine aside.

Chocolate Sponge: Melt the butter in a saucepan over low heat; set aside. Place the sugar and eggs in a heatproof bowl; whisk to combine. Stand the bowl over a bain-marie and whisk continuously for 5–8 minutes, or until the batter becomes light and thick and falls in an unbroken ribbon from the whisk or beater. Do not allow it to become too hot. Remove the bowl from the bain-marie and continue whisking quickly by hand, or with an electric beater on high speed, until cool. Gently fold in the flour and cocoa powder, adding them in 2 or 3 batches. Quickly add the melted butter. Pour the batter into the oven tray and smooth with a palette knife. Bake approximately 8 minutes, or until the surface of the sponge is firm but springy to the touch and it starts to pull away from the parchment. Slide the cooked sponge, with the parchment attached, onto a rack. Place a sheet of baking parchment and a rack on the sponge and turn everything over, remove the rack; cool. Peel off the cooking parchment. Cut the sponge in strips and use to line the terrine, placing the crusty side against the walls and base. Reserve a piece of sponge, the same dimensions as the terrine, for the final assembly.

Milk Chocolate Mousse: Chop the chocolate and melt over a bain-marie. Whisk the cream until stiff peaks cling to the whisk; refrigerate. Whisk the egg yolks in a large bowl until pale yellow. Put the water and sugar into a saucepan and stir over low heat until the sugar dissolves; bring to the boil and cook for 2 minutes. Pour the syrup slowly down the side of the bowl into the egg yolks, whisking continuously until the mixture thickens and cools. Using a spatula, gradually blend in the melted chocolate then fold in the whipped cream.

Dark Chocolate Mousse: Repeat the previous step using dark chocolate instead of milk chocolate.

Pour the milk chocolate mousse into the sponge-lined terrine then add the dark chocolate mousse on top. Cover with the reserved piece of sponge. Refrigerate for 2 hours or freeze for 1 hour. Serve cold.

Chocolate-Coffee Dessert

SERVES 6–8

DIFFICULTY ★ ★ ★

PREPARE: 1 hour

COOK: 15 minutes

REFRIGERATE: 2 hours

Chocolate Cake
- 50 g dark (70%) chocolate
- 50 g soft unsalted butter
- 2 egg yolks
- 2 egg whites
- 20 g caster sugar
- 25 g flour, sifted

Coffee Syrup
- 50 ml water
- 40 g caster sugar
- 1 tsp instant coffee

Coffee Mousse
- 85 g dark (55%) chocolate
- 175 ml whipping cream
- 3 egg yolks
- 40 g caster sugar
- 4 tsp (20 ml) coffee extract

Chocolate Glaze
- 65 g dark chocolate
- 75 ml whipping cream
- 15 g mild honey

Decoration (Optional)
- Chocolate coffee beans

Preheat the oven to 180°C (350°F). Line a baking tray with baking parchment. Butter an 18-cm square cake frame; place it on the baking tray.

Chocolate Cake: Finely chop the chocolate and melt over a bain-marie. Remove from the heat, add the butter, stir until smooth; add the egg yolks. In a separate bowl, whisk the egg whites gradually adding the sugar until the egg whites are smooth, shiny and stiff peaks form. Whisk a third of the egg whites into the chocolate mixture to lighten it. Using a flexible spatula, carefully fold in the remainder then add the flour. Pour the batter into the cake frame and bake for 15 minutes. Cool in the cake frame.

Coffee Syrup: Put the water and sugar into a saucepan and stir over low heat until the sugar dissolves completely, increase the heat and boil for 2 minutes, add the coffee; cool.

Coffee Mousse: Finely chop the chocolate and melt over a bain-marie; cool. Beat the cream until firm peaks cling to the whisk; refrigerate. Whisk the egg yolks and sugar in a bowl until pale yellow and creamy; add the coffee extract. Use a spatula and gradually blend in the chocolate, then fold in the whipped cream.

Sprinkle or brush the chocolate cake with the coffee syrup and pour the coffee mousse over the top filling the cake frame. Smooth the surface with a palette knife; refrigerate 1 hour.

Chocolate Glaze: Finely chop the chocolate and place in a bowl. Heat the cream and honey until simmering, pour over the chocolate and stir until smooth.

Remove the cake from the refrigerator, spread the glaze evenly over the surface; refrigerate for 1 hour. Remove the frame when the glaze is firm. Decorate with the chocolate coffee beans, if desired.

Chocolate and Yuzu Dessert

SERVES 6–8

DIFFICULTY ★ ★ ★

PREPARE: 1½ hours

COOK: 30 minutes

REST: 30 minutes

REFRIGERATE: 3 hours

FREEZE: 5 hours

Macarons
- 85 g ground almonds, sifted
- 140 g icing sugar, sifted
- 2 egg whites
- 20 g caster sugar

Yuzu Crème Brûlée
- 1 leaf gelatine
- 1 egg yolk
- 20 g caster sugar
- 80 ml whipping cream
- 60 g candied yuzu (can be found in Asian (Korean) supermarkets)

Chocolate Mousse
- 75 g dark chocolate
- 2 egg yolks
- 25 g caster sugar
- 150 ml whipping cream

Glaze
- 2½ leaves gelatine
- 50 ml water
- 40 ml whipping cream
- 100 g caster sugar
- 60 g glucose
- 10 g cocoa butter
- 50 g unsweetened cocoa powder

Preheat the oven to 180°C (350°F). Line two 30 x 38 cm baking trays with baking parchment.

Macarons: Follow the recipe on page 288 but without adding the cocoa powder. Pipe two 14 cm spiral discs onto one of the baking trays. Bake for 18 minutes. Pipe 15 x 2 cm balls onto the second tray. Leave to rest at room temperature for 20-30 minutes, then bake for 10 to 15 minutes. Half way through baking, lower the oven temperature to 120-130°C (250-275°F). Take out the macarons and refrigerate as soon as the domed tops harden.

Yuzu Crème Brûlée: Soften the gelatine leaf in cold water. Make a crème Anglaise following the recipe on page 208. Squeeze excess water from the gelatine leaf, then mix into the crème Anglaise together with the candied yuzu. Leave to cool, then refrigerate. Whisk the mixture, then pour into a piping bag fitted with a plain nozzle.

Chocolate Mousse: Chop the chocolate and melt over a bain-marie. Whisk the egg yolks in a bowl with the sugar until pale and thick. Whip the cream to stiff peaks. Quickly whisk ⅓ of the cream into the egg yolk-sugar mixture, then gently fold in the remaining cream.

Line a baking tray with baking parchment. Place a 16 cm diameter circle on the tray and line with the chocolate mousse. Place a macaron disc in the base of the circle. Cover with a layer of chocolate mousse. Spread a layer of yuzu crème brûlée over it and top with the second macaron disc. Cover with chocolate mousse and smooth with a palette knife. Freeze for 5 hours.

Glaze: Soften the gelatine leaves in cold water. Bring the water, cream, sugar, glucose and cocoa butter to the boil. Squeeze the excess water from the gelatine leaves. Whisk in the gelatine and cocoa powder off the heat. Pour into a bowl and cover with cling film. Leave to cool to 30-32°C.

Remove the dessert from the mould and glaze as indicated on page 14. Attach the macaron shells to the side of the dessert and refrigerate for 3 hours before serving.

Chocolate-Raspberry Mogador

SERVES 10

DIFFICULTY ★ ★ ★

PREPARE: 1 hour

COOK: 35 minutes

Raspberry Chocolate Cake
- 100 g dark chocolate
- 100 g unsalted butter
- 4 egg yolks
- 4 egg whites
- 40 g caster sugar
- 50 g flour, sifted
- 100 g frozen raspberries

Raspberry Syrup
- 50 ml water
- 50 g caster sugar
- 2 tbsp (30 ml) raspberry eau-de-vie

Chocolate Mousse
- 75 g dark (55%) chocolate
- 200 ml whipping cream
- 3 egg yolks
- 25 ml water
- 50 g caster sugar

Decoration
- 100 g raspberry jam
- 125 g raspberries
- 100 g chocolate shavings (p.397)

Preheat the oven to 165°C (325°F). Line a baking tray with baking parchment. Butter a 22 cm tart ring and place it on the baking tray.

Raspberry Chocolate Cake: Finely chop the chocolate and melt over a bain-marie. Remove from the heat, add the butter, stir until smooth; add the egg yolks. In a separate bowl, whisk the egg whites, gradually adding the sugar until smooth, shiny and stiff peaks form. Whisk a third of the egg whites into the chocolate mixture to lighten it. Using a flexible spatula, carefully fold in the remainder in two batches then add the sifted flour. Pour the batter into the tart ring, arrange the raspberries on the surface and bake for 35 minutes. Cool in the tart ring.

Raspberry Syrup: Put the water and sugar into a saucepan, stir over low heat until the sugar dissolves, increase the heat and boil for 2 minutes; cool. Add the raspberry eau-de-vie to the cold syrup.

Chocolate Mousse: Chop the chocolate and melt over a bain-marie. Beat the cream until stiff peaks cling to the whisk; refrigerate. Whisk the egg yolks in a large bowl until light and creamy. Put the water and sugar into a saucepan and stir over low heat until the sugar dissolves; bring to the boil and cook for 2 minutes. Carefully pour the syrup down the side of the bowl into the egg yolks, whisking continuously until the mixture thickens and cools. Using a spatula, gradually mix in the melted chocolate then fold in the whipped cream. Fit a piping bag with a plain nozzle and fill with the mousse; set aside.

Put the cake onto a plate and remove the tart ring. Sprinkle or brush with the raspberry syrup; spread with the raspberry jam. Pipe touching balls of chocolate mousse in decreasing layers to form a pyramid. Decorate with raspberries and chocolate shavings.

Chocolate-Mascarpone Dessert

SERVES 8–10

DIFFICULTY ★ ★ ★

PREPARE: 30 minutes

INFUSE: 30 minutes

COOK: 20 minutes

REFRIGERATE: Overnight

- 600 ml milk
- 1 vanilla pod, split
- 50 g semolina
- 50 g caster sugar
- 225 g dark chocolate, chopped
- 4 tbsp (60 ml) rum
- 225 g mascarpone

Decoration
- Strawberries
- Mascarpone

◊ This recipe must be prepared the day before serving.

Pour the milk into a saucepan. Using the point of a knife, scrape the seeds from the vanilla pod into the milk, add the pod and bring to the boil. Remove from the heat, cover and infuse for 30 minutes.

Discard the vanilla pod and bring the milk to the boil again. Remove the saucepan from the heat and stirring continuously, add the semolina in a thin, steady stream. Continue stirring, add the sugar and return the pan to the heat and bring to the boil. Reduce the heat to low and cook for about 20 minutes, stirring often to stop the semolina sticking. Remove from the heat, add the chopped chocolate and stir until melted. Blend in the rum and mascarpone.

Rinse a 25 x 8 cm loaf pan with cold water (do not dry) then fill with the mascarpone-chocolate mixture. Cover with cling film; refrigerate overnight.

Just before serving, turn the dessert out; decorate with fresh strawberries and mascarpone.

CHEF'S TIP: When cooking the semolina, add some raisins, if desired.

Creole Chocolate Flan with Guava Caramel

SERVES 8

DIFFICULTY: ★ ★ ★

PREPARE: 30 minutes

COOK: 30 minutes

REFRIGERATE: 2 hours

Guava Caramel
• 100 ml water
• 200 g caster sugar
• 160 g guava purée

Creole Chocolate Flan
• 120 g dark chocolate
• 5 eggs
• 400 ml milk
• 150 g dulce de leche
• 100 ml sweetened condensed milk
• 1 tsp vanilla extract
• 1 pinch ground cinnamon

Preheat the oven to 150°C (300°F).

Guava Caramel: Heat the water and sugar in a saucepan; stir until the sugar dissolves. Increase the heat and boil (without stirring) for about 10 minutes, or until the syrup becomes a golden caramel colour. Remove from the heat and add the guava purée; take care as the caramel will spit violently when the liquid is added. Into 8 small bowls or ramekins pour an equal amount of the guava caramel.

Creole Chocolate Flan: Finely chop the chocolate and place in a large bowl. Whisk the eggs in a separate bowl. Combine the milk, dulce de leche and sweetened condensed milk in a saucepan; heat until simmering. Pour the milk mixture over the chocolate and stir until smooth. Stir the chocolate mixture into the whisked eggs, then add the vanilla extract and ground cinnamon. Strain the flan mixture through a sieve over a bowl and distribute between the bowls of guava caramel.

Stand the bowls in a large roasting tin and half-fill the tin with boiling water. Transfer to the oven and cook for 30 minutes, or until the flans are firm. Remove the bowls from the roasting tin, cool and refrigerate for 2 hours before serving.

Chocolate Fondant with Praline Cream

SERVES 10

DIFFICULTY ★ ★ ★

PREPARE: 1 hour

REFRIGERATE: 4 – 5 hours

Chocolate Fondant
- 270 g dark chocolate
- 165 g soft unsalted butter
- 4 egg yolks
- 4 egg whites
- 60 g caster sugar

Praline Cream
- 250 ml milk
- 3 egg yolks
- 70 g caster sugar
- 100 g praline paste (p.325)

◇See p.208: Making a crème Anglaise.

Line a 25 x 10 cm loaf tin with baking parchment.

Chocolate Fondant: Chop the chocolate and melt over a bain-marie. Remove from the heat and add the butter, stir until smooth; blend in the egg yolks. Put the egg whites into a bowl and whisk until frothy. Add 20 g of the sugar a little at a time, whisking until the egg whites are smooth and shiny. Gradually add the remaining sugar, whisking until stiff peaks form. Whisk $1/3$ of the egg whites into the chocolate mixture to lighten it. Using a spatula, carefully fold in the remainder in two batches. Pour the mixture into the prepared loaf tin and refrigerate for 4– 5 hours, or until firm.

Praline Cream: Bring the milk to the boil. Beat the egg yolks and sugar until pale yellow and creamy. Whisk in $1/3$ of the hot milk and mix well to combine; pour the mixture into the remaining hot milk. Stirring constantly with a wooden spoon, cook over low heat until the cream is thickened and coats the back of the spoon. (Do not allow to boil!) Remove from the heat immediately, strain into a bowl and blend in the praline paste. Cool the cream then refrigerate until required.

Dip the bottom of the loaf tin into very hot water momentarily to loosen. Place a serving platter on top and turn the tin upside down so the cake is turned out onto the platter. Serve the praline cream separately.

CHEF'S TIP: You can also prepare individual fondants by using small ramekins or moulds instead of the loaf tin.

Chocolate Fondue

SERVES 4

DIFFICULTY ★ ★ ★

PREPARE: 20 minutes

- 500 g dark chocolate
- 300 ml whipping cream
- 50 ml milk
- 1 vanilla pod, split
- 1 banana
- 3 kiwis
- 3–4 slices pineapple, fresh or tinned
- 250 g strawberries

Chop the chocolate and set aside. Put the cream and milk into a saucepan. Using the point of a knife, scrape the seeds from the vanilla pod into the saucepan, add the pod and heat slowly until simmering. Remove from the heat and discard the vanilla pod. Add the chopped chocolate to the cream and milk mixture and stir until completely melted. Place over a bain-marie to keep warm.

Slice or cut the fruit in pieces but leave the strawberries whole.

Thread the fruit on 4 metal skewers and serve with individual bowls of melted chocolate. Or, place a larger bowl of the chocolate, along with the fruit and skewers in the centre of the table and let the guests help themselves.

CHEF'S TIP: Vary your choice of fruit, according to the season.

Chocolate Hedgehog

SERVES **8**

DIFFICULTY ★ ★ ★

PREPARE: 1 hour

COOK: 20 minutes

Chocolate Sponge
• 3 egg yolks
• 75 g caster sugar
• 3 egg whites
• 70 g flour, sifted
• 15 g unsweetened cocoa
  powder, sifted

Syrup
• 50 ml water
• 50 g caster sugar

Chocolate Whipped Cream
• 125 g dark chocolate
• 300 g whipping cream

Decoration
• 50 g flaked almonds
• Unsweetened cocoa powder,
  sifted

◊ See p.211: Making
meringue, batter or pastry
discs.

Preheat the oven to 165°C (325°F). Prepare 2 baking trays and 2 pieces of baking parchment. Trace 3 circles – 16 cm, 14 cm and 12 cm – on the paper; turn the marked sides over onto the baking trays.

Chocolate Sponge: Whisk the egg yolks and 40 g of the sugar until pale yellow and creamy. Whisk the egg whites in a separate bowl, gradually adding the remaining sugar until the egg whites are smooth, shiny and stiff peaks form. Gently fold in the egg yolk-sugar mixture then the sifted flour and cocoa powder. Fit a piping bag with a plain nozzle, and fill with the batter. Start piping in the centre of each traced circle, working outwards in a spiral until filled. Bake the layers for 15 minutes then set aside. (Do not turn off the oven; maintain it at the same temperature.)

Syrup: Heat the water and sugar in a saucepan over low heat until the sugar dissolves then increase the heat and boil for 2 minutes; cool.

Chocolate Whipped Cream: Chop the chocolate and melt over a bain-marie. Beat the cream until stiff peaks cling to the whisk. Quickly whisk in the warm melted chocolate. Fit a piping bag with a plain nozzle and fill with the chocolate whipped cream; set aside.

Line a baking tray with baking parchment and sprinkle the almonds over it. Toast the almonds in the oven for about 5 minutes, or until lightly golden.

Place the 16 cm sponge layer on a plate and sprinkle or brush with syrup. Pipe touching balls of chocolate whipped cream over the surface. Put the 14 cm layer on top, repeat the syrup and the cream; repeat the operation for the 12 cm layer. Pipe further chocolate whipped cream balls over the surface of the cake to form a pyramid. Dust with sifted cocoa powder and insert the flaked almonds to resemble 'spikes'.

Chocolate Marquise

SERVES 12

DIFFICULTY ★ ★ ★

PREPARE: 1 hour

FREEZE: 30 minutes

REFRIGERATE: 1 hour
20 minutes

Chocolate Discs
• 150 g dark chocolate
• 200 g praline paste
• 120 g dentelle crêpes, lightly crushed

Chocolate Mousse
• 275 g dark chocolate
• 550 ml whipping cream

Dark Chocolate Glaze
• 150 g dark chocolate
• 150 ml whipping cream
• 75 g mild honey
• 20 g unsalted butter

Decoration (optional)
• Chocolate wafers

◊ See p.14: Glazing a cake or entremets.

Chocolate Discs: Trace two 20 cm circles on baking parchment. Finely chop the chocolate and melt over a bain-marie. Add the praline paste (see p. 325), stir until smooth then add the crushed dentelle crêpes. Spread a 0.5 cm thick layer of the mixture in each of the traced circles; freeze the discs for 30 minutes.

Chocolate Mousse: Place the chocolate in a bowl and melt over a slowly simmering bain-marie until the temperature reaches approximately 45°C on a digital thermometer. Beat the cream until firm peaks cling to the whisk. Whisking quickly, add about $1/3$ of the whipped cream to the hot chocolate. Pour the mixture over the remaining cream and fold in gently with the whisk or a spatula to evenly blend the ingredients; set aside.

Place a 3 x 22 cm pastry ring on a plate; put a chocolate disc into it. Fit a piping bag with a plain nozzle, and fill with the mousse. Pipe a 1 cm layer of chocolate mousse over the disc. Place the other disc on top, press down lightly and pipe on enough chocolate mousse to fill the pastry ring; smooth with a spatula. Refrigerate the cake for 1 hour, or until firm.

Dark Chocolate Glaze: Finely chop the chocolate and place in a large bowl. Heat the cream and honey in a saucepan until simmering and pour over the chocolate; stir until smooth. Add the butter and set aside at room temperature.

Remove the cake from the refrigerator. Warm the pastry ring by running a hot, damp tea towel around it and slide it off the cake. Put the cake back into the refrigerator for 10 minutes. Put a rack over a bowl, place the cake on it and pour the glaze over the entire surface; smooth with a palette knife. When the glaze stops trickling into the bowl, transfer the marquise to a serving platter; if desired, cut chocolate wafers in half and press into the side as decoration. Refrigerate for about 10 minutes until firm. Cut into individual portions; serve.

CHEF'S TIP: The praline paste can be replaced with a chocolate-hazelnut spread.

Chocolate Meringues

SERVES 10

DIFFICULTY ★ ★ ★

PREPARE: 30 minutes

COOK: 1 hour

COOL: 1 hour

Chocolate Meringues
- 4 egg whites
- 120 g caster sugar
- 100 g icing sugar, sifted
- 20 g unsweetened cocoa powder, sifted

Chocolate Chantilly Cream
- 100 g dark (66%) chocolate, chopped
- 200 ml whipping cream
- 20 g icing sugar

Decoration
- 200 g raspberries
- Icing sugar

◇ See p.211: Making meringue, batter or pastry discs.

Preheat the oven to 100°C (215°F). Trace ten 8 cm circles on baking parchment and turn the marked sides over onto the baking tray(s).

Chocolate Meringues: Put the egg whites into a bowl and whisk until frothy. Add 40 g of the caster sugar a little at a time, whisking until the egg whites are smooth and shiny. Gradually add the remaining sugar, whisking until stiff peaks form. Carefully fold in the sifted icing sugar and cocoa powder. Fit a piping bag with a star nozzle and fill with the chocolate meringue. Start piping in the centre of the traced circles, working outwards in a spiral until filled. Pipe a raised border on each edge to form a 'nest'. Bake the meringues for 1 hour, or until crisp. Remove from the baking tray(s); cool on a rack at room temperature for 1 hour.

Chocolate Chantilly Cream: Melt the chocolate over a bain-marie. Whisk the cream until it begins to firm, add the icing sugar and continue whisking until stiff peaks cling to the whisk. Quickly whisk in the warm melted chocolate.

Divide the chocolate Chantilly cream evenly between the meringue nests. Decorate with raspberries and dust with sifted icing sugar.

CHEF'S TIP: You can make the meringues several weeks in advance if you store them in a dry place.

Chocolate Mousse

SERVES 8

DIFFICULTY ★ ★ ★

PREPARE: 30 minutes

REFRIGERATE: 3 hours min.

- 125 g dark (55%) chocolate
- 50 g unsalted butter
- 150 ml whipping cream
- 2 egg yolks
- 3 egg whites
- 45 g caster sugar

Chop the chocolate and melt over a bain-marie, add the butter; stir until smooth. Set aside to cool.

Whisk the cream in a large bowl until stiff peaks cling to the whisk. Beat the egg yolks and blend into the cream. Refrigerate.

Put the egg whites into a bowl and whisk until frothy. Add 15 g of the sugar a little at a time, whisking until the egg whites are smooth and shiny. Gradually add the remaining sugar, whisking until stiff peaks form.

Whisk $1/3$ of the egg whites into the cream-egg yolk mixture to lighten it. Using a spatula, carefully fold in the remainder in 2 separate batches. Quickly whisk in the melted chocolate mixture, making sure it is thoroughly incorporated. Refrigerate the chocolate mousse for at least 3 hours, or until firm before serving.

CHEF'S TIP: To obtain a lighter mousse, remove the eggs from the refrigerator well before starting the recipe.

White Chocolate Mousse

SERVES **10**

DIFFICULTY ★ ★ ★

PREPARE: 20 minutes

REFRIGERATE: 3 hours min.

White Chocolate Mousse
- 600 ml whipping cream
- 300 g white chocolate

Decoration
- 150 g dark chocolate
  shavings (p.397)

Beat the cream until firm peaks cling to the whisk. Set aside ½ cup in a bowl and refrigerate the rest. Finely chop the chocolate and melt over a slowly simmering bain-marie until the temperature reaches no more than 40°C on a digital thermometer. Whisking quickly, pour the melted chocolate over the whisked cream. Then, using a whisk or spatula, fold in the refrigerated whipped cream gently until the ingredients are evenly blended.

Divide the mousse equally between 10 dessert glasses and refrigerate for at least 3 hours, or until firm.

About 30 minutes before serving, remove the mousse-filled glasses from the refrigerator, to take the chill off them; decorate with dark chocolate shavings.

CHEF'S TIP: To whisk cream more easily, refrigerate it for 15 minutes in the bowl you are going to use.

Darjeeling Infused Chocolate Mousse, Columbian Coffee Cream

SERVES 4

DIFFICULTY ★ ★ ★

PREPARE: 50 minutes

REFRIGERATE: 3 hours min.

Darjeeling Infused Chocolate Mousse
- 50 ml water
- 1 Darjeeling tea bag
- 200 g dark chocolate
- 25 g unsalted butter
- 75 g caster sugar
- 60 g toasted hazelnuts, crushed (optional)
- 3 egg yolks
- 3 egg whites

Columbian Coffee Cream
- 250 ml milk
- 1 tsp instant Columbian coffee
- 3 egg yolks
- 70 g caster sugar

Chantilly Cream
- 200 ml whipping cream
- 1 or 2 drops vanilla extract
- 20 g icing sugar

Decoration
- Mint leaves

Darjeeling Infused Chocolate Mousse: Boil the water then add the tea bag; infuse for 10 minutes then discard the bag. Chop the chocolate and place in a bowl with the butter and 35 g of the sugar; melt over a bain-marie without stirring. Add the hazelnuts (if desired) and pour in the tea. Remove the mixture from the bain-marie and add the egg yolks; set aside to cool. In a separate bowl, whisk the egg whites, gradually adding the remaining sugar until the whites are smooth, shiny and stiff peaks form. Whisk $1/3$ of the egg whites into the chocolate mixture to lighten it, gently fold in the remainder in 2 separate batches. Divide the mousse evenly between 4 dessert bowls; refrigerate for at least 3 hours, or until firm.

Columbian Coffee Cream: Bring the milk and coffee slowly to the boil. Beat the egg yolks and sugar until pale yellow and creamy. Stir in $1/3$ of the hot milk and mix well to combine; pour the mixture into the remaining hot milk. Stir constantly with a wooden spoon over low heat until the cream is thickened and coats the back of the spoon. (Do not allow to boil!) Remove from the heat immediately, strain into a bowl and cool; refrigerate.

Chantilly Cream: Combine the cream and vanilla extract; whisk until the cream begins to firm. Add the icing sugar and continue whisking until firm peaks cling to the whisk. Fit a piping bag with a plain round nozzle and fill with the Chantilly.

Decorate the surfaces of the mousses with Chantilly and mint leaves. Serve the Columbian coffee cream separately.

Hazelnut and Whisky Chocolate Mousse

SERVES 8–10

DIFFICULTY ★ ★ ★

PREPARE: 30 minutes

COOK: 10 minutes

REFRIGERATE: 3 hours min.

- 200 g blanched hazelnuts, crushed
- 450 g dark (55%) chocolate
- 30 g unsalted butter
- 200 g caster sugar
- 6 egg yolks
- 85 ml whisky
- 6 egg whites

Decoration
- Chocolate shavings (p.397)

Preheat the oven to 180°C (350°F).

Cover a baking tray with baking parchment. Spread the crushed hazelnuts on it, transfer to the oven for about 5 minutes and toast until fragrant and golden.

Chop the chocolate and place in a bowl with the butter and 100 g of the sugar; melt over a bain-marie without stirring. Remove from the heat and stir in the egg yolks, then add 60 g of the toasted hazelnuts and the whisky.

Put the egg whites into a separate bowl and whisk until frothy. Add 30 g of the remaining sugar a little at a time whisking until the egg whites are smooth and shiny. Gradually blend in the remaining sugar, whisking until stiff peaks form. Whisk $1/3$ of the egg whites into the chocolate mixture to lighten it, gently fold in the remainder in 2 separate batches.

Divide the mousse evenly between 8–10 dessert bowls; refrigerate for at least 3 hours, or until firm. Just before serving, decorate with the remaining hazelnuts and chocolate shavings.

Chocolate-Praline Mousse

SERVES 10

DIFFICULTY ★ ★ ★

PREPARE: 1 hour

REFRIGERATE: 3 hours min.

Almond-Hazelnut Praline Paste
- 30 ml water
- 150 g caster sugar
- 75 g blanched almonds
- 75 g blanched hazelnuts

Dark Chocolate Mousse
- 300 g dark (55%) chocolate
- 350 ml whipping cream
- 6 egg yolks
- 6 egg whites
- 80 g caster sugar

◊ See p.325: Making praline paste.

Almond-Hazelnut Praline Paste: Put the water and sugar in a medium saucepan over low heat and stir until the sugar dissolves completely. Increase the heat and bring to the boil. Stir in the blanched almonds and hazelnuts using a wooden spoon. Remove from the heat and continue stirring until the sugar crystallises covering the nuts with a white powder. Return the saucepan to the heat until the sugar melts and the nuts turn golden brown. Spread the mixture on an oiled baking tray; cool. When cold, break the praline in pieces, place in a food processor and grind, first to a powder then to a creamy paste. To do so, it will be necessary to stop the food processor often, and stir the powder with a spatula. (To avoid overworking the food processor, grind the praline in several batches.) Set the praline paste aside in a bowl.

Dark Chocolate Mousse: Chop the chocolate and melt over a bain-marie; cool. Whisk the cream until stiff peaks cling to the whisk, blend in the egg yolks; refrigerate. Put the egg whites into a bowl and whisk until frothy. Add 25 g of the sugar a little at a time, whisking until the egg whites are smooth and shiny. Gradually add the remaining sugar, whisking until stiff peaks form. Whisk $1/3$ of the egg whites into the whipped cream and egg mixture to lighten it. Using a flexible spatula, carefully fold in the remainder in 2 separate batches. Quickly whisk in the melted chocolate.

Blend the praline paste into the dark chocolate mousse using a spatula. Refrigerate for at least 3 hours before serving.

Chocolate-Orange Mousse

MAKES 6

DIFFICULTY ★ ★ ★

PREPARE: 45 minutes

COOK: 15 minutes

REFRIGERATE: 3 hours min.

Glazed Orange Zests
• 2 oranges
• 100 ml water
• 100 g caster sugar

Chocolate Mousse
• 150 g dark chocolate
• 200 ml whipping cream
• 3 egg yolks
• 3 egg whites
• 50 g caster sugar

Glazed Orange Zests: Zest the oranges using a vegetable peeler to remove strips of rind (without the pith). Cut the zest into long thin shreds. Bring a small saucepan of water to the boil. Add the zests, blanch for 1 minute, drain and rinse under cold water. Heat the water and sugar over low heat, and stir until the sugar dissolves; increase the heat and boil for 2 minutes. Lower the heat, add the orange zests and simmer for 15 minutes until tender; drain and set aside.

Chocolate Mousse: Chop the chocolate and melt over a bain-marie; cool. Whisk the cream until stiff peaks cling to the whisk, blend in the egg yolks; refrigerate. Put the egg whites into a bowl and whisk until frothy. Add 20 g of the sugar little by little, whisking until the egg whites are smooth and shiny. Gradually blend in the remaining sugar, whisking until stiff peaks form. Whisk $1/3$ of the egg whites into the whipped cream-egg yolk mixture to lighten it; carefully fold in the remainder in 2 separate batches. Quickly whisk in the melted chocolate, making certain it is thoroughly incorporated.

Set a few glazed orange zests aside for decoration. Add the remainder to the chocolate mousse; refrigerate for at least 3 hours until firm. Before serving, decorate with the reserved glazed orange zests.

Frozen Chocolate Mousse

SERVES 10

DIFFICULTY ★ ★ ★

PREPARE: 10 minutes

REFRIGERATE: 45 minutes

FREEZE: 3 hours

- 190 g dark chocolate
- 1 egg yolk
- 40 g caster sugar
- 250 ml milk
- 50 ml whipping cream
- 15 g powdered milk
- 30 g honey

Decoration
- 100 g dark chocolate shavings (see p.397)
- Icing sugar

Chop the chocolate and place in a bowl. In a separate bowl, whisk the egg yolk with the sugar until pale and creamy.

Bring the milk, cream, powdered milk and honey to the boil in a saucepan. Quickly whisk $^1/_3$ of this liquid into the egg yolk-sugar mixture. Return to the saucepan and cook over a low heat, stirring constantly with a wooden spoon, until the cream thickens and coats the back of the spoon (take care not to boil the cream). Pour the cream over the chocolate and gently fold in with a flexible spatula.

Pour into a Chantilly siphon, insert two gas cartridges, then shake vigorously to combine the gas with the mixture to make it light and airy.

Refrigerate for 45 minutes. Once the mousse is cold, hold the siphon upside down and dispense the mousse into 4 cm high, 5 cm diameter moulds. Decorate with chocolate shavings and freeze for 3 hours before serving. You can also dust the frozen mousses with icing sugar before serving.

Nutty Chocolate Spread

SERVES 8

DIFFICULTY ★ ★ ★

PREPARE: 40 minutes

- 80 g dark chocolate
- 20 g mild honey
- 160 ml whipping cream

Hazelnut-Almond Praline Paste

- 60 ml water
- 200 g caster sugar
- 150 g blanched hazelnuts
- 50 g blanched almonds
- 2 tbsp (30 ml) hazelnut oil

◇ See p.325: Making praline paste.

Finely chop the chocolate and place in a bowl with the honey. Heat the cream until simmering, pour over the chocolate and honey; stir to combine. Set aside.

Hazelnut-Almond Praline Paste: Put the water and sugar into a saucepan over low heat and stir until the sugar is completely melted. Increase the heat and bring to the boil without stirring. Using a wooden spoon, stir in the hazelnuts and almonds. Remove from the heat and continue stirring until the sugar crystallises covering the nuts with a white powder. Return the saucepan to the heat until the sugar melts and the nuts turn golden brown. Spread the mixture on an oiled baking tray; cool. When cold, break the praline into pieces, place in a food processor and grind – first to a powder then to a creamy paste. To do so, it will be necessary to stop the food processor often, and stir the powder with a flexible spatula. (To avoid overworking the food processor, grind the praline in several batches.) Set the praline paste aside in a bowl.

Add a little praline paste to the chocolate mixture using a spatula, then add the remainder and the hazelnut oil. Cut down to the bottom of the mixture with the spatula, lift up the contents, and bring the spatula up the side of the bowl; continue until the mixture is shiny. Transfer to the bowl of a food processor and pulse or process until smooth. Store in a glass container for 2–3 weeks at room temperature.

CHEF'S TIP: The dark chocolate in this recipe can be replaced with milk chocolate. Also, the hazelnut oil could be substituted with walnut oil.

Little Chocolate Pots

MAKES 6

DIFFICULTY ★ ★ ★

PREPARE: 15 minutes

COOK: 25–30 minutes

- 150 g dark (66%) chocolate
- 200 ml milk
- 300 ml whipping cream
- 4 egg yolks
- 60 g caster sugar

Preheat the oven to 170°C (335°F).

Chop the chocolate and place in a saucepan; add the milk and cream. Heat slowly until the chocolate melts and the mixture barely simmers. Remove from the heat. Beat the egg yolks and sugar until pale yellow and creamy. Stir in the chocolate mixture using a wooden spoon; strain into a bowl. Skim the froth from the surface of the chocolate cream with a spoon.

Divide the chocolate cream equally between six 9 cm ramekins (125 ml capacity). Stand the ramekins in a large roasting tin half filled with boiling water. Transfer to the oven and cook for 25–30 minutes, or until the chocolate creams puff very slightly and still tremble in the middle. Remove from the roasting tin and cool. Serve the chocolate pots cold.

CHEF'S TIP: The little chocolate pots can be kept refrigerated for 2–3 days. If desired, decorate with Chantilly cream and grated chocolate.

Coffee, Chocolate and Vanilla Cream Pots

MAKES 12

DIFFICULTY ★ ★ ★

PREPARE: 10 minutes

COOK: 20–25 minutes

- 1 tsp instant coffee
- 2 tbsp unsweetened cocoa powder
- 750 ml milk
- 150 g caster sugar
- 1 vanilla pod, split
- 3 eggs
- 2 egg yolks

Preheat the oven to 170°C (335°F).

Prepare 3 large bowls: Place the instant coffee in one, the cocoa powder in another and leave the third bowl empty.

Place the milk and 75 g of the sugar in a saucepan. Using the point of a knife, scrape the seeds from the vanilla pod into the milk and sugar mixture, add the pod and bring to the boil. Remove from the heat.

Beat the whole eggs, egg yolks and remaining sugar until pale yellow and creamy; whisk into the hot milk. Strain and divide the mixture equally between the three large bowls. Whisk the coffee and cocoa mixtures to blend the flavours.

Set aside 12 x 7 cm ramekins (100 ml capacity).

Fill 4 ramekins with the coffee cream, another 4 with the chocolate cream and the remaining 4 with the vanilla cream. If necessary, skim the froth from the surface of the creams with a spoon. Stand the ramekins in a large roasting tin half filled with boiling water. Transfer to the oven and cook for 20 – 25 minutes, or until the point of a knife, inserted into centre of the cream(s) comes out clean. Remove from the roasting tin, cool then refrigerate. Serve the little pots of cream cold – 1 of each of the creams per person.

CHEF'S TIP: If you line the bottom of the roasting tin with absorbent paper, it will stop bubbles from forming in the creams giving them a smooth rather than a grainy texture.

Chocolate Soufflé

SERVES 8

DIFFICULTY ★ ★ ★

PREPARE: 30 minutes

COOK: 45 minutes

Chocolate Pastry Cream
- 115 g dark chocolate
- 500 ml milk
- 1 vanilla pod, split
- 4 egg yolks
- 80 g caster sugar
- 60 g flour
- 6 egg whites
- 30 g caster sugar

Decoration
- Unsweetened cocoa powder, sifted

◇ See p.139: Preparing soufflé dishes.

Chocolate Pastry Cream: Finely chop the chocolate, place in a bowl and melt over a bain-marie. Pour the milk into a saucepan. Using the point of a knife, scrape the seeds from the vanilla pod into the milk, add the pod and bring to the boil; remove from the heat. Put the eggs and sugar into a bowl and beat until pale yellow, thick and creamy; blend in the flour. Remove the vanilla pod and stir half the hot milk quickly into the eggs-sugar-flour mixture, mix well to combine; add the remaining milk. Cook over low heat, stirring continuously with a whisk until the cream thickens. Boil for 1 minute while continuing to stir. Remove from the heat and pour the pastry cream into the melted chocolate; stir until smooth. Cover the surface of the chocolate pastry cream with cling film; cool.

Preheat the oven to 180°C (350°F). Brush a 23 cm soufflé dish with butter and dust evenly with caster sugar, tipping out the excess.

Put the egg whites into a bowl and whisk until frothy. Add 10 g of the sugar a little at a time, whisking until the egg whites are smooth and shiny. Gradually add the remaining sugar, whisking until stiff peaks form.

Whisk a third of the egg whites into the pastry cream to lighten it. Using a spatula, carefully fold in the remainder in 2 separate batches. Pour the mixture into the prepared soufflé dish, filling it completely; smooth the surface with the spatula. Run your thumb around the top of the dish to open a narrow (5 mm) channel between the mixture and the rim. (This will allow the soufflé to rise cleanly and evenly.) Cook for 45 minutes, or until the soufflé has risen. As soon as it comes out of the oven, dust with sifted cocoa powder; serve immediately.

Bitter Chocolate Soufflés

SERVES 6

DIFFICULTY ★ ★ ★

PREPARE: 30 minutes

COOK: 15 minutes

Chocolate Soufflé
- 30 g (55–70%) chocolate
- 30 g unsweetened cocoa powder
- 120 ml water
- 1 egg yolk
- 20 g cornflour
- 6 egg whites
- 90 g caster sugar

Decoration
- Icing sugar, sifted

◊ See p.139: Preparing soufflé dishes.

Preheat the oven to 180°C (350°F). Brush six 8 cm ramekins with butter and dust evenly with caster sugar, tipping out the excess.

Chocolate Soufflé: Finely chop the chocolate and place in a bowl. Put the cocoa powder and water into a saucepan, stir to combine and bring to the boil. Pour the hot mixture over the chocolate, stirring until smooth; set aside until cool. Blend in the egg yolk then the cornflour.

Put the egg whites into a bowl and whisk until frothy. Add 30 g of the sugar a little at a time, whisking until the egg whites are smooth and shiny. Gradually add the remaining sugar, whisking until stiff peaks form.

Whisk $1/3$ of the egg whites into the chocolate mixture to lighten it. Use a spatula and carefully fold in the remainder in two separate batches. Divide the mixture evenly between the ramekins; smooth the surface with the spatula. Run the thumb around the tops of the ramekins to open a narrow (5 mm) channel between the mixture and the rim. (This will allow the soufflés to rise cleanly and evenly.) Cook for 15 minutes, or until risen. As soon as the soufflés come out of the oven, dust with sifted icing sugar; serve immediately.

Chocolate-Coffee Soufflés

SERVES 6

DIFFICULTY ★ ★ ★

PREPARE: 1 hour

FREEZE: 2 hours

COOK: 15 minutes

Coffee Ganache Discs
- 75 g dark chocolate
- 75 ml whipping cream
- ½ tsp instant coffee

Chocolate Soufflé
- 60 g dark chocolate
- 60 g unsweetened cocoa powder
- 240 ml water
- 2 egg yolks
- 4 egg whites
- 50 g caster sugar

◇ See p.139: Preparing soufflé dishes.

Coffee Ganache Discs: Cover a baking tray with baking parchment. Coarsely chop the chocolate and place in a bowl. Heat the cream and instant coffee until simmering, pour over the chocolate; stir until smooth. Use a teaspoon to form 24 small discs on the baking tray; freeze for 2 hours.

Preheat the oven to 180°C (350° F). Brush six 8 cm ramekins with butter and dust evenly with caster sugar, tipping out the excess.

Chocolate Soufflé: Finely chop the chocolate and place in a bowl. Put the cocoa powder and water into a saucepan, stir to combine and bring to the boil. Pour the hot mixture over the chocolate, stirring until smooth; set aside until cold then blend in the egg yolks.

Put the egg whites into a bowl and whisk until frothy. Add 15 g of the sugar a little at a time, whisking until the egg whites are smooth and shiny. Gradually add the remaining sugar, whisking until stiff peaks form.

Whisk $1/3$ of the egg whites into the chocolate mixture to lighten it. Use a spatula and carefully fold in the remainder in 2 separate batches. Pour the mixture into the ramekins, filling them to the half-way mark. Place 4 ganache discs in each ramekin then fill with the remaining soufflé mixture; smooth the surface with the spatula. Run your thumb around the tops of the ramekins to open a narrow (5 mm) channel between the mixture and the rim. (This will allow the soufflés to rise cleanly and evenly.) Cook for 15 minutes, or until risen. As soon as the soufflés come out of the oven, dust with icing sugar; serve immediately.

White Chocolate Soufflés

SERVES 6

DIFFICULTY ★ ★ ★

PREPARE: 30 minutes

COOK: 20 minutes

White Chocolate Pastry Cream
- 125 g white chocolate
- 300 ml milk
- 4 egg yolks
- 80 g caster sugar
- 20 g flour

- 10 egg whites
- 80 g caster sugar

Decoration
- Icing sugar, sifted

◊ See p.139: Preparing soufflé dishes.

Preheat the oven to 180°C (350°F). Brush twelve 8 cm ramekins with butter and dust evenly with caster sugar, tipping out the excess.

White Chocolate Pastry Cream: Finely chop the chocolate and place in a bowl. Pour the milk into a saucepan and bring to the boil; remove from the heat. Put the eggs and sugar into a bowl and beat until pale yellow and creamy; add the flour. Whisk one half of the hot milk quickly into the egg yolk-sugar-flour mixture; add the remaining milk. Return to the heat and cook over low heat, whisking continuously until the cream thickens. Boil for 1 minute while continuing to whisk. Remove from the heat and pour the mixture over the chopped chocolate; stir until smooth. Cover the surface of the chocolate pastry cream with cling film; cool.

Put the egg whites into a bowl and whisk until frothy. Add 25 g of the sugar a little at a time, whisking until the egg whites are smooth and shiny. Gradually add the remaining sugar, whisking until stiff peaks form.

Whisk $1/3$ of the egg whites into the chocolate mixture to lighten it. Using a spatula, carefully fold in the remainder in 2 separate batches. Divide the mixture evenly between the ramekins, filling them completely; smooth the surface with the spatula. Run the thumb around the tops of the ramekins to open a narrow (5 mm) channel between the mixture and the rim. (This will allow the soufflés to rise cleanly and evenly.) Cook for 15 minutes, or until risen. As soon as the soufflés come out of the oven, dust with icing sugar; serve immediately.

Chocolate Duo...

SERVES 6

DIFFICULTY ★ ★ ★

PREPARE: 45 minutes

COOK: 15 minutes

FREEZE: 1½ hours approx

Chocolate Sorbet
• 200 g dark chocolate
• 250 ml water
• 250 ml milk
• 170 g caster sugar
• 25 g unsweetened cocoa powder

Moist Chocolate Soufflés
• 100 g dark chocolate
• 60 g unsalted butter
• 4 egg yolks
• 4 egg whites
• 50 g caster sugar

Decoration
• Icing sugar, sifted

◊ See p.139: Preparing soufflé dishes.

Chocolate Sorbet: Finely chop the chocolate and place in a bowl. Put the water, milk, sugar and cocoa powder in a saucepan, stir until the sugar dissolves and bring to the boil. Pour over the chopped chocolate, stirring until smooth and strain. Stand the bowl in crushed ice until the mixture is cold. Pour the mixture into an ice-cream maker (pre-frozen, if necessary) and freeze-churn according to the manufacturer's instructions (about 30 minutes). Remove the sorbet from the machine and transfer it to the freezer to harden for a minimum of 1 hour before using.

Preheat the oven to 180°C (350°F). Brush six 8 cm ramekins with butter and dust evenly with caster sugar, tipping out the excess.

Moist Chocolate Soufflés: Finely chop the chocolate and melt with the butter over a bain-marie. Remove from the heat and when cool, add the egg yolks; set aside until cold. Put the egg whites into a bowl and whisk until frothy. Add 20 g of the sugar a little at a time, whisking until the egg whites are smooth and shiny. Gradually add the remaining sugar, whisking until stiff peaks form. Whisk 1/3 of the egg whites into the chocolate mixture to lighten it. Use a spatula and carefully fold in the remainder, in 2 separate batches. Divide the mixture evenly between the ramekins; smooth the surface with the spatula. Run the thumb around the tops of the ramekins to open a narrow (5 mm) channel between the mixture and the rim. (This will allow the soufflés to rise cleanly and evenly.) Cook for about 15 minutes, or until risen. As soon as the soufflés come out of the oven, dust with icing sugar; serve immediately with the chocolate sorbet in separate bowls.

Chocolate and Matcha Tea Verrines

SERVES 10

DIFFICULTY ★ ★ ★

PREPARE: 40 minutes

COOK: 10– 15 minutes

REFRIGERATE: 1¾ hours

Crumble
- 60 g caster sugar
- 40 g raw cane sugar
- 100 g ground unskinned hazelnuts
- 100 g flour
- ½ tsp salt
- 100 g soft unsalted butter

Matcha Tea Cream
- 1 leaf gelatine
- 4 egg yolks
- 55 g caster sugar
- 25 ml whipping cream
- 2 tsp matcha tea powder

Chocolate Mousse
- 225 g dark chocolate
- 6 eggs
- 45 g soft unsalted butter
- 90 g caster sugar

Decoration
- Icing sugar

◇ See p.208: Make a crème Anglaise

Preheat the oven to 160°C (325°F). Line a 30 cm x 38 cm baking tray with baking parchment.

Crumble: Combine all the ingredients together in a large bowl and rub together until sandy and crumbly in texture. Spread onto a baking tray about 6 mm thick. Refrigerate for 10 minutes. Crumble the dough, then bake for 10– 15 minutes.

Matcha Tea Cream: Soften the gelatine leaf in cold water. Whisk the egg yolks and sugar in a bowl until pale and thick. Bring the cream and matcha powder to the boil in a saucepan. Pour $1/3$ of this liquid into the egg yolk-sugar mixture while whisking rapidly. Return to the saucepan and cook over a low heat. Stir constantly with a wooden spoon until the cream thickens and coats the back of the spoon (take care not to boil the cream). Pour the crème Anglaise into a bowl. Squeeze excess water from the gelatine leaf and mix into the crème Anglaise. Stir and pour into a piping bag fitted with a plain nozzle. Fill 10 x 100 ml verrines $1/3$ of the way up with the matcha tea cream. Refrigerate for 30 minutes.

Chocolate Mousse: Chop the chocolate and melt over a bain-marie. Separate the eggs. Stir the butter into the chocolate, then add the egg yolks and mix well. In a separate bowl, whisk the egg whites until slightly frothy. Gradually add $1/3$ of the sugar, continuing to whisk the egg whites until smooth and glossy. Add the remaining sugar and whisk to stiff peaks. Fold a third of the egg whites into the chocolate mixture with a flexible spatula, then fold in the remainder. Transfer the mousse to a piping bag fitted with a plain nozzle. Pipe the mousse into the verrines until $2/3$ full.

Dust the crumble with icing sugar, then distribute among the verrines. Refrigerate for 1 hour before serving.

Iced desserts
& sweet drinks

The best way to prepare crème Anglaise

Adapt this version of crème Anglaise using the ingredients listed in the recipe of your choice (see pp.220 or 234).

① Beat 5 egg yolks and 125 g sugar until pale yellow and creamy.

② Using the point of a knife, scrape the seeds from a vanilla pod into 500 ml milk; add the pod and bring the milk slowly to the boil. Beating quickly, pour a third of the hot milk onto the egg yolk-sugar mixture.

③ Pour the mixture into the remaining hot milk. Stirring constantly with a wooden spoon, cook over low heat until the cream is thickened and coats the back of the spoon. (Do not allow to boil!) Remove from the heat immediately and strain into a bowl. Set in a container of crushed ice to cool; stir from time to time.

The best way to prepare choux pastry dough

Adapt this version of choux pastry dough using the ingredients shown in the recipe of your choice (see, for example, pp.234, 264 or 310).

① Cook 50 g unsalted butter, 120 ml water, ½ tsp salt and ½ tsp sugar in a saucepan over low heat. When the butter melts, bring the mixture to the boil; remove from the heat immediately. Tip 75 g of flour into the hot liquid. Stir with a wooden spoon until a firm, smooth paste forms. Return the saucepan to low heat to dry out the paste; continue beating until it forms a ball and pulls away cleanly from the sides of the saucepan.

② Transfer the paste to a bowl; cool for 5 minutes. One by one, add 3 eggs to the paste, beating vigorously after each addition. Beat a fourth egg separately in a bowl and add half to the paste. The paste should be smooth and shiny.

③ The paste is ready to be used, when it falls from the spoon in a point. If it doesn't, add half of another beaten egg. Depending on the egg size and/or flour quality it may be necessary to use all of the egg.

The best way to shape quenelles

Follow the recipe of your choice to create the mixture (see pp.220, 222 or 224); then shape the quenelles as set out below.

① Place 2 tablespoons (or teaspoons) in a glass of hot water. Set out the mixture, serving dishes and/or pastry shells.

② Using one spoon, scoop out a mound of the mixture. Invert the second spoon over the top and shape it into an oval (a quenelle). Slide the top spoon under the quenelle and repeat the operation until the quenelle is smooth and oval.

③ Slide the quenelle off the spoon, into the serving dish or pastry shell.

The best way to make meringue, batter or pastry discs

Prepare the meringue, batter or pastry, following the recipe of your choice, for example, on p.34.

(1) Place a pastry ring or tart tin of the appropriate size on a sheet of baking parchment and using it as a guide, trace a circle on the paper.

(2) Turn the marked side of the baking parchment over onto a baking tray. Fit a piping bag with a round nozzle, pushing it right through to the end of the bag to prevent it leaking when piping.

Twist the bag just above the nozzle to seal it. Make a collar by folding the top of the bag over your hand and fill using a spatula.

(3) Clear any air pockets by twisting the bag until the mixture is visible in the nozzle. Start piping in the centre of the circle, working outwards in a spiral until the circle is filled. Bake according to the directions indicated in the chosen recipe.

Iced Chocolate Log

SERVES 12

DIFFICULTY ★ ★ ★

PREPARE: 1¼ hours

COOK: 12 minutes

FREEZE: 3 hours

Chocolate Sponge
- 100 g dark (70%) chocolate
- 100 g soft unsalted butter
- 4 egg yolks
- 4 egg whites
- 40 g caster sugar
- 50 g flour, sifted

Chocolate Syrup
- 70 ml water
- 75 g caster sugar
- 10 g unsweetened cocoa powder

Dark Chocolate Parfait
- 100 g dark chocolate
- 300 ml whipping cream
- 5 egg yolks
- 40 ml water
- 45 g caster sugar

Chocolate Chantilly Cream
- 100 g dark chocolate
- 200 ml whipping cream
- 20 g icing sugar

Chocolate Shards
- 250 g dark chocolate

◊ You will need a 6 x 35 cm log mould.

Chocolate Sponge: Preheat the oven to 180°C (350°F). Line a 30 x 38 cm oven tray with baking parchment. Chop the chocolate and melt over a bain-marie. Remove from the heat; add the butter then the egg yolks. In a separate bowl, whisk the egg whites, gradually adding the sugar until the whites are smooth, shiny and stiff peaks form; gently fold into the chocolate mixture. Blend in the sifted flour, stirring to combine. Pour a 1 cm layer of the batter into the oven tray, smooth with a palette knife. Bake for 12 minutes. Cool on a rack.

Chocolate Syrup: Combine the water, sugar and cocoa powder in a saucepan and stir over low heat until the sugar dissolves, bring to the boil; cool.

Dark Chocolate Parfait: Chop the chocolate and melt over a bain-marie. Beat the cream until firm and clinging to the whisk; refrigerate. Whisk the egg yolks in a large bowl until pale yellow. Put the water and sugar into a saucepan and stir over low heat until the sugar dissolves; increase the heat and boil for 2 minutes. Pour the syrup slowly down the side of the bowl into the egg yolks, whisking continuously until the mixture thickens and cools. Using a spatula, gradually blend in the melted chocolate then fold in the whipped cream.

Pour the parfait into the log mould, filling it to the ⅓ mark. Cut the chocolate sponge into two rectangles, one measuring 3 x 35 cm and the other, 5 x 35 cm. Place the smaller rectangle on the parfait and brush with chocolate syrup; pour on the remaining parfait. Brush it with chocolate syrup and place the rectangle, syrup side down, on the parfait. Freeze for 3 hours.

Chocolate Chantilly Cream: Melt the chopped chocolate over a bain-marie. Whisk the cream until it begins firm, add the icing sugar and continue whisking until stiff peaks cling to the whisk. Quickly whisk in the warm melted chocolate. Fit a piping bag with a star nozzle and fill with the chocolate Chantilly cream; refrigerate.

Chocolate Shards: Temper the chocolate (pp.320-324) and spread it on a baking tray covered with baking parchment; refrigerate. When hardened, remove from the refrigerator, bring to room temperature and break in large pieces. Pipe chocolate Chantilly rosettes on top and decorate with chocolate shards.

Chocolate Ice Cream Sundae

SERVES 8

DIFFICULTY ★ ★ ★

PREPARE: 45 minutes

FREEZE: 30 minutes

Chocolate Ice Cream
- 120 g dark (55-70%) chocolate
- 30 g unsweetened cooking chocolate
- 500 ml milk
- 6 egg yolks
- 100 g caster sugar

Chocolate Sauce
- 250 g dark chocolate
- 150 ml milk
- 120 ml whipping cream

Chantilly Cream
- 400 ml whipping cream
- 40 g icing sugar

Decoration
- Chocolate shavings (see p.397)

Chocolate Ice Cream: Finely chop the chocolates; place in a large bowl. Bring the milk slowly to the boil. In a separate bowl, beat the egg yolks and sugar until pale yellow and creamy. Whisk in $1/3$ of the hot milk and mix well to combine; pour the mixture into the remaining hot milk. Stirring constantly with a wooden spoon, cook over low heat until the mixture is thickened and coats the back of the spoon. (Do not allow to boil!) Remove from the heat immediately. Pour over the chopped chocolate and stir until smooth; strain into a bowl. Stand the bowl in crushed ice until the mixture is cold. Pour the mixture into an ice-cream maker (pre-frozen, if necessary) and freeze-churn according to the manufacturer's instructions (about 30 minutes). Remove the ice cream from the machine and transfer it to the freezer before serving.

Chocolate Sauce: Chop the chocolate and place in a bowl. Heat the milk and cream until simmering and pour over the chopped chocolate; stir until smooth.

Chantilly Cream: Whisk the cream until it begins to stiffen, add the icing sugar and continue whisking until firm peaks cling to the whisk. Fit a piping bag with a star nozzle and fill with the Chantilly cream.

Place 3 scoops of chocolate ice cream in each glass and pour in a ribbon of chocolate sauce. Pipe a large rosette of Chantilly cream on top, and decorate with chocolate shavings.

CHEF'S TIP: If you can't find unsweetened cooking chocolate, use chocolate with a high percentage of cocoa, 72% for example.

Chocolate Ice Cream topped with Hot Chocolate Sauce

SERVES 8

DIFFICULTY ★ ★ ★

PREPARE: 30 minutes

FREEZE: 30 minutes

Chocolate Ice Cream

- 120 g dark (55-70%) chocolate
- 30 g unsweetened cooking chocolate
- 500 ml milk
- 6 egg yolks
- 100 g caster sugar

Chocolate Sauce

- 250 g dark chocolate
- 150 ml milk
- 120 ml whipping cream

◇ See p.208: Making a crème Anglaise.

Chocolate Ice Cream: Finely chop the chocolates and place in a large bowl. Bring the milk slowly to the boil. In a separate bowl, beat the egg yolks and sugar until pale yellow and creamy. Whisk in $1/3$ of the hot milk and mix well to combine; pour the mixture into the remaining hot milk. Stirring constantly with a wooden spoon, cook over low heat until thickened and the mixture coats the back of the spoon. (Do not allow to boil!) Remove from the heat immediately. Pour over the chopped chocolate and stir until smooth; strain into a bowl. Stand the bowl in crushed ice until the mixture is cold. Pour the mixture into an ice-cream maker (pre-frozen, if necessary) and freeze-churn according to the manufacturer's instructions (about 30 minutes). Remove the ice cream from the machine and transfer it to the freezer before serving.

Chocolate Sauce: Chop the chocolate and place in a bowl. Heat the milk and cream until simmering and pour over the chopped chocolate; stir until smooth.

Place 3 scoops of chocolate ice cream in each bowl and pour over the hot chocolate sauce.

Chocolate Ice Cream Dessert with Hot Coffee Sabayon

SERVES 4

DIFFICULTY ★ ★ ★

PREPARE: 1½ hours

COOK: 8 minutes

FREEZE: 30 minutes

Chocolate Ice Cream
- 120 g dark (55-70%) chocolate
- 30 g unsweetened cooking chocolate
- 500 ml milk
- 6 egg yolks
- 100 g caster sugar

Sponge
- 3 egg yolks
- 3 egg whites
- 75 g caster sugar
- 75 g flour, sifted

Coffee Syrup
- 50 ml water
- 50 g caster sugar
- 2 tbsp rum
- 1 tbsp coffee liqueur

Coffee Sabayon
- 1½ tsp instant coffee
- 100 ml water
- 4 egg yolks
- 100 g caster sugar
- 1 tsp coffee liqueur

Decoration
- 100 ml Chantilly cream (p.214)
- Unsweetened cocoa powder

Chocolate Ice Cream: Prepare as in the recipe on page 214. Pour the mixture into an ice-cream maker (pre-frozen, if necessary) and freeze-churn according to the manufacturer's instructions (about 30 minutes). Remove the ice cream from the machine and transfer it to the freezer before serving.

Preheat the oven to 180°C (350°F). Prepare 1 or 2 baking tray(s), depending on the oven size. Trace four 8 cm circles on baking parchment and turn the marked side over onto the baking tray(s).

Sponge: Beat the egg yolks until pale yellow. In a separate bowl, whisk the egg whites until frothy. Add 25 g of the sugar a little at a time, whisking until the egg whites are smooth and shiny. Gradually add the remaining sugar, whisking until stiff peaks form. Gently fold in the egg yolks, then the sifted flour. Fit a piping bag with a plain round nozzle and fill it with the batter. Start piping in the centre of each traced circle, working outwards in a spiral until filled. Bake for approximately 8 minutes; set aside until required.

Coffee Syrup: Put the water and sugar into a saucepan and stir over low heat until the sugar dissolves, increase the heat and boil; cool. When cold, add the rum and coffee liqueur.

Coffee Sabayon: Dissolve the instant coffee in the water; set aside. Place the egg yolks and sugar in a heatproof bowl over a bain-marie; whisk until pale and creamy. Pour in the coffee and continue whisking until thick and light and the sabayon falls in a ribbon trail from the whisk; add the coffee liqueur.

Place a 10 cm (depth 4.5 cm) pastry ring on each plate. Put a sponge disc (p.13) into the ring and sprinkle or brush with coffee syrup. Fill with chocolate ice cream and return to the freezer briefly until firm. To serve, remove the pastry rings, decorate with Chantilly cream, pour the hot coffee sabayon over; dust with sifted cocoa powder.

Vanilla Ice Cream in Hot Chocolate Sauce, with Crunchy Spice Biscuits

SERVES 8

DIFFICULTY ★ ★ ★

PREPARE: 1½ hours

REFRIGERATE: Overnight

FREEZE: 30 minutes

COOK: 20 minutes

Crunchy Spice Biscuits

- 100 g caster sugar
- 25 g soft brown sugar
- 200 g flour, sifted
- 100 g unsalted butter
- 1 pinch salt
- ½ tsp baking powder
- 2 pinches ground nutmeg
- ½ tsp ground cinnamon
- 20 ml milk
- 1 egg

Vanilla Ice Cream

- 5 egg yolks
- 125 g caster sugar
- 500 ml milk
- 1 vanilla pod, split
- 50 ml whipping cream

Hot Chocolate Sauce

- 250 g dark chocolate
- 50 g praline paste (p.325)
- 500 ml milk
- 200 ml whipping cream

◊ This recipe must be started a day before serving.

Crunchy Spice Biscuits: The day before serving, put the sugars, sifted flour and unsalted butter into a bowl. Rub the butter into the dry ingredients with your fingertips until the mixture resembles fine breadcrumbs. Blend in the salt, baking powder, nutmeg and cinnamon. Add the milk and egg and mix gently until the dough forms a ball, being careful not to overwork it. Wrap in cling film and refrigerate overnight.

Vanilla Ice Cream: The following day, beat the egg yolks with 60 g of the sugar until pale yellow and creamy. Place the milk and remaining sugar in a saucepan. Using the point of a knife, scrape the seeds from the vanilla pod into the milk and sugar mixture, add the pod and bring slowly to the boil. Whisk $1/3$ of the hot milk into the egg yolk-sugar mixture, mixing well to combine; pour the mixture into the remaining hot milk. Stirring constantly with a wooden spoon, cook over low heat until the mixture is thickened and coats the back of the spoon. (Do not allow to boil!) Stir in the cream and remove from the heat immediately; strain into a bowl. Stand the bowl in crushed ice until the mixture is cold. Pour the mixture into an ice-cream maker (pre-frozen, if necessary) and freeze-churn according to the manufacturer's instructions (about 30 minutes). Remove the ice cream from the machine and transfer it to the freezer before serving.

Preheat the oven to 170°C (335°F). Line a baking tray with baking parchment. Roll out the biscuit dough and cut it in 2 x 10 cm rectangles. Transfer to the baking tray and bake for 20 minutes; cool on a rack.

Hot Chocolate Sauce: Coarsely chop the chocolate and place in a bowl with the praline paste. Heat the milk and cream slowly until simmering. Pour the hot mixture over the chocolate and praline paste, whisking quickly to combine. Use a fine-meshed sieve and strain the sauce into a bowl.

Divide the hot chocolate sauce between 8 rimmed soup dishes. Form the ice cream into quenelles using 2 large spoons (p.210). Place two quenelles in each dish; serve the crunchy spice biscuits on the rim.

White Chocolate Islands in Strawberry Soup

SERVES 8

DIFFICULTY ★ ★ ★

PREPARE: 30 minutes

INFUSE: 30 minutes

REFRIGERATE: 6 hours 30 minutes

White Chocolate Islands
• 150 g white chocolate
• 1 vanilla pod, split
• 150 ml passion fruit juice
• 250 ml coconut milk

Strawberry Soup
• 700 g strawberries
• 2 lemongrass stalks

Decoration
• Reserved vanilla pods

◊ See p.210: Shaping quenelles.

White Chocolate Islands: Chop the white chocolate and place in a bowl. Combine the passion fruit juice and coconut milk in a saucepan. Using the point of a knife, scrape the seeds from a vanilla pod into the saucepan, add the pod and heat slowly until simmering. Remove the saucepan from the heat; infuse for 30 minutes. Remove and rinse the vanilla pod; set aside for decoration. Pour the passion fruit mixture over the chopped chocolate, stir until smooth; let cool. Then place in the refrigerator for 6 hours.

Strawberry Soup: Wash the strawberries. Coarsely chop the lemongrass stalks and 200 g of the strawberries. Place in the bowl of a food processor and process; strain the juice into a bowl using a fine-meshed strainer. Hull and cut the remaining strawberries into quarters and add to the strawberry juice. Refrigerate for at least 30 minutes, or until cold.

Divide the strawberry soup between 8 small dishes. Use 2 spoons to form the white chocolate into quenelles; place 4 in each dish. Use the reserved vanilla pod, along with any extra vanilla pods, to decorate.

White Chocolate-Aniseed Ice Cream topped with Pecans

SERVES 8

DIFFICULTY ★ ★ ★

PREPARE: 35 minutes

FREEZE: 1½ hours

White Chocolate-Aniseed Ice Cream
- 150 g white chocolate
- 6 egg yolks
- 100 g caster sugar
- 500 ml milk
- ½ tsp pastis (or ouzo)

Decoration
- Chopped pecans

◊ See p.210: Shaping quenelles.

White Chocolate-Aniseed Ice Cream: Finely chop the chocolate and place in a large bowl. In a separate bowl, beat the egg yolks and sugar until pale yellow and creamy. Bring the milk slowly to the boil. Whisk $1/3$ of the hot milk into the egg yolk-sugar mixture, mixing well to combine; pour the mixture into the remaining hot milk. Stirring constantly with a wooden spoon, cook over low heat until the mixture is thickened and coats the back of the spoon. (Do not allow to boil!) Remove from the heat immediately. Pour over the chopped chocolate and stir until smooth; strain into a bowl. Stand the bowl in crushed ice until the ice-cream mixture is cold. Add the pastis. Pour the mixture into an ice-cream maker (pre-frozen, if necessary) and freeze-churn according to the manufacturer's instructions (about 30 minutes). Remove the ice cream from the machine and transfer it to the freezer before serving.

Prepare 8 rimmed soup dishes. Use 2 spoons to form the white chocolate-aniseed ice cream into quenelles; place three in each dish. Sprinkle over the chopped pecans.

CHEF'S TIP: This ice cream is delicious with caramelised pecans incorporated into it. Heat 50 g sugar in a saucepan. When it starts to melt and turns a golden colour, add 160 g pecans and cook for 1–2 minutes, stirring with a wooden spoon. Add 15 g unsalted butter and set aside. When you take the ice cream out of the maker and before you freeze it, add ½ of the nuts. Use the other ½ as decoration.

Chocolate Granita

SERVES 4

DIFFICULTY ★ ★ ★

PREPARE: 10 minutes

FREEZE: 2 hours

- 50 g dark chocolate
- 200 ml water
- 40 g caster sugar

Chop the chocolate and place in a bowl. Combine the water and sugar in a saucepan and stir over low heat until the sugar dissolves completely then bring to the boil. Pour over the chopped chocolate; stir until smooth.

Pour a shallow (1 cm) layer of the chocolate mixture into a large container and freeze. Stir with a fork from time to time, crushing the crystals and scraping the bottom and sides of the container so the mixture will freeze evenly (about 2 hours).

Divide the chocolate granita evenly between mugs or glasses; serve immediately.

Iced Chocolate Nougat Mousse

SERVES 6

DIFFICULTY ★ ★ ★

PREPARE: 45 minutes

COOK: 5 minutes

FREEZE: 1 hour

Nougatine
- 70 g flaked almonds
- 95 g caster sugar

Chocolate Mousse
- 2 egg whites
- 125 g caster sugar
- 85 g dark (66%) chocolate
- 250 ml whipping cream
- 75 g mixed glacé fruits, chopped
- 1 tbsp Kirsch

Chantilly Cream
- 200 ml whipping cream
- 20 g icing sugar

Decoration
- 6 Amarena (or Maraschino) cherries

Preheat the oven to 150°C (300°F). Line a baking tray with baking parchment. Prepare a 5 x 22 cm terrine.

Nougatine: Place the flaked almonds on the baking tray. Toast in the oven for 5 minutes until lightly coloured, remove from the lined baking tray; set aside. Place the sugar in a saucepan and cook over medium heat (do not stir) for about 10 minutes until it melts and becomes a golden caramel colour. Remove from the heat immediately and carefully stir in the toasted almonds. Pour onto the lined baking tray and cover with another piece of parchment. Using a rolling pin, spread the nougatine into a 2 mm thick layer. When cool, break in large pieces, wrap in a tea towel and crush coarsely using the rolling pin.

Chocolate Mousse: Whisk the egg whites until frothy. Add 40 g of the sugar a little at a time, whisking until the egg whites are smooth and shiny. Gradually add the remaining sugar, whisking until stiff peaks form; refrigerate until required.

Chop the chocolate and melt over a bain-marie. Beat the cream until firm and clinging to the whisk; carefully blend in the melted chocolate. Quickly whisk 1/3 of the chocolate cream into the whisked egg whites. Using a spatula, carefully fold in the remainder, in 2 separate batches. Add the crushed nougatine, chopped glacé fruits then the Kirsch. Pour the mixture into the terrine; freeze for 1 hour.

Chantilly Cream: Whisk the cream until it begins to stiffen, add the icing sugar and continue whisking until firm peaks cling to the whisk. Fit a piping bag with a star nozzle and fill with the cream.

Remove the terrine from the freezer and place it briefly in hot water then invert the iced chocolate nougat mousse onto a platter. Cut into 6 slices. Top each slice with a piped rosette of Chantilly cream and an Amarena cherry; serve immediately.

CHEF'S TIP: If you do not have Amarena cherries, use other cherries in syrup for the decoration. The nougat mousse could also be served with a cherry coulis.

Iced Chocolate Parfait with Orange-Basil Cream

SERVES 6

DIFFICULTY ★ ★ ★

PREPARE: 1¼ hours

FREEZE: 2 hours

Dark Chocolate Parfait
- 100 g dark chocolate
- 300 ml whipping cream
- 5 egg yolks
- 50 ml water
- 45 g caster sugar

Orange-Basil Cream
- 1 bunch basil
- 4 egg yolks
- 90 g caster sugar
- 350 ml orange juice

Citrus Fruit Segments
- 2 oranges
- 1 pink grapefruit

Decoration
- Small basil leaves

Chocolate Parfait: Chop the chocolate and melt over a bain-marie. Beat the cream until firm and clinging to the whisk; refrigerate. Whisk the egg yolks in a large bowl until pale yellow. Put the water and sugar into a saucepan and stir over low heat until the sugar dissolves completely; increase the heat and boil for 2 minutes. Pour the syrup slowly down the side of the bowl into the egg yolks, whisking continuously until the mixture thickens and cools. Using a spatula, gradually blend in the melted chocolate then fold in the whipped cream. Pour the mixture into an 18 x 7 cm porcelain terrine; freeze for 2 hours.

Orange-Basil Cream: Wash and dry the basil. In a separate bowl, beat the egg yolks and sugar until pale yellow and creamy. Place the basil and orange juice in a saucepan and bring slowly to the boil. Whisk 1/3 of the hot juice into the egg yolk-sugar mixture, mixing well to combine; pour the mixture into the remaining juice. Stirring constantly with a wooden spoon, cook the mixture over low heat until thickened and it coats the back of the spoon. (Do not allow to boil!) Remove from the heat immediately. Strain the orange-basil cream into a bowl; cool and then refrigerate.

Citrus Fruit Segments: Using a very sharp knife, cut a small slice off both ends of the fruit. Stand the fruit on a board and cut off the peel and all the pith in wide strips, working from top to bottom. Hold the peeled fruit, and insert the knife between the membrane and the flesh cutting towards the centre without cutting the membrane. Then, cut on the other side of the segment in the same way and ease it out. Continue until all the segments have been removed; set aside.

Remove the terrine from the freezer, wrap it in a hot, damp tea towel then turn the parfait out. Spoon the orange-basil cream into six dessert bowls and place a slice of parfait in each bowl. Top with citrus segments and decorate with basil leaves.

Pears Belle-Hélène

SERVES 6

DIFFICULTY ★ ★ ★

PREPARE: 1 hour

REFRIGERATE: 2 hours

FREEZE: 30 minutes

Poached Pears
- 6 small pears
- ½ lemon
- 700 ml water
- 250 g caster sugar
- ½ vanilla pod, split

Vanilla Ice Cream
- 5 egg yolks
- 125 g caster sugar
- 500 ml milk
- 1 vanilla pod, split
- 50 ml whipping cream

Chocolate Sauce
- 135 g dark chocolate
- 15 g unsalted butter
- 150 ml crème fraîche

◊ See p.208: Making a crème Anglaise.

Poached Pears: Peel and cut the pears in half; remove the cores. Rub the pears with the lemon to prevent darkening. Combine the water and sugar in a saucepan. Using the point of a knife, scrape the seeds from the vanilla pod into the sugared water; add the pod. Stir over low heat until the sugar dissolves then bring to the boil. Lower the heat, add the pears and poach for 20 minutes, or until tender when pierced with the point of a knife. Transfer the poached pears and syrup to a bowl to cool then refrigerate for 2 hours.

Vanilla Ice Cream: Beat the egg yolks and 60 g of the sugar until pale yellow and creamy. Pour the milk into a saucepan; add the remaining sugar. Using the point of a knife, scrape the seeds from the vanilla pod into the milk, add the pod and bring the sugared milk slowly to the boil. Whisk $^1/3$ of the hot mixture into the egg yolk-sugar mixture, stirring well to combine; pour the mixture into the remaining hot milk. Stirring constantly with a wooden spoon, cook over low heat until the mixture is thickened and coats the back of the spoon. (Do not allow to boil!) Stir in the cream and remove from the heat immediately; strain into a bowl. Stand the bowl in crushed ice until the mixture is cold. Pour the mixture into an ice-cream maker (pre-frozen, if necessary) and freeze-churn according to the manufacturer's instructions (about 30 minutes). Remove the ice cream from the machine and transfer it to the freezer before serving.

Warm Chocolate Sauce: Finely chop the chocolate and melt over a bain-marie with the butter and crème fraîche. Stir well until smooth; keep warm.

Place one scoop of vanilla ice cream and two pear halves in each footed ice-cream dish; pour the warm chocolate sauce over the top. Serve immediately.

Iced Profiteroles with Hot Chocolate Sauce

SERVES 6

DIFFICULTY ★ ★ ★

PREPARE: 45 minutes

COOK: 25 minutes

Choux Pastry Dough
- 50 g unsalted butter
- 125 ml water
- ½ tsp salt
- ½ tsp caster sugar
- 75 g flour, sifted
- 2 eggs
- 1 beaten egg, for glazing

Hot Chocolate Sauce
- 100 g dark chocolate
- 60 ml milk
- 50 g unsalted butter

Filling
- ½ litre vanilla ice cream (p.232)

◇ See p.209: Making choux pastry dough.

Choux Pastry Dough: Preheat the oven to 180°C (350°F). Put the butter, water, salt and sugar in a saucepan over low heat. When the butter melts, bring the mixture to the boil; remove from the heat immediately. Tip the sifted flour into the hot liquid. Stir with a wooden spoon until a firm smooth dough forms. Return the saucepan to low heat to dry out the dough; continue beating until it forms a ball and pulls away cleanly from the sides of the saucepan. Transfer the dough to a bowl; cool for 5 minutes. Then add an egg, little by little, beating energetically with a wooden spoon. Beat the second egg apart in a bowl. Stir half into the dough, continuing to beat until the dough is smooth and shiny. At this point, check that the dough is ready to use: take a little with the wooden spoon, then lift it. If the dough drops into a 'V', it is ready. If not, add a little of the remaining beaten egg and repeat the test.

Fit a piping bag with a plain nozzle, and spoon in the choux pastry dough. Take a baking tray and grease it with butter. Pipe small mounds, 2–3 cm in diameter, on the baking tray. Brush the tops with the egg glaze and flatten slightly with the back of a fork. Transfer to the oven and bake for 15 minutes without opening the door. Then, lower the oven temperature to 165°C (325°F) and continue baking for another 10 minutes, or until the choux are golden and sound hollow when tapped. Cool on a wire rack.

Hot Chocolate Sauce: Finely chop the chocolate. Bring the milk to the boil, remove from the heat and add the chocolate; stir until smooth. Add the butter and keep the sauce hot.

Cut the top third off the choux buns. Place a scoop of vanilla ice cream in each base; replace the tops and pour the hot chocolate sauce over. Serve immediately.

Chocolate Sorbet on a Raspberry Coulis

SERVES 8

DIFFICULTY ★ ★ ★

PREPARE: 30 minutes

REFRIGERATE: 10 minutes

FREEZE: 30 minutes

Chocolate Sorbet
- 200 g dark chocolate
- 80 g unsweetened cocoa powder
- 500 ml water
- 120 g caster sugar

Raspberry Coulis
- 200 g raspberries, fresh or frozen
- 2 or 3 drops lemon juice
- 30 g icing sugar

Decoration (Optional)
- Fresh raspberries

◇ See p.210: Shaping quenelles.

Chocolate Sorbet: Finely chop the chocolate and place in a bowl. Dissolve the unsweetened cocoa powder in 125 ml of the water. Add the remaining water and sugar into a saucepan. Stir over low heat to blend in the cocoa powder and dissolve the sugar; bring to the boil. Pour the syrup over the chopped chocolate, stir until smooth and strain the mixture into a bowl; cool. Pour the mixture into an ice-cream maker (pre-frozen, if necessary) and freeze-churn according to the manufacturer's instructions (about 30 minutes). Remove the sorbet from the machine and transfer it to the freezer before serving.

Raspberry Coulis: Puree the raspberries with the lemon juice in a food processor. Add the icing sugar, to taste. Strain the coulis into a bowl through a fine-meshed sieve; refrigerate for 10 minutes.

Spoon the raspberry coulis into 8 small bowls. Use 2 spoons to form the chocolate sorbet into quenelles and place one in each bowl. If desired, decorate with fresh raspberries.

CHEF'S TIP: If you like, you can make the coulis with other berries.

Iced Chocolate Soufflés

SERVES 4

DIFFICULTY ★ ★ ★

PREPARE: 30 minutes

FREEZE: 6 hours

REFRIGERATE: 15 minutes

Chocolate Cream
- 300 g dark chocolate
- 7 egg yolks
- 225 g caster sugar
- 250 ml milk
- 400 ml whipping cream

French Meringue
- 4 egg whites
- 80 g caster sugar

Decoration
- Icing sugar, sifted

Prepare four 8 cm soufflé dishes or ramekins. Create collars from doubled over, baking parchment paper rectangles that extend 3 cm above the rim of the dish. Secure with adhesive tape.

Chocolate Cream: Finely chop the chocolate and melt over a bain-marie. Beat the egg yolks and sugar until pale yellow and creamy. Bring the milk to the boil and whisk $1/3$ into the egg yolks and sugar, mixing well to combine; pour the mixture into the remaining hot milk. Stirring constantly with a wooden spoon, cook over low heat until the mixture is thickened and coats the back of the spoon. (Do not allow to boil!) Remove from the heat immediately, strain into a bowl and blend in the melted chocolate; cool. Beat the cream until firm and clinging to the whisk, then carefully fold into the chocolate mixture.

Divide the chocolate cream between the prepared soufflé dishes. Fill to within 0.5 cm of the top of the collar, leaving sufficient space for the French meringue; freeze for 6 hours.

French Meringue: Whisk the egg whites until frothy. Add $1/3$ of the sugar a little at a time, whisking until the egg whites are smooth and shiny. Gradually add the remaining sugar, whisking until stiff peaks form.

Remove the soufflés from the freezer and spread with a 0.5 cm layer of French meringue. Dip a serrated knife (or a fork) in hot water and make wavy lines in the meringue to decorate the tops of the soufflés; refrigerate for 15 minutes until firm.

Preheat the oven grill to the maximum temperature.

Place the soufflés briefly under the grill until the meringue is lightly coloured. Discard the paper collars. Sprinkle with icing sugar; serve immediately.

Triple Chocolate Iced Terrine

SERVES 8

DIFFICULTY ★ ★ ★

PREPARE: 45 minutes

FREEZE: 3 hours

White Chocolate Mousse
- 50 g white chocolate
- 1 leaf gelatine
- 150 ml whipping cream
- 20 g sugar
- 20 ml water

Milk Chocolate Mousse
- 50 g milk chocolate
- 1 leaf gelatine
- 150 ml whipping cream
- 20 g sugar
- 20 ml water

Dark Chocolate Mousse
- 150 ml whipping cream
- 60 g dark chocolate

White Chocolate Mousse: Chop the white chocolate and melt over a bain-maire. Soften the leaf gelatine in cold water. Whisk the cream until firm and clinging to the whisk; refrigerate. Place the sugar and water in a saucepan and swirl over low heat until the sugar dissolves, bring to the boil; add the leaf gelatine. Pour into the melted chocolate whisking quickly; carefully fold in the whipped cream. Pour the white chocolate mousse into a 25 x 10 cm terrine, smooth the surface with a rubber spatula and transfer to the freezer.

Milk Chocolate Mousse: Repeat the preceding step replacing the white chocolate with the milk chocolate. Remove the terrine from the freezer and pour the milk chocolate mousse on top of the white chocolate mousse; smooth the surface with a spatula and return the terrine to the freezer.

Dark Chocolate Mousse: Whisk the cream until firm and clinging to the whisk; refrigerate. Chop the dark chocolate and melt over a bain-marie; carefully fold in the whipped cream. Remove the terrine from the freezer, fill with the dark chocolate mousse and smooth the surface with a rubber spatula; freeze for 3 hours.

When ready to serve, remove the terrine from the freezer and cut slices. Or, place the terrine briefly in very hot water and turn the dessert out onto a serving platter.

Chilled Chocolate Truffles

MAKES 12

DIFFICULTY ★ ★ ★

PREPARE: 30 minutes

FREEZE: 1½ hours

Chocolate Ice Cream
- 60 g (55-70%) chocolate
- 15 g unsweetened cooking chocolate
- 250 ml milk
- 3 egg yolks
- 50 g caster sugar

Ganache Coating
- 250 g dark chocolate
- 250 ml whipping cream
- 45 g caster sugar
- Unsweetened cocoa powder, sifted

Line a baking tray with baking parchment; transfer to the freezer to chill.

Chocolate Ice Cream: Finely chop the chocolates and place in a large bowl. Bring the milk slowly to the boil. In a separate bowl, beat the egg yolks and sugar until pale yellow and creamy. Whisk in $1/3$ of the hot milk, mixing well to combine; pour the mixture into the remaining hot milk. Stirring constantly with a wooden spoon, cook over low heat until the mixture is thickened and coats the back of the spoon. (Do not allow to boil!) Remove from the heat immediately. Pour over the chopped chocolate and stir until smooth; strain into a bowl. Stand the bowl in crushed ice until the mixture is cold. Pour the mixture into an ice-cream maker (pre-frozen, if necessary) and freeze-churn according to the manufacturer's instructions (about 30 minutes). Remove the ice cream from the machine.

Use a spoon to form 12 balls of chocolate ice cream. Transfer to the chilled baking tray; freeze for 1 hour.

Ganache Coating: Chop the chocolate and place in a large bowl. Heat the cream and sugar until simmering, stir until the sugar dissolves completely. Pour the mixture over the chopped chocolate; stir until smooth. Then stir every 10 minutes until the ganache cools.

Spread the sifted cocoa powder on a large plate. When the ice cream balls are hard, immerse each one individually in the ganache coating then roll in the cocoa powder. Transfer to the freezer for at least 30 minutes before serving.

CHEF'S TIP: You can keep the chocolate-coated ice cream balls frozen in an air-tight container for 15 days; just before serving, roll them in cocoa powder. Take care when coating the ice cream balls; the ganache must not be warm, or the ice cream will melt. On the other hand, if it is too cold the coating will become very thick.

Iced Chocolate Creams with Apricot Compote and Almond Crumble

SERVES 10

DIFFICULTY ★ ★ ★

PREPARE: 45 minutes

FREEZE: 30 minutes

COOK: 20 minutes

Chocolate Cream
- 80 g dark chocolate
- 200 ml whipping cream
- 3 egg yolks
- 20 g caster sugar

Almond Crumble
- 50 g salted butter
- 50 g caster sugar
- 50 g flour
- 1 pinch baking powder
- 50 g ground almonds

Apricot Compote
- 20 g unsalted butter
- 40 g caster sugar
- 12 tinned apricot halves in syrup
- 1 or 2 drops vanilla extract

Decoration
- Icing sugar, sifted

Chocolate Cream: Chop the chocolate and place in a bowl. Heat the cream until simmering. In a separate bowl, beat the egg yolks and sugar until thick and creamy. Whisk $1/3$ of the hot cream into the egg yolks and sugar, mixing well to combine; pour the mixture into the remaining hot cream. Stirring constantly with a wooden spoon, cook over low heat until the mixture is thickened and coats the back of the spoon. (Do not allow to boil!) Remove from the heat immediately, strain over the chopped chocolate; stir until smooth.

Pour a 2 cm layer of the chocolate cream into each of 10 dessert glasses; transfer to the freezer for 30 minutes.

Preheat the oven to 165°C (325°F). Line a baking tray with baking parchment.

Almond Crumble: Put all the crumble ingredients into a bowl; rub the butter into the dry ingredients until the mixture resembles breadcrumbs. Spread the mixture on the baking tray and bake for 20 minutes; cool. Break or crush the cooked crumble in small pieces; set aside.

Apricot Compote: Place the butter and sugar in a saucepan and heat over low heat. Add the apricots, 100 ml of the syrup and the vanilla extract. Cook until the compote is smooth and thick; set aside until cold.

Remove the dessert glasses from the freezer and spoon a 2 cm layer of cold apricot compote into each. Divide the crumble between the glasses and sprinkle with icing sugar; serve immediately.

CHEF'S TIP: If you don't have salted butter, use a pinch of sea salt flakes or fleur de sel in the crumble.

Creamy Hot Chocolate

SERVES 6

DIFFICULTY ★ ★ ★

PREPARE: 15 minutes

- 1 L milk
- 250 ml crème fraîche
- 120 g dark chocolate
- 1 tsp ground cinnamon
- 1 black peppercorn
- 2 tbsp (30 g) caster sugar

Decoration (Optional)
- 6 marshmallows

Chop the chocolate. Heat the milk and crème fraîche in a saucepan until simmering.

Add the chopped chocolate, ground cinnamon, peppercorn and sugar to the hot milk and cream mixture. Place the saucepan over low heat for about 10 minutes; stir from time to time using a wooden spoon.

Strain the hot chocolate mixture then divide it between six mugs. Decorate each with a marshmallow, if desired; serve immediately.

CHEF'S TIP: The taste of the hot chocolate will be richer if it is refrigerated for several hours, or even up to three days and reheated before serving.

Iced Chocolate Milk, with Chantilly Cream

SERVES 6

DIFFICULTY ★ ★ ★

PREPARE: 20 minutes

FREEZE: 30 minutes

Iced Chocolate Milk
- 80 g dark chocolate
- 500 ml milk

Chantilly Cream
- 100 ml whipping cream
- 10 g icing sugar

Prepare six martini glasses.

Iced Chocolate Milk: Chop the chocolate and place in a bowl. Bring the milk to the boil and pour over the chopped chocolate; stir until smooth. Divide the mixture between six martini glasses. Transfer to the freezer for 30 minutes.

Chantilly Cream: Whisk the cream until it begins to stiffen, add the sugar and continue whisking until firm peaks cling to the whisk. Fit a piping bag with a star nozzle and fill with the Chantilly cream. Remove the glasses of iced chocolate milk from the freezer and pipe rosettes of Chantilly on each one. Serve immediately.

CHEF'S TIP: If you have a Chantilly siphon in your kitchen, you could make Chantilly foam. Pour the cream and 10 g icing sugar into the siphon and insert the gas cartridge. Shake it vigorously to combine the ingredients and to make the mixture light and airy.

Chocolate Milkshake

SERVES 6–8

DIFFICULTY ★ ★ ★

PREPARE: 20 minutes

REFRIGERATE: 1 hour

- 200 ml milk
- 3 tsp unsweetened cocoa powder
- 2 tsp caster sugar
- 6 scoops vanilla ice cream (p. 220)
- 6 scoops chocolate ice cream (p.218)
- 6 ice cubes

Pour 100 ml milk into a saucepan, add the cocoa powder and sugar and bring to the boil. Add the remaining milk, stir well to combine; remove from the heat. When cold, refrigerate the chocolate milk for 1 hour.

Place the vanilla and chocolate ice creams, ice cubes and cold chocolate milk in a food processor, or blender, and process on maximum speed for 1–2 minutes.

Divide the chocolate milkshake between 6–8 tall glasses; serve immediately.

CHEF'S TIP: If you like, you can use ready-prepared ice creams.

Chocolate Soup, Pineapple Brochette Macerated in Star Anise and Dried Pineapple

SERVES 6

DIFFICULTY: ★ ★ ★

PREPARE: 30 minutes

CHILL: Overnight

COOK: 4–5 hours

INFUSE: 30 minutes

Pineapple Macerated in Star Anise and Dried Pineapple

- 1 pineapple
- 500 ml water
- 150 g caster sugar
- 4 star anise
- Icing sugar

Chocolate Soup

- 150 ml milk
- 10 g mild honey
- ½ vanilla pod
- 100 g dark chocolate, chopped

◊ This recipe needs to be started one day ahead.

The day before, prepare the star anise-macerated pineapple: Remove the pineapple skin and cut in half horizontally. Take one half and cut into pieces (set aside the other half to make the dried pineapple). Bring the water, sugar and star anise to a boil in a saucepan. Pour this syrup over the pineapple pieces and macerate in the fridge overnight.

Preheat the oven to 80°C (175°F). Line a baking tray with baking parchment.

For the dried pineapple: Finely slice the other pineapple half. Place on the baking tray, dust with icing sugar and dry in the oven for 4–5 hours.

The next day, make the chocolate soup: Bring the milk to a boil in a saucepan with the honey and the half vanilla pod, cut in two. Scrape out the vanilla seeds with the tip of a knife. Infuse for 30 minutes off the heat, then remove the vanilla pod. Pour the hot liquid over the chopped chocolate and mix well. Leave to cool.

Thread the pineapple pieces onto 6 skewers, alternating pieces of star-anise macerated pineapple with dried pineapple. Pour the chocolate soup into 6 ramekins. Lay 1 pineapple brochette over the top and accompany with a slice of dried pineapple.

Teatime treats to share

The best way
to fill éclairs

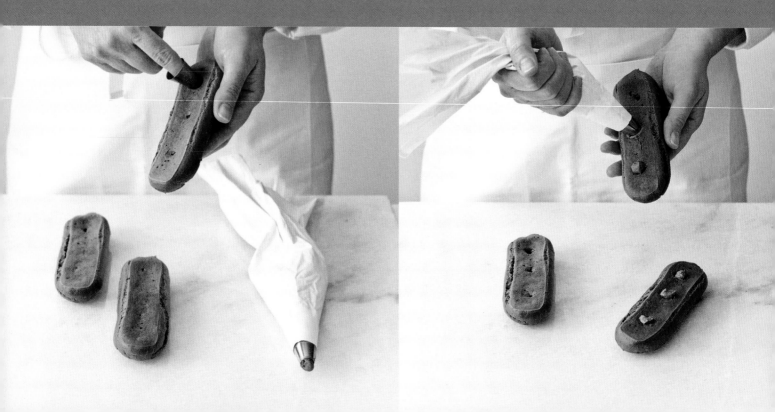

Make the éclairs and cream filling using the recipe of your choice, for example, on pp.276 or 298.

(1) Set aside a fine-tipped nozzle. Fit a piping bag with a larger plain round nozzle and fill with the cream to be used. Place the éclairs side by side on a work surface, flat side up.

(2) Holding one éclair in the palm of your hand, pierce two or three small holes in the flat side, using the fine-tipped nozzle.

(3) Continue holding the éclair and place the nozzle of the filled piping bag over each hole and squeeze it, filling the éclair with the cream.

The best way to prepare chocolate containers

You can adapt this technique when using the chocolate design of your choice (cones, bowls, cases...) depending on the recipe chosen, see p.272.

(1) Prepare a pastry brush, a small knife, a bowl of tempered chocolate (p.320) and some cone-shaped paper cups.

(2) Brush a thin coat of tempered chocolate on the inside of the cone then invert it, placing the opening on your work surface, so the excess chocolate will run out. Set the cones aside at room temperature for 30 minutes, until firm. Then, apply a second coat of chocolate in the same manner. A third coat may be necessary.

(3) When the chocolate is hard, carefully peel off the paper. If necessary, use the knife. Store the chocolate containers in a cool location until required.

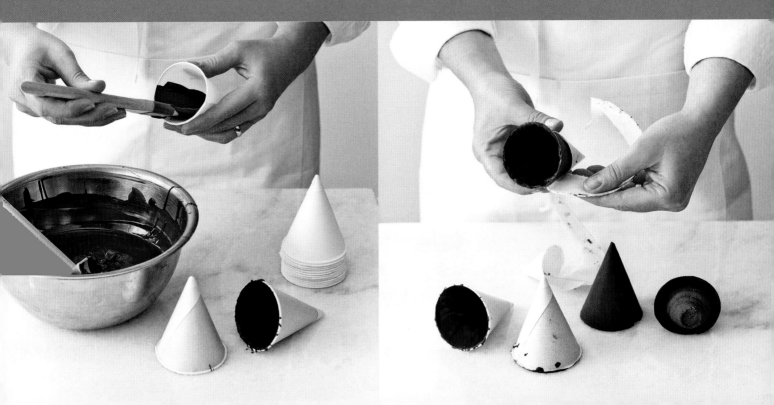

Field Marshal's Batons

MAKES 60

DIFFICULTY ★ ★ ★

PREPARE: 1 hour

COOK: 8-10 minutes

- 5 egg whites
- 30 g caster sugar
- 125 g ground almonds, sifted
- 125 g icing sugar, sifted
- 25 g flour, sifted
- 70 g chopped almonds

Decoration
- 250 g dark chocolate

◊ See pp.320-324: Tempering chocolate.

Preheat the oven to 170°C (335°F). Line a baking tray with baking parchment.

Whisk the egg whites until frothy. Add $^1/3$ of the sugar a little at a time, whisking until the egg whites are smooth and shiny. Gradually add the remaining sugar, whisking until stiff peaks form. Gradually add the ground almonds, sifted icing sugar and flour, and gently incorporate with a flexible spatula. Fit a piping bag with a medium round nozzle and fill with the mixture. Pipe small batons – 6 cm long – on the baking tray continuing until all the mixture is used; sprinkle with the chopped almonds. Bake for 8– 10 minutes, or until the batons are lightly golden. Remove from the oven and cool. When cold, peel off the baking parchment and store the batons at room temperature.

Decoration: Lay a sheet of thick plastic on the worktop. Temper the chocolate by following each of these steps, in order to obtain a good crystallisation of the chocolate: coarsely chop the dark chocolate. Melt two-thirds in a bain-marie up to 45°C on the digital thermometer. When the chocolate reaches this temperature, remove it from the bain-marie. Add the remaining chocolate stirring until the temperature drops to 27°C. Return the bowl to the bain-marie, stir and reheat the chocolate to 32°C. Transfer the chocolate to a pastry bag fitted with a very small plain nozzle and pipe lines 5 cm long on the thick plastic sheet. Place the batons on top and refrigerate for 10 minutes so that the chocolate hardens, before lifting from the thick plastic sheet.

Place on a rack, chocolate-coated side up; cool at room temperature until firm.

CHEF'S TIP: The Field Marshal's Batons can be kept several days in an airtight container.

Chocolate Fritters

MAKES **25–30** FRITTERS

DIFFICULTY ★ ★ ★

PREPARE: 40 minutes + 30 minutes

REFRIGERATE: 1 hour

FREEZE: Overnight

COOK: 45 minutes

Chocolate Cream

- 200 g dark (55–70%) chocolate
- 140 ml whipping cream
- Unsweetened cocoa powder

Batter

- 125 g flour, sifted
- 1 tbsp cornflour, sifted
- 1 tbsp vegetable oil
- 2 pinches salt
- 1 egg
- 120 ml beer
- 1 egg white
- 20 g caster sugar
- Vegetable oil for frying
- Flour
- Unsweetened cocoa powder, sifted (optional)

◇ This recipe needs to be started one day ahead.

Chocolate Cream: The day before, chop the chocolate and melt over a bain-marie. Heat the cream in a saucepan until simmering, pour over the chocolate and stir until smooth. Cover and refrigerate until the cream is firm enough to pipe. Fit a piping bag with a round nozzle and fill with the chocolate cream. On a baking tray lined with baking parchment, pipe 25–30 neat mounds on the baking tray. Refrigerate for 1 hour, or until firm. Wearing rubber gloves, roll the mounds by hand to form balls, dust with cocoa powder; freeze overnight.

Batter: The next day, place the sifted flour and cornflour in a large bowl; make a well in the centre. Put the oil, salt and egg into the well and gradually blend in the sifted ingredients, stir until the mixture is smooth then add the beer a little at a time.

Whisk the egg white, gradually adding the sugar until it is smooth and shiny and stiff peaks form. Gently fold it into the batter.

Pour the frying oil into a deep fat fryer (or heavy-bottomed saucepan) to a depth of approx. $7^1/2$ cm; heat to 200°C (400°F).

Remove 2 or 3 balls of chocolate from the freezer and roll them lightly in flour. Immerse in the batter then, using tongs, in the hot oil; deep fry for 3–5 minutes, or until lightly golden. Drain the fritters on kitchen paper and dust with cocoa powder, if desired. Repeat for the remaining chocolate balls; serve.

Brownies

SERVES 10

DIFFICULTY ★ ★ ★

PREPARE: 30 minutes

COOK: 30 minutes

- 125 g dark (55-70%) chocolate
- 225 g unsalted butter
- 4 eggs
- 125 g unrefined cane sugar
- 125 g caster sugar
- 50 g flour, sifted
- 20 g unsweetened cocoa powder, sifted
- 100 g pecans, crushed

Preheat the oven to 170°C (335°F). Line a 20 cm square cake tin with parchment paper.

Chop the chocolate and melt over a bain-marie with the butter; stir with a spatula until smooth.

In a separate bowl, combine the eggs, unrefined cane and caster sugars and beat until thick and creamy; add to the chocolate-butter mixture. Then, using a spatula, fold in the sifted flour and cocoa powder followed by the crushed pecans; mix well.

Pour the mixture into the prepared cake tin and bake for 30 minutes, or until the point of a knife inserted into the centre comes out clean. Cool on a rack and cut the brownies into squares to serve.

Chocolate and Raspberry Cream Puffs

MAKES 8–10 PUFFS

DIFFICULTY ★ ★ ★

PREPARE: 35 minutes

COOK: 30 minutes

Choux Pastry Dough
- 100 g unsalted butter
- 250 ml water
- 1 tsp salt
- 1 tsp caster sugar
- 150 g flour, sifted
- 4 eggs
- 1 beaten egg for glazing

Chocolate Chantilly Cream
- 125 g dark chocolate
- 300 ml whipping cream
- 30 g icing sugar, sifted

Decoration
- 500 g raspberries
- Icing sugar, sifted

◇ See p.209: Making choux pastry dough.

Preheat the oven to 180°C (350°F). Butter a baking tray.

Choux Pastry Dough: Cook the butter, water, salt and sugar in a saucepan over low heat. When the butter melts, bring the mixture to the boil; remove from the heat immediately. Tip the sifted flour into the hot liquid. Stir with a wooden spoon until a firm, smooth paste forms. Return the saucepan to low heat to dry out the paste; continue beating until it forms a ball and pulls away cleanly from the sides of the saucepan. Transfer the paste to a bowl; cool for 5 minutes.

Then add 3 eggs, one by one, beating energetically with the spoon. Beat the fourth egg apart in a bowl. Stir in half to the dough while continuing to beat until the dough is smooth and shiny. At this point, check that the dough is ready to use: take a little with the spoon, then lift it. If the dough drops into a 'V', it is ready. If not, add a little more beaten egg and repeat the test. Fit a piping bag with a plain round nozzle, and spoon in the choux paste; pipe mounds, 4–5 cm in diameter, onto the baking tray. Brush the tops with the egg glaze and flatten slightly with the back of a fork. Transfer to the oven and bake for 15 minutes without opening the door. Lower the oven temperature to 165°C (325°F) and continue baking for another 15 minutes, or until the puffs are golden and sound hollow when tapped. Cool on a rack.

Chocolate Chantilly Cream: Chop the chocolate and melt over a bain-marie. Whisk the cream until it begins to stiffen, add the icing sugar and continue whisking until the cream is firm and clinging to the whisk. Quickly whisk in the melted chocolate. Fit a piping bag with a star nozzle and fill with the chocolate Chantilly cream; set aside.

Cut the top $1/3$ off each puff. Pipe the chocolate Chantilly cream into the bases, decorate with fresh raspberries and replace the tops; dust with sifted icing sugar.

Chocolate Cigarettes

MAKES 45 CIGARETTES

DIFFICULTY ★ ★ ★

PREPARE: 30 minutes

REFRIGERATE: 20 minutes

COOK: 6–8 minutes

- 80 g soft unsalted butter
- 120 g icing sugar
- 4 egg whites (130 g)
- 90 g flour, sifted
- 20 g unsweetened cocoa powder, sifted

Beat the butter and icing sugar until creamy. Add the egg whites, a little at a time, mixing well after each addition. Blend in the sifted flour and cocoa powder; refrigerate the paste for 20 minutes.

Preheat the oven to 200°C (400°F). Line a baking tray with baking parchment.

On a piece of cardboard trace an 8 cm circle. Cut out and discard the circle leaving a round hole in the cardboard. This is your template. Place it on the baking tray, put a spoonful of the chocolate paste into the centre of the hole and spread the mixture out to form an 8 cm disc. Pick up the template and continue making paste discs, leaving only a few millimetres between each one, until the baking tray is covered. Bake for 6–8 minutes.

Set out a wooden spoon (or spatula) with a round handle to use for rolling the cigarettes. As soon as discs come out of the oven, roll each one around the handle of the spoon, waiting for a couple of seconds until it hardens. Slide each one off onto a rack. Store the chocolate cigarettes in a cool dry place.

Chocolate Chip Cinnamon Biscuits

MAKES 40

DIFFICULTY ★ ★ ★

PREPARE: 15 minutes

REFRIGERATE: 1 hour

COOK: 10 minutes

- 2 egg yolks
- 1 tsp vanilla extract
- 2 tbsp water
- 150 g soft unsalted butter
- 100 g icing sugar
- 300 g flour, sifted
- 1½ tsp baking powder, sifted
- 1 large pinch salt
- 1½ tsp ground cinnamon
- 120 g chocolate chips
- Icing sugar, sifted

Combine the egg yolks, vanilla extract and water. In a separate bowl, beat the butter and icing sugar until creamy. Add the egg-yolk mixture a little at a time, beating after each addition. Blend in the sifted flour and baking powder, salt and cinnamon. Fold in the chocolate chips being careful not to over-mix the dough.

Divide the dough in two even portions. Roll each one into a cylinder about 3 cm in diameter. Roll the cylinders in icing sugar and wrap in cling film. Roll again before chilling to ensure they are evenly shaped; refrigerate for at least 1 hour.

Preheat the oven to 160°C (325°F). Butter a baking tray.

Remove and discard the cling film from the dough cylinders. Cut the dough into slices 1 cm thick and place on the baking tray. Bake for about 10 minutes, or until the biscuits are golden; cool on a rack.

CHEF'S TIP: For a variation, you could also roll the dough cylinders in unsweetened cocoa powder.

Chocolate-Orange Biscuits

MAKES 20 BISCUITS

DIFFICULTY ★ ★ ★

PREPARE: 15 minutes

REFRIGERATE: 15 minutes

COOK: 7–8 minutes

• 100 g soft unsalted butter
• 40 g caster sugar
• Zest of ½ orange, finely grated
• 125 g flour, sifted
• ½ tsp baking powder, sifted
• 100 g dark chocolate

Preheat the oven to 190°C (375°F). Butter a baking tray.

Place the butter in a bowl and beat until creamy. Add the sugar and grated orange zest, a little at a time, beating until the mixture is light. Blend in the sifted flour and baking powder. Using two teaspoons, form the dough into balls about the size of a walnut and place on the baking tray. Dip a fork in cold water and use the back of it to flatten the dough.

Put the baking tray into the oven and bake for 7–8 minutes, or until the biscuits are golden. Remove from the oven and cool on a rack.

Chop the chocolate and melt slowly over a bain-marie; remove from the heat. Put a sheet of baking parchment on the work surface. Using your fingers or plastic-coated tongs, dip each biscuit halfway into the melted chocolate and place it on the parchment; repeat until all the biscuits have been dipped. Refrigerate for 15 minutes, or until the chocolate hardens.

Chocolate Cases, Bowls and Cones

MAKES **10** CONTAINERS

DIFFICULTY ★ ★ ★

PREPARE: **45** MINUTES

• 500 g dark chocolate

◇ See pp.320-324: Tempering chocolate.

◇ See p.257: Preparing chocolate containers.

Temper the chocolate: Coarsely chop the chocolate. Place $2/3$ (330 g) in a bowl; melt over a simmering bain-marie until the temperature reaches 45°C on a digital thermometer. Remove the bowl from the heat and add the remaining chocolate, stirring until the temperature drops to 27°C. Return the bowl to the bain-marie, stir gently and reheat the chocolate to 32°C.

Chocolate Cases: Use either large (cupcake) or small (petites fours) individual paper baking cases. If the paper is flimsy, put one case inside another. Using a pastry brush, apply a thin coat of tempered chocolate to the inside of the case. Set aside at room temperature for 30 minutes, or until firm. Then apply a second coat of chocolate in the same manner. If necessary, apply a third coat. When the chocolate is hard, carefully remove the paper cases. Store the small chocolate cases in a cool, dry place until required.

Chocolate Bowls: Inflate and tie-off 10 small balloons. Dip the bottom half of each balloon into the tempered chocolate and place on a baking tray covered with baking parchment. Refrigerate for 15 minutes, or until the chocolate firms. When the chocolate is hard, pierce the balloons with a needle and carefully peel them away. Store the chocolate bowls in a cool, dry place until required.

Chocolate Cones: Use small paper cups. Apply a thin coat of tempered chocolate on the inside of the cone then invert and place the opening on the work surface, so the excess chocolate will run out. Set the cones aside at room temperature for 30 minutes, or until firm. Then apply a second coat of chocolate in the same manner. It may be necessary to apply a third coat. When the chocolate is hard, carefully peel off the paper; use the knife if necessary. Store the chocolate cones in a cool dry place until required.

CHEF'S TIP: Use the differently shaped containers to serve your desserts. Fill with ice cream, mousse or fruits.

Chocolate Crêpes

MAKES 15 CRÊPES

DIFFICULTY ★ ★ ★

PREPARE: 10 minutes

REFRIGERATE: 2 hours

COOK: 45 minutes

Crêpe Batter
- 150 g flour, sifted
- 30 g unsweetened cocoa powder, sifted
- 2 eggs
- 450 ml milk
- 10 g caster sugar

Clarified Butter
- 125 g unsalted butter

Garnish
- Chantilly cream (p.214) and caster sugar, or chocolate-hazelnut spread

Crêpe Batter: Tip the sifted flour and cocoa powder into a large bowl; make a well in the centre. Put the eggs and 125 ml of the milk into the well and gradually blend in the sifted ingredients, stirring until the mixture is smooth. Continue stirring, gradually adding the remaining milk. Cover the batter and refrigerate for 2 hours.

Clarified Butter: Place the butter in a saucepan and melt completely over low heat. Remove from the heat and let stand for several minutes, allowing the milk solids to settle on the bottom. Skim the froth from the top of the melted butter and pour only the clear yellow liquid butter into a bowl; discard the milk solids left in the saucepan.

Put a little clarified butter into a crêpe or small frying pan and pour out or wipe away the excess with kitchen paper. Heat the pan over medium heat until a drop of water sizzles in it. Using a small ladle, pour in about 30 ml of batter. Tilt and swivel the pan to thinly coat the bottom. Cook 1–2 minutes, or until the crêpe bottom is pale and golden. Flip or turn using a spatula and cook the other side. Turn the crêpe out onto a warmed plate; cover with an upturned plate to keep warm. Continue cooking until all the batter is used; re-butter the pan only if the crêpes start to stick.

Serve the crêpes sprinkled with sugar and garnished with Chantilly cream or even covered with chocolate-hazelnut spread and folded.

CHEF'S TIP: Your crêpes can be prepared several hours in advance and reheated quickly in a lightly buttered or oiled pan. The clarified butter, which has its milk solids removed, can be heated more easily without burning and refrigerated for longer without becoming rancid, than non-clarified butter.

All-Chocolate Éclairs

MAKES 15 ÉCLAIRS

DIFFICULTY ★ ★ ★

PREPARE: 1 hour

COOK: 25 minutes

REFRIGERATE: 25 minutes

Chocolate Choux Pastry Dough

- 250 ml water
- 100 g unsalted butter
- 1 tsp salt
- 1 tsp caster sugar
- 130 g flour, sifted
- 20 g unsweetened cocoa powder, sifted
- 4 eggs
- 1 beaten egg for glazing

Chocolate Pastry Cream

- 150 g dark chocolate
- 500 ml milk
- 1 vanilla pod, split
- 4 egg yolks
- 125 g caster sugar
- 40 g cornflour

Chocolate Glaze

- 100 g dark chocolate
- 100 g icing sugar
- 40 ml water

◊See p.256: The best way to fill éclairs.

Preheat the oven to 180°C (350°F). Butter a baking tray.

Chocolate Choux Pastry Dough: Using the ingredients listed, prepare as indicated on p.209, adding the sifted cocoa powder at the same time as the flour. When the paste is ready to be used, fit a piping bag with a plain round nozzle, and spoon in the paste; pipe fingers of choux, 3 x 10 cm long, on the baking tray. Brush the tops with the egg glaze. Transfer to the oven and bake for 15 minutes without opening the door. Then, lower the oven temperature to 165°C (325°F) and continue baking for another 10 minutes, until the éclairs are firm and sound hollow when tapped. Cool on a rack.

Chocolate Pastry Cream: Finely chop the chocolate and place in a bowl. Pour the milk into a saucepan. Using the point of a knife, scrape the seeds from the vanilla pod into the milk, add the pod and bring to the boil; remove from the heat. Put the egg yolks and sugar into a bowl and beat until pale yellow, thick and creamy; add the cornflour. Remove the vanilla pod and whisk one half of the hot milk quickly into the egg yolk-sugar-cornflour mixture; add the remaining milk. Cook over low heat, whisking continuously until the cream thickens. Boil for 1 minute while continuing to whisk. Remove from the heat and pour the pastry cream over the chopped chocolate; stir until smooth. Cover the surface of the cream with cling film; refrigerate for 25 minutes.

Chocolate Glaze: Melt the chocolate over a bain-marie. Combine the icing sugar and water and blend into the melted chocolate. Heat the mixture until it registers 40°C on a digital thermometer.

Fit a piping bag with a plain round nozzle and fill it with pastry cream. Pierce 2 or 3 small holes in the flat side of each éclair and fill with chocolate pastry cream. Spread a layer of chocolate glaze on the top of the éclairs using a spatula; set aside to dry before serving.

Mini Muffins topped with Milk Chocolate Mousse

MAKES 15 MUFFINS

DIFFICULTY ★ ★ ★

PREPARE: 40 minutes

COOK: 10 – 15 minutes

REFRIGERATE: overnight plus 10 minutes

Chocolate-Chip Muffins
- 170 g unsalted butter
- 100 g flour, sifted
- 125 g ground almonds, sifted
- 250 g caster sugar
- 7 egg whites (200 g)
- 40 g mild honey
- 90 g chocolate chips

Milk Chocolate Mousse
- 220 g milk chocolate
- 320 ml whipping cream
- ½ vanilla pod, split

Decoration
- Milk chocolate

◊ See p.329: Making a paper piping bag

◊ The recipe must be started a day ahead. You will need a silicone mini-muffin mould producing 15 muffins 3 x 4.5 cm.

Chocolate-Chip Muffins: On the day of serving, preheat the oven to 180°C (350°F). Heat the butter until it turns golden brown and the milk solids colour and stick to the bottom of the saucepan (this is known as a "beurre noisette"). Remove from the heat immediately and strain through a fine-meshed wire strainer; set aside to cool. Tip the sifted flour and almonds into a large bowl. Add the sugar, egg whites and honey and whisk until creamy. Blend in the "beurre noisette" little at a time until the mixture increases in volume; fold in the chocolate chips; refrigerate overnight. Fill the muffin imprints to the ¾ mark, using a piping bag or spoon, and bake for 10– 15 minutes, or until the point of a knife inserted in the centre of a muffin comes out clean. Cool for several minutes before turning out onto a rack.

Milk Chocolate Mousse: Chop the chocolate and melt over a slowly simmering bain-marie until the temperature registers approximately 45°C on a digital thermometer. Using the point of a knife, scrape the seeds from the vanilla pod into the cream. Beat the cream until firm peaks cling to the whisk. Whisking quickly, add about $1/3$ of the whipped cream to the hot chocolate to lighten it. Pour the mixture over the remaining cream and fold in gently with the whisk or a spatula to evenly blend the ingredients. Fit a piping bag with star nozzle and fill with the milk chocolate mousse; pipe rosettes of mousse on each muffin; refrigerate for 10 minutes.

Decoration: Melt the chocolate over a bain-marie; cool. Fill a small paper piping bag with the cooled chocolate, folding the top over until the chocolate is squeezed into the nose. Snip off the tip and streak the muffins with fine lines of chocolate.

CHEF'S TIP: You can also use dark or white chocolate to make the mousse and for the decoration.

Chocolate-Orange Financiers

MAKES 12

DIFFICULTY ★ ★ ★

PREPARE: 30 minutes

COOK: 10 – 15 minutes

REFRIGERATE: Overnight

Chocolate-Orange Financiers

• 75 g unsalted butter
• 40 g candied orange peel
• 50 g flour, sifted
• 120 g icing sugar, sifted
• 50 g ground almonds, sifted
• 4 egg whites
• 30 g chocolate chips

Chocolate Ganache

• 100 g dark chocolate
• 100 ml whipping cream
• 20 g unsalted butter

◊ This recipe must be started one day ahead. You will need financier moulds or mini loaf tins measuring 5 x 10 cm.

Chocolate-Orange Financiers: Heat the butter until it turns golden brown and the milk solids colour and stick to the bottom of the saucepan (this is known as "beurre noisette"). Remove from the heat immediately and strain through a fine-meshed wire strainer; set aside to cool. Finely dice the candied orange peel. Tip the sifted flour, icing sugar and almonds into a large bowl. Add egg whites and whisk until creamy. Blend in the "beurre noisette" a little at a time until the mixture increases in volume; fold in the chocolate chips and the diced candied orange peel. Refrigerate overnight.

On the day of serving, preheat the oven to 180°C (350°F). Brush 12 small rectangular financier moulds or mini loaf tins with butter, dust with flour and tap out the excess.

Fill the moulds to the ¾ mark, using a piping bag or spoon, and bake for 10– 15 minutes, or until the point of a knife inserted in the centre of a financier comes out clean. Cool for several minutes before turning out onto a rack.

Chocolate Ganache: Chop the chocolate and place in a bowl. Heat the cream until simmering and pour it over the chocolate, stir until smooth; blend in the butter. Fit a piping bag with a plain round nozzle and fill with the chocolate ganache; decorate the tops of the financiers. Serve three per person.

Florentines

MAKES **40**

DIFFICULTY ★ ★ ★

PREPARE: 45 minutes

COOK: 30 minutes

COOL: 30 minutes

• 50 g mixed glacé fruit
• 50 g candied orange peel
• 35 g glacé cherries
• 100 g flaked almonds
• 25 g flour sifted
• 100 ml whipping cream
• 85 g caster sugar
• 30 g mild honey
• 300 g dark chocolate

◇ See pp.320-324: Tempering chocolate.

Preheat the oven to 170°C (335°F). Butter a baking tray.

Finely chop the mixed glacé fruit, orange peel and cherries and place in a bowl; add the almonds. Tip the flour into the bowl and stir carefully by hand to separate the pieces of fruit.

Heat the cream, sugar and honey until simmering; stir over low heat for 2–3 minutes, or until the sugar dissolves. Using a wooden spoon, carefully blend the hot cream mixture into the glacé fruit and flour. (If desired, the Florentine mixture could be kept refrigerated for 2 days.)

Using a teaspoon, put small mounds of the mixture on the baking tray placing them well apart. Flatten with the back of the spoon into thin 3 cm discs. Transfer to the oven and when the discs start to bubble, remove and cool for about 30 minutes. Lower the oven temperature to 160°C (325°F) and bake the discs for another 10 minutes. Cool and transfer to a rack.

Temper the chocolate: Coarsely chop the chocolate. Place ²/3 (200 g) of the chopped chocolate in a bowl; melt over a bain-marie until the temperature reaches 45°C on a digital thermometer. Remove the bowl from the heat and add the remaining chocolate, stirring until the temperature drops to 27°C. Return the bowl to the bain-marie, stir gently and reheat the chocolate to 32°C.

Using a pastry brush, apply a layer of tempered chocolate to the flat side of each Florentine; tap each one on the work surface to release any air bubbles in the chocolate. Spread with a second layer, using a spatula to remove any excess chocolate. Harden the Florentines at room temperature.

CHEF'S TIP: Make sure that you spread the dough out thinly on the baking tray otherwise the Florentines will not be easy to eat when cooked.

Chocolate-Cinnamon Chews

MAKES 45

DIFFICULTY ★ ★ ★

PREPARE: 15 minutes

REFRIGERATE: 45–60 minutes

COOK: 12–15 minutes

Chocolate Dough
- 180 g soft unsalted butter
- 100 g icing sugar
- 1 egg yolk
- 200 g flour, sifted
- 10 g unsweetened cocoa powder, sifted

Cinnamon Dough
- 140 g soft unsalted butter
- 75 g icing sugar
- ½ tsp vanilla extract
- ½ tsp ground cinnamon
- 1 egg yolk
- 200 g flour, sifted

Decoration
- 2 egg whites, beaten
- 100 g desiccated coconut

Chocolate Dough: Beat the butter with the icing sugar until smooth and creamy. Add the egg yolk then the sifted flour and cocoa powder; mix until smooth. Refrigerate the dough for 15–20 minutes.

Cinnamon Dough: Beat the butter with the icing sugar until smooth and creamy. Blend in the vanilla extract and cinnamon. Add the egg yolk then the sifted flour and mix until smooth. Refrigerate the dough for 15–20 minutes.

Roll out the chocolate dough to a thickness of 1 cm. Form the cinnamon dough by hand into a cylinder, 3 cm in diameter, and wrap the chocolate dough around it, retaining the cylinder shape; refrigerate for 15–20 minutes.

Preheat the oven to 160°C (325°F). Butter 2 baking trays.

Brush the chocolate-cinnamon dough with egg white and roll in the desiccated coconut. Using a sharp knife dipped in hot water and wiped dry between each slice, cut the dough into 1 cm thick slices. Transfer to the buttered baking trays and bake for 12–15 minutes. Cool on a rack.

Chocolate Macarons

MAKES 30

DIFFICULTY ★ ★ ★

PREPARE: 30 minutes

REST: 20 – 30 minutes

COOK: 10 – 15 minutes

REFRIGERATE: 24 hours

Macarons
- 125 g ground almonds, sifted
- 200 g icing sugar, sifted
- 30 g unsweetened cocoa powder, sifted
- 5 egg whites (150 g)
- 75 g caster sugar

Ganache
- 150 g dark chocolate
- 200 ml whipping cream
- 20 g mild honey

◊ This recipe must be prepared a day before serving.

Macarons: Tip the sifted almonds, icing sugar and cocoa powder into a bowl; set aside. In a separate bowl, whisk the egg whites until frothy. Add 25 g of the sugar a little at a time, whisking until the egg whites are smooth and shiny. Gradually add the remaining sugar whisking until stiff peaks form. Slowly fold in ¼ of the almond-icing sugar-cocoa mixture, cutting straight down to the bottom of the bowl with a spatula, and lifting up the contents, bring the spatula up the side of the bowl while giving it a quarter turn. Add the remainder in the same manner, in 3 separate batches. Stop folding as soon as the mixture is smooth and shiny. Fit a piping bag with a 4-mm round nozzle and fill with the macaron batter. Cover a baking tray with baking parchment; pipe 60 small rounds of batter, 2 cm in diameter, on it. Set aside at room temperature for 20– 30 minutes.

Preheat the oven to 160°C (325°F).

Bake the macarons for 5– 7 minutes then lower the oven temperature to 120– 130°C (250– 265°F) and continue baking for a further 5– 7 minutes. Remove from the baking tray and cool on a rack; refrigerate when the rounded part of the macaron is hard.

Ganache: Chop the chocolate and place in a bowl. Heat the cream and honey slowly until simmering. Pour half of the hot liquid over the chocolate and whisk to combine, add the remainder little by little, whisking gently; set aside until cold.

Spread the flat side of 30 macarons with ganache and sandwich with the remaining halves. Refrigerate for 24 hours, when the centres will become moist.

CHEF'S TIP: Use a raspberry jam or chocolate-hazelnut spread as an alternative filling. Macarons can be frozen after being baked.

Chocolate Macarons with Fleur de Sel

MAKES 8

DIFFICULTY ★ ★ ★

PREPARE: 30 minutes

REST: 20 – 30 minutes

COOK: 18 minutes

REFRIGERATE: 24 hours

Chocolate Macarons

- 180 g ground almonds, sifted
- 270 g icing sugar, sifted
- 30 g unsweetened cocoa powder, sifted
- 5 egg whites (150 g)
- 30 g caster sugar
- Sea salt flakes or fleur de sel

Ganache

- 150 g dark chocolate
- 2 egg yolks
- 100 g caster sugar
- 100 ml whipping cream
- 1 vanilla pod, split

◊ This recipe must be prepared a day before serving.

Chocolate Macarons: Tip the sifted almonds, icing sugar and cocoa powder into a bowl; set aside. In a separate bowl, whisk the egg whites until frothy. Add 10 g of the sugar a little at a time, whisking until the egg whites are smooth and shiny. Gradually add the remaining sugar, whisking until stiff peaks form. Slowly fold in ¼ of the almond-icing sugar-cocoa mixture, cutting straight down to the bottom of the bowl with a spatula, and lifting up the contents, bring the spatula up the side of the bowl while giving it a quarter turn. Add the remainder in the same manner, in three separate batches. Stop folding as soon as the mixture is smooth and shiny. Fit a piping bag with a plain round nozzle and fill with the macaron batter. Cover a baking tray with baking parchment; pipe 16 rounds of batter, 4– 5 cm diameter, on it. Set aside at room temperature for 20 – 30 minutes.

Preheat the oven to 160°C (325°F). Sprinkle a few sea salt flakes on the rounds of batter. Bake for 9 minutes then lower the oven temperature to 120– 130°C (250– 265°F) and continue baking for a further 9 minutes. Remove from the baking tray and cool on a rack; refrigerate when the rounded part of the macaron is hard.

Ganache: Chop the chocolate and place in a bowl. Beat the egg yolks and the sugar until pale yellow and creamy. Put the cream into a saucepan. Using the point of a knife, scrape the seeds from the vanilla pod into the cream; add the pod and heat until simmering. Quickly whisk $1/3$ of the hot cream into the egg yolk-sugar mixture. Pour into the remaining hot cream. Stirring constantly with a wooden spoon, cook over low heat until the cream is thickened and coats the back of the spoon. (Do not allow to boil!) Remove from the heat immediately. Strain over the chopped chocolate; stir until smooth. Set aside until cold; stir from time to time.

Fit a piping bag with a plain round nozzle, fill with the ganache; pipe balls of ganache onto the flat side of 8 macarons; top with the remaining halves. Refrigerate for 24 hours when the centres will become moist.

Marbled Chocolate-Lemon Madeleines

MAKES 48 MADELEINES

DIFFICULTY ★ ★ ★

PREPARE: 30 minutes

REFRIGERATE: Overnight

COOK: 10 – 12 minutes

Chocolate Dough

- 85 g unsalted butter
- 2 eggs
- 130 g caster sugar
- 35 ml milk
- 150 g flour, sifted
- 30 g unsweetened cocoa powder, sifted
- 1 tsp baking powder, sifted

Lemon Dough

- 85 g unsalted butter
- 2 eggs
- 130 g caster sugar
- 35 ml milk
- 150 g flour, sifted
- 1 tsp baking powder, sifted
- Grated zest of 2 lemons

◇ This recipe must be started one day ahead. You will need 4 regular-sized Madeleine sheet moulds (12 Madeleines) or you will have to cook 4 batches.

Chocolate Dough: Heat the butter until it turns golden brown and the milk solids colour and stick to the bottom of the saucepan (this is known as "beurre noisette"). Remove from the heat immediately and strain through a fine-meshed wire strainer; set aside to cool. Beat the eggs and sugar until pale yellow and creamy. Add the milk then the sifted flour and baking powder; stir to combine. Gradually blend in the "beurre noisette" until the batter starts to become foamy and increases in volume. Cover the bowl with cling film; refrigerate overnight.

Lemon Dough: Repeat the preceding step replacing the cocoa powder with the grated lemon zest.

The next day, preheat the oven to 200°C (400°F). Brush a Madeleine mould with butter, dust with flour and tip out the excess.

Spoon or pipe the chocolate batter into the imprints to the halfway mark. Then, fill with the lemon batter. Bake for 5 minutes, or until the Madeleines start to colour; lower the oven temperature to 180°C (350°F) and continue cooking for 5– 7 minutes. Remove from the oven, turn out immediately and cool on a rack.

If you are using a single mould, you will have enough dough for 4 batches.

CHEF'S TIP: For a little variation, you could cook the batters separately and have all chocolate or all lemon Madeleines.

Chocolate-Dipped Honey Madeleines

MAKES 24 MADELEINES

DIFFICULTY ★ ★ ☆

PREPARE: 30 minutes

REFRIGERATE: Overnight

COOK: 10 – 12 minutes

- 85 g unsalted butter
- 2 eggs
- 130 g mild honey
- 35 ml milk
- 170 g flour, sifted
- 1 tsp (5.5 g) baking powder, sifted
- 200 g dark chocolate

◊ This recipe must be started one day ahead. You will need 2 regular-sized Madeleine sheet moulds (12 Madeleines) or you will have to cook 2 batches.

◊ See pp.320-324: Tempering chocolate.

Heat the butter until it turns golden brown and the milk solids colour and stick to the bottom of the saucepan (this is known as "beurre noisette"). Remove from the heat immediately and strain through a fine-meshed wire strainer; set aside to cool.

Beat the egg yolks and the honey. Add the milk then the sifted flour and baking powder; stir to combine. Gradually blend in the "beurre noisette" until the batter starts to become foamy and increases in volume. Cover the bowl with cling film; refrigerate overnight.

The next day, preheat the oven to 200°C (400°F). Brush the mould with butter, dust with flour and tip out the excess.

Fill the imprints with the batter using a spoon or piping bag. Bake for 5 minutes, or until the Madeleines start to colour; lower the oven temperature to 180°C (350°F) and continue cooking for 5–7 minutes. Remove from the oven, turn out immediately and cool on a rack.

If you are using one mould, you'll have enough for a second batch.

Temper the chocolate: Coarsely chop the chocolate. Place ²/3 (140 g) in a bowl; melt over a simmering bain-marie until the temperature reaches 45°C on a digital thermometer. Remove the bowl from the heat and add the remaining chocolate, stirring until the temperature drops to 27°C. Return the bowl to the bain-marie, stir gently and reheat the chocolate to 32°C.

Using a fork, dip the lined side of the Madeleines into the chocolate; set aside on baking parchment. Let the chocolate harden at room temperature before serving.

CHEF'S TIP: When buttering the mould, brush it twice with soft, creamy butter, letting it harden between each coat. Dust with flour and refrigerate for a few minutes before filling with the batter. This way, your Madeleines will be much easier to turn out after they are baked.

Chocolate-Orange Bites

MAKES 12

DIFFICULTY ★ ★ ★

PREPARE: 45 minutes

REFRIGERATE: Overnight
+ 1 hour

COOK: 25 minutes

Orange Compote
• 1 orange
• 50 g caster sugar
• 50 g unrefined cane sugar
• 35 g mild honey

Chocolate-Orange Batter
• 50 g chocolate
• 60 g soft unsalted butter
• 100 g ground almonds
• 70 g caster sugar
• 2 eggs, beaten
• 10 g mild honey
• 2 tsp Cointreau

Decoration
• Icing sugar (optional)

◇ This recipe must be started
a day ahead. You will need a
silicone mini-muffin mould.

Orange Compote: Peel and segment the orange (p.312). Place the orange segments, caster and unrefined cane sugars and honey in a saucepan. Over low heat, cook for 25 minutes, or until the fruit becomes stewed; cool and refrigerate overnight.

Chocolate-Orange Batter: The next day, chop the chocolate and melt over a bain-marie. Beat the butter until creamy then add the melted chocolate, a little at a time. Place the almonds and sugar in the bowl of a mixer. Beating continuously, gradually add the eggs until the mixture is thick and smooth; add the honey. Blend in the chocolate-butter mixture then the Cointreau. Continue beating until the batter is smooth and velvety; refrigerate for 1 hour.

Preheat the oven to 180°C (350°F). Brush the mini-muffin mould with butter.

Fit a piping bag with a plain round nozzle and fill with the chocolate-orange batter; pipe a 1 cm layer in the bottom of each imprint. Use a teaspoon to place a little orange compote on the batter; reserve the remainder for decoration. Fill the imprints with batter to come to the 2/3 mark. Bake for 10 minutes, lower the oven temperature to 160°C (325°F), and continue baking for another 15 minutes.

Cool the chocolate-orange bites then turn out onto a rack. Decorate the top of each with the reserved orange compote. If desired, dust lightly with icing sugar.

Chocolate-Vanilla Millefeuilles

SERVES **6–8**

DIFFICULTY ★ ★ ★

PREPARE: 3 hours + 1 hour

REFRIGERATE: Overnight

COOK: 45 minutes

Chocolate Puff Pastry
- 50 g unsalted butter
- 225 g flour, sifted
- 25 g unsweetened cocoa powder, sifted
- 8 g salt
- 15 g caster sugar
- 120 ml water
- 250 g cold unsalted butter

Vanilla Pastry Cream
- 750 ml milk
- 2 vanilla pods, split
- 6 egg yolks
- 225 g caster sugar
- 50 g cornflour
- 25 g flour

Decoration
- Unsweetened cocoa powder, sifted

◇ This recipe must be started a day ahead.

Chocolate Puff Pastry: Heat the butter until it turns golden brown and the milk solids colour and stick to the bottom of the saucepan. Remove from the heat immediately and strain through a fine meshed wire strainer; set aside to cool. Tip the sifted flour and cocoa powder, salt and sugar into a large bowl; make a well in the centre. Pour in the water and melted butter and mix with the fingers. Pull the flour gradually into the well, mixing until blended to form a smooth ball. (If needed, sprinkle in a little water to moisten the dough.) Cut an 'X' into the top to stop the dough shrinking and wrap in cling film; refrigerate for 1 hour.

Lightly flour the work surface, place the dough on it; flatten slightly. Roll out into a cross shape, leaving a mound in the centre large enough for the butter. Sandwich the 250 g cold unsalted butter between 2 sheets of baking parchment and tap with a rolling pin until it is the same consistency as the dough; form into a square 2 cm thick. Place the butter on the mound in the centre of the dough; fold the extended sections of dough up and over, enclosing it completely. Dust the dough and rolling pin lightly with flour then lightly roll it over the dough to seal in the butter. Dust the work surface with flour and roll out the dough into a 12 x 36 cm rectangle (think of it as 3 square sections). Fold the top third over the middle section. Then, fold the bottom third over the middle to form a square; make sure all the edges are aligned. Give the dough a 45° turn to the right. Lightly press the rolling pin along the edges to seal, then roll out into a 12 x 36 cm rectangle again, folding as before; refrigerate 30 minutes. Roll and turn the dough twice again, as previously described and refrigerate for another 30 minutes. Roll and fold the dough twice more. (At this point, it should have been rolled and folded 6 times.) Refrigerate overnight.

The next day, preheat the oven to 145°C (295°F). Butter a 30 x 38 cm baking tray and lightly sprinkle with water. Roll the dough out to a thickness of 1–2 mm, cutting it to the same dimensions as the baking tray. Transfer to the baking tray, place a rack on top and bake for 45 minutes. Cool the puff pastry on a rack.

Vanilla Pastry Cream: Using only the ingredients listed, follow the instructions for Chocolate Pastry Cream on p.298; refrigerate 25 minutes.

Cut the puff pastry into 3 rectangles each 10 x 38 cm long. Spread or pipe the vanilla pastry cream onto one rectangle, place another rectangle on top and repeat with the pastry cream; finish with the remaining rectangle. Use a serrated knife and gently cut into 6–8 portions; dust with sifted cocoa powder.

Mini Chocolate Éclairs

MAKES 20 MINI ÉCLAIRS

DIFFICULTY ★ ★ ★

PREPARE: 1 hour

COOK: 16 minutes

REFRIGERATE: 25 minutes

Choux Pastry Dough
• 125 ml water
• 50 g unsalted butter
• ½ tsp salt
• ½ tsp caster sugar
• 75 g flour, sifted
• 2 eggs
• 1 beaten egg for glazing

Chocolate Pastry Cream
• 75 g dark chocolate
• 250 ml milk
• 1 vanilla pod, split
• 2 egg yolks
• 65 g caster sugar
• 20 g cornflour

Chocolate Glaze
• 50 g dark chocolate
• 50 g icing sugar
• 2 tsp water

◊ See p.256: The best way to fill éclairs.

Preheat the oven to 180°C (350°F). Butter a baking tray.

Choux Pastry Dough: Using the ingredients listed, follow the instructions on p.209. When the paste is ready to be used, fit a piping bag with a plain round nozzle, and spoon in the paste. Pipe fingers of choux, 5–6 cm long, on the baking tray. Brush the tops with the egg glaze. Transfer to the oven and bake for 8 minutes without opening the door. Then lower the oven temperature to 165°C (325°F) and continue baking for another 8 minutes, or until the éclairs are golden and sound hollow when tapped. Cool on a rack.

Chocolate Pastry Cream: Finely chop the chocolate and place in a bowl. Pour the milk into a saucepan. Using the point of a knife, scrape the seeds from the vanilla pod into the milk, add the pod and bring to the boil; remove from the heat. Beat the egg yolks and sugar until pale yellow, thick and creamy; add the cornflour. Discard the vanilla pod and quickly whisk half the hot milk into the egg yolk-sugar-cornflour mixture; add the remaining milk. Cook over low heat, whisking continuously until the cream thickens then boil for 1 minute while continuing to whisk. Remove from the heat and pour the pastry cream over the chopped chocolate; stir until smooth. Cover the surface of the chocolate pastry cream with cling film; set aside to cool then refrigerate for 25 minutes.

Chocolate Glaze: Melt the chocolate over a bain-marie. Combine the icing sugar and water and blend into the melted chocolate. Heat until the temperature of the mixture registers 40°C on a digital thermometer.

Fit a piping bag with a plain round nozzle and fill it with pastry cream. Pierce a small hole in the flat side of each éclair and fill with chocolate pastry cream. Spread a layer of chocolate glaze on the top of the éclairs using a spatula and set aside to dry before serving.

Passion Fruit Muffins with Chocolate Chips

MAKES 5

DIFFICULTY ★ ★ ★

PREPARE: 15 minutes

COOK: 15 minutes

Muffin Batter
- 50 g crème fraîche
- A few drops of lemon juice
- 2 eggs
- 140 g caster sugar
- 3 passion fruits
- 2 pinches of salt
- 110 g flour, sifted
- ½ tsp baking powder, sifted
- 50 g unsalted butter, melted
- 50 g chocolate chips

Glaze
- Neutral glaze
- 1 passion fruit

Preheat the oven to 170°C (335°F).

Muffin Batter: Combine the crème fraîche and a few drops of lemon juice in a bowl. Add the eggs, sugar, the pulp from the passion fruits and the salt. Whisk together, then fold in the sifted flour and baking powder. Stir in the melted butter and chocolate chips. Transfer to a piping bag fitted with a plain nozzle and pipe into 5 muffin cases. Bake for 15 minutes. Allow to cool before glazing.

Glaze: Mix the neutral glaze with the passion fruit pulp. Brush the tops of the muffins with the glaze. Serve immediately.

Chocolate Butter Biscuits with Lemon Cream

MAKES 20–30 BISCUITS

DIFFICULTY ★ ★ ★

PREPARE: 55 minutes

REFRIGERATE: Overnight

COOK: 15 – 20 minutes

Chocolate Butter Biscuits
- 210 g unsalted butter
- 180 g caster sugar
- ¼ tsp sea salt flakes or fleur de sel
- 5 egg yolks
- 250 g flour, sifted
- 3 tsp baking powder, sifted
- 30 g unsweetened cocoa powder, sifted

Lemon Cream
- 2 leaves gelatine
- 4 eggs
- 175 g caster sugar
- 150 ml lemon juice
- 300 g soft unsalted butter

Garnish
- 200 g raspberries
- 200 g strawberries

◊ This recipe must be started a day ahead.

Chocolate Butter Biscuits: Place the butter, sugar and sea salt flakes in a large bowl and beat until creamy. Add the egg yolks, one at a time, beating after each addition. Blend in the sifted flour, baking and cocoa powders, and form the dough into a ball. Wrap in cling film and refrigerate overnight.

Lemon Cream: On the day of serving, soften the gelatine leaves in ice-cold water. Beat the eggs. Heat the sugar and lemon juice over a bain-marie then whisk in the beaten eggs. Whisk briskly for 10–15 minutes, or until thickened. Squeeze the excess water from the gelatine. Remove the lemon-juice mixture from the bain-marie, add the gelatine; stir to dissolve. Pour the mixture into a separate bowl and blend in half the soft butter; refrigerate for 15 minutes. Gradually add the remaining butter, whisking until the mixture is smooth and shiny. Fit a piping bag with a plain round nozzle and fill with the lemon cream; refrigerate until required.

Preheat the oven to 180°C (350°F). Line a baking tray with baking parchment. Brush a 7 cm round pastry cutter with butter.

Dust the work surface with flour and roll the dough out to a thickness of 5 mm. Cut out discs of dough with the pastry cutter and place on the baking tray using a palette knife; leave a few centimetres between one. Bake for 15– 20 minutes, or until firm to the touch. Remove from the oven; cool on a rack.

Pipe mounds of lemon cream on each of the biscuits; refrigerate until required. Serve with fresh raspberries and strawberries.

CHEF'S TIP: If desired, you could replace the lemon juice with grapefruit, lime or passion fruit juice.

Chocolate-Raspberry Biscuits

MAKES 35 BISCUITS

DIFFICULTY ★ ★ ★

PREPARE: 1 hour

REFRIGERATE: 40 minutes

COOK: 10 minutes

Biscuits
- 160 g soft salted butter
- 140 g icing sugar
- 3 egg yolks
- 210 g flour, sifted
- 1 tsp baking powder, sifted

Chocolate Mousse
- 150 g dark (70%) chocolate
- 270 ml whipping cream
- 75 g caster sugar
- 4 egg yolks

Decoration
- Raspberry jam
- 250 g raspberries

Biscuits: Place the butter and icing sugar in a large bowl and beat until creamy. Add the egg yolks, one at a time, beating after each addition. Blend in the sifted flour and baking powder. Form the dough into a ball and wrap in cling film; refrigerate 20 minutes.

Preheat the oven to 180°C (350°F). Line a baking tray with baking parchment.

Brush a 6 cm round pastry cutter with butter. Dust the work surface with flour and roll the dough out to a thickness of 2 mm. Cut out discs of dough using the pastry cutter and place on the baking tray using a palette knife; leave a few centimetres between each one. Bake for 10 minutes, or until firm to the touch. Remove from the oven; cool on a rack.

Chocolate Mousse: Chop the chocolate and melt over a bain-marie; remove from the heat. Whisk the cream with the sugar until firm peaks cling to the whisk. Beating quickly, add $1/3$ of the cream and the egg yolks to the melted chocolate. Fold in the remaining cream with a spatula. Fit a piping bag with a star nozzle and fill with the chocolate mousse; refrigerate for about 20 minutes.

Using a teaspoon, spread a little raspberry jam on each biscuit, pipe with a rosette of chocolate mousse and top with a raspberry. Refrigerate the biscuits until required.

CHEF'S TIP: In place of the raspberry jam, you could use a seedless raspberry jelly.

Chocolate Biscuits

MAKES 35 BISCUITS

DIFFICULTY ★ ★ ★

PREPARE: 30 minutes

REFRIGERATE: 20 minutes

COOK: 15 minutes

- 200 g salted butter, chilled
- 50 g dark chocolate
- 200 g flour, sifted
- 25 g unsweetened cocoa powder, sifted
- 80 g unrefined cane sugar
- 1 egg yolk

Preheat the oven to 180°C (350°F). Line a baking tray with baking parchment.

Cut the chilled butter into small cubes. Finely chop the chocolate. Tip the sifted flour, cocoa powder and unrefined cane sugar into a large bowl. Add the butter cubes rubbing them into the dry ingredients with your fingertips until the mixture resembles fine breadcrumbs. Blend in the egg yolk and the chopped chocolate.

Divide the dough in two even portions. Roll each one into a cylinder about 3 cm in diameter. Refrigerate for 20 minutes. Cut the dough into slices 1 cm thick and place on the baking tray. Bake for about 15 minutes, or until firm to the touch; cool on a rack.

CHEF'S TIP: For a sweeter biscuit, use half dark and half white chocolate.

Chocolate-Mascarpone Semolina Fritters

MAKES 12

DIFFICULTY ★ ★ ★

PREPARE: 2½ hours

REFRIGERATE: 2 hours

INFUSE: 30 minutes

COOK: 45 minutes

Chocolate-Mascarpone Filling
• 100 g dark chocolate
• 100 g mascarpone

Semolina
• 300 ml milk
• 1 vanilla pod, split
• 25 g semolina
• 25 g caster sugar
• 2 – 3 drops bitter almond extract
• Ground almonds

Coating
• 100 g blanched almonds
• 100 g breadcrumbs
• 2 eggs, beaten

• Vegetable oil for frying
• Caster sugar

Chocolate-Mascarpone Filling: Melt the chocolate over a bain-marie. When cooled, blend in the mascarpone. Refrigerate the mixture until firm enough to be rolled into 12 small balls, then refrigerate again for 1 hour.

Semolina: Pour the milk into a saucepan. Using the point of a knife, scrape the seeds from the vanilla pod into the milk; add the pod and heat until almost simmering. Remove from the heat, cover and infuse for 30 minutes. Discard the vanilla pod and bring the milk to the boil. Remove the saucepan from the heat and stirring continuously, add the semolina in a thin, steady stream. Continue stirring and add the sugar; bring the mixture to the boil. Cook over low heat for about 20 minutes, stirring often to stop the semolina sticking. Pour the mixture, in an even layer, into a Swiss roll tin or shallow gratin dish; set aside until cold.

Divide the semolina into 12 portions. Cover each chocolate-mascarpone ball with a layer of cooked semolina and roll in ground almonds to stop the semolina balls sticking to the fingers or hands.

Coating: Coarsely chop the blanched almonds and combine with the breadcrumbs. Dip the semolina balls into the beaten egg then roll in the breadcrumb mixture; refrigerate for at least 30 minutes.

Pour the vegetable oil into a deep fat fryer (or heavy-bottomed saucepan), to a depth of approximately 7½ cm; heat to 200°C (400°F). Use tongs to immerse 3 or 4 balls in the hot oil then deep fry for 3– 5 minutes, or until lightly golden. Drain on kitchen paper and roll the fritters in sugar. Repeat for the remaining semolina balls; serve.

CHEF'S TIP: To make it easier to coat the chocolate-mascarpone balls with the semolina mixture, they could be frozen for 2 hours.

Chocolate and Mango Religieuses

MAKES 12

DIFFICULTY ★ ★ ★

PREPARE: 1½ hours

COOK: 1 hour

REFRIGERATE: 30 minutes

Choux Pastry Dough
- 125 ml water
- 50 g unsalted butter
- ½ tsp salt
- ½ tsp caster sugar
- 75 g flour, sifted
- 2 eggs + 1 beaten egg for the glazing

Jellied Mango Coulis
- 2½ leaves gelatine
- 350 g mango purée
- 75 g caster sugar

Chocolate Pastry Cream
- 180 g dark chocolate
- 500 ml milk
- 30 g unsalted butter
- 5 egg yolks
- 125 g caster sugar
- 30 g flour
- 30 g cornflour
- 180 ml whipping cream

Ganache
- 75 g dark chocolate
- 75 ml whipping cream

Glaze
- 400 g fondant icing
- 50 ml water
- Orange food colouring

◊ See p.209: Preparing choux pastry dough.

◊ See p.256: The best way to fill éclairs.

Preheat the oven to 180°C (350°F). Line a 30 cm x 38 cm baking tray with baking parchment.

Choux Pastry Dough: Make according to the recipe on page 209. Use a piping bag fitted with a plain nozzle to pipe 12 x 4 cm diameter choux balls and 12 x 1 cm diameter choux balls onto the baking tray. Brush with egg glaze and bake for 15 minutes without opening the oven door. Then lower the temperature to 165°C (325°F). Leave the door partially open and continue baking for 15 minutes. Take the smaller choux puffs out after 10 minutes. Cool on a rack.

Jellied Mango Coulis: Soften the gelatine leaves in a bowl of cold water. Bring the mango purée and sugar to the boil in a saucepan. Squeeze excess water from the leaves of gelatine and whisk into the purée. Leave to cool, then transfer to a piping bag fitted with a small plain nozzle.

Chocolate Pastry Cream: Prepare as indicated on page 298 heating the butter in the milk, and adding the flour with the cornflour. Whip the cream until it forms stiff peaks and clings to the tip of the whisk. Whisk the chocolate pastry cream until smooth and gently fold in the whipped cream. Transfer to a piping bag fitted with a plain nozzle.

Ganache: Prepare as indicated on page 12. Transfer the ganache to a piping bag fitted with a star nozzle.

Cut the larger choux puffs in half and pipe in the chocolate pastry cream. Next, place a small amount of jellied mango coulis in the middle of the cream and put the two choux halves back together. Fill the small choux puffs from the bottom, as indicated on page 256.

Glaze: Warm the fondant icing and soften with the water. Add the food colouring. Glaze the choux puffs by dipping them halfway into the fondant. Remove any excess fondant and smooth using your finger. Leave to dry.

Pipe a ganache rosette on top of the larger choux puffs and top each one with a smaller choux puff. Finish by decorating the smaller choux puffs with a ganache rosette.

Chocolate 'Tagliatelle' in Orange Salad

SERVES 4

DIFFICULTY ★ ★ ★

PREPARE: 1 hour

REFRIGERATE: 1½ hours

REST: 30 minutes

COOK: 10 minutes

Chocolate 'Tagliatelle'
- 200 g flour, sifted
- 1 pinch salt
- 2 eggs
- 40 g icing sugar
- 40 g unsweetened cocoa powder
- 2– 3 tbsp water

Orange Salad
- 4 oranges
- 2 tbsp caster sugar
- 2 tbsp grenadine syrup
- 1 tbsp orange marmalade
- 2 tbsp Cointreau

- 1½ L water
- 200 g caster sugar
- ¼ tsp vanilla essence

Decoration
- Mint leaves

Chocolate 'Tagliatelle': Tip the sifted flour and salt into a bowl and make a well in the centre. Beat the eggs in a separate bowl. Sift the icing sugar and cocoa powder into the beaten eggs, stir to combine then blend in the water. Pour the mixture into the well and slowly draw in the flour to form a ball. Knead until the dough no longer sticks to the fingers, wrap in cling film; refrigerate for $1^{1}/2$ hours.

Dust the work surface with flour. Divide the dough into 3 pieces and roll out each one into a rectangle 3 mm thick. Lightly dust each rectangle with flour and place one on top of the other then cut to form an even rectangle. Roll up the rectangle of dough fairly tightly so it forms a cylinder; use a sharp knife to cut slices 1 cm thick to obtain 'tagliatelle'. Spread out a clean tea towel, dust it lightly with flour and place the tagliatelle on it to dry for about 30 minutes.

Orange Salad: Squeeze 2 of the oranges and put the juice into a saucepan. Add the sugar and bring to the boil. Remove from the heat, stir in the grenadine syrup, orange marmalade and Cointreau; set aside until cold.

Segment the remaining oranges: Using a very sharp knife, cut a small slice off both ends of the orange. Stand it on a cutting board and, working from top to bottom, cut off the peel and all the pith in wide strips. Hold the peeled orange in the palm of your hand. Insert the knife between the membrane and the flesh, cutting towards the centre without cutting the membrane. Then cut on the other side of the segment and ease it out. Continue until all the segments have been removed; repeat for the remaining orange. Transfer the segments to the syrup; refrigerate the orange salad until required.

Bring the water, sugar and the vanilla to the boil. Add the 'tagliatelle' and cook for 10 minutes. Drain in a colander then carefully combine with the orange salad. Divide between 4 rimmed soup dishes and decorate with mint leaves.

Chocolate Tuile Biscuits

MAKES 15

DIFFICULTY ★ ★ ★

PREPARE: 35 minutes

COOL: 15– 25 minutes

- 250 g dark chocolate
- 100 g flaked almonds, toasted

◇ See pp.320-324: Tempering chocolate.

Cut five rectangles of acetate 12 x 30 cm long. Prepare a pastry brush, a rolling pin and some adhesive tape.

Temper the chocolate: Coarsely chop the dark chocolate. Place 2/3 (160 g) of the chopped chocolate in a bowl; melt over a bain-marie until the temperature reaches 45°C on a digital thermometer. Remove the bowl from the heat and add the remaining chocolate, stirring until the temperature drops to 27°C. Return the bowl to the bain-marie, stir gently and reheat the chocolate to 32°C.

Work quickly and use a pastry brush to form three chocolate discs, 8 cm in diameter and 2– 3 mm thick on one of the rectangles; sprinkle with toasted almonds. Place it on the rolling pin and gently curl the chocolate discs around the pin; secure the acetate with adhesive tape. Repeat the operation 4 more times, placing one acetate rectangle on top of the other. Cool at room temperature for 15– 25 minutes, or until the chocolate hardens. Lift off the rectangles one by one; gently remove the chocolate discs. Place in an airtight container and store in a cool location (12°C maximum).

CHEF'S TIP: Chocolate is easier to work with when the weather is mild. You could also make the tuiles using either white or milk chocolate but be sure to follow the tempering instructions given on pp.320-324.

Chocolate-Hazelnut Tuile Biscuits

MAKES 30

DIFFICULTY ★ ★ ★

PREPARE: 30 minutes

REFRIGERATE: 20 minutes

COOK: 6–8 minutes

- 50 g soft unsalted butter
- 100 g icing sugar
- 2 egg whites
- 40 g flour, sifted
- 10 g unsweetened cocoa powder, sifted
- 200 g hazelnuts, toasted and chopped

Preheat the oven to 180°C (350°F). Line a baking tray with parchment paper. Lightly brush a rolling pin with butter or oil.

Beat the butter and icing sugar until creamy. Add the egg whites little by little, mixing well after each addition. Then, blend in the sifted flour and cocoa powder. Refrigerate for 20 minutes.

Use a spoon to thinly spread out the mixture on the baking tray forming discs about 6 cm in diameter. Leave sufficient space between each one to allow for spreading during cooking. Sprinkle with chopped hazelnuts and bake for 6–8 minutes.

Loosen the tuiles from the baking tray (using a metal scraper) and, working very quickly (the tuiles may shatter if allowed to harden), curl them over the rolling pin while still warm and pliable. When firm, slip off and cool completely on a rack. Repeat until all the tuiles have been formed.

CHEF'S TIP: Pastry chefs often have among their tools, a triangular metal paint scraper which makes lifting tuiles off the baking tray much easier. To prevent the tuiles becoming too hard to fashion, you may prefer to make them in batches.

Delicious mouthfuls

The best way to temper chocolate over a bain-marie

The following steps will ensure a glossy and crisp finish. If you are tempering milk chocolate, melt to 45°C, cool to 26°C, and reheat to 29°C. If you are tempering white chocolate, melt to 40°C, cool to 25°C and reheat to 28°C.

① Coarsely chop 300 g dark (preferably couverture) chocolate or the amount specified in your choice of recipe (see pp. 336 or 368). Place 2/3 of the chocolate in a bowl; melt over a bain-marie of gently simmering water. The bottom of the bowl should not touch the water; shine and smoothness may be lost.

② Heat until the temperature reaches 45°C on a digital thermometer. Remove the bowl from the heat and stir in the remaining chocolate; stir with a spatula from time to time.

③ As soon as the temperature cools to 27°C, return the bowl to the bain-marie and reheat, stirring gently until the chocolate reaches 32°C (maximum). When the chocolate is smooth and shiny, it is ready to be used for chocolate shavings or as a coating.

The best way to temper chocolate with Mycryo®

Adapt the amount of dark chocolate used according to your chosen recipe.

(1) Chop 300 g of dark chocolate (preferably couverture chocolate). Melt the chocolate over a bain-marie. The water should simmer, not boil, and should never come into contact with the chocolate as the chocolate will become dull and less fluid. The temperature of the chocolate should reach 45°C on a digital thermometer.

(2) Once the chocolate reaches a temperature of 45°C, remove it from the heat and place on the work surface. Leave to cool to 35°C, stirring from time to time.

(3) Once it has reached 35°C, position a fine mesh china cap sieve over the bowl of chocolate and sprinkle in the Mycryo® butter (1% of the chocolate mass). Mix well. Leave the chocolate to cool to 31°C. It should be smooth and glossy.

The best way to temper chocolate on a marble work surface

Adapt the amount of dark chocolate used according to your chosen recipe.

(1) Chop 300 g of dark chocolate (preferably couverture chocolate). Melt the chocolate over a bain-marie. The water should simmer, not boil, and should never come into contact with the chocolate as the chocolate will become dull and less fluid. The temperature of the chocolate should reach 45°C on a digital thermometer.

(2) Once the chocolate reaches a temperature of 45°C, remove it from the heat and pour three-quarters onto the cold marble.

(3) Use a stainless-steel chocolate scraper to spread out the chocolate, using an up and down movement and from left to right.

④ Bring the chocolate to the centre using the chocolate scraper. Use a stainless-steel palette knife to scrape off the chocolate that accumulates on the scraper.

⑤ Repeat steps 3 and 4 several times until the chocolate begins to thicken.

⑥ When the chocolate starts to thicken, immediately return to the bowl containing the remaining chocolate. Reheat over the bain-marie, stirring gently several times so that the bowl does not increase the temperature of the chocolate too much or too quickly. Once the chocolate reaches 32°C (maximum), remove from the bain-marie immediately. It should be smooth and glossy.

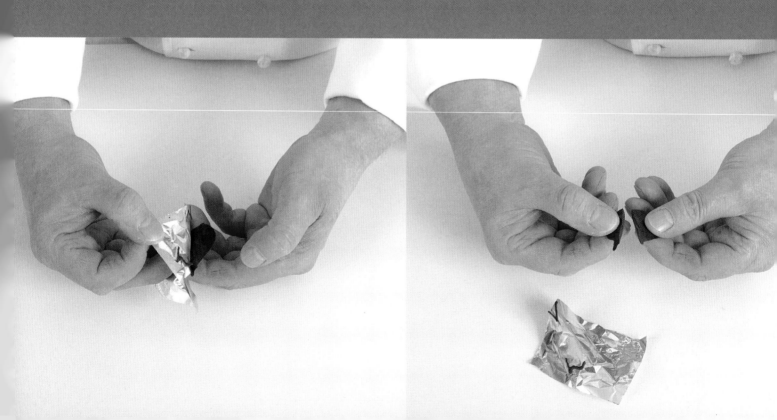

The best way to check if chocolate is tempered

1. Pour a small amount of chocolate onto a piece of aluminium foil.

2. Leave the chocolate to harden in the refrigerator for 7 minutes, then remove from the aluminium foil.

3. The tempered chocolate is ready to be used if the piece of chocolate is smooth, glossy and snaps easily. For milk chocolate: Melt to 45°C, cool to 26°C, then reheat to 29°C. For white chocolate: Melt to 40°C, cool to 25°C, then reheat to 28°C.

The best way to make praline paste

The following will produce 230 g praline paste. Any paste greater than the quantity necessary for the recipe of your choice can be stored in a glass jar in a cool, dry location for 3 weeks. Before using, stir well.

(1) Heat 30 ml of water and 150 g of sugar in a medium saucepan over low heat, stirring until the sugar dissolves completely; increase the heat and boil for 2 minutes without stirring. Stir in 75 g almonds and 75 g hazelnuts using a wooden spoon. Remove from the heat and continue stirring until the sugar crystallises cover-ing the nuts with a white powder. Return the saucepan to the heat until the sugar melts and the nuts turn golden brown.

(2) Spread the caramelised nuts on an oiled baking tray; set aside until cold.

(3) Break the praline in pieces, place in a food processor and grind, first to a powder then to a creamy paste. To avoid overworking the food processor, stop the food processor often and mix with a spatula or grind the praline in several batches.

The best way to mould chocolates

Temper the chocolate, prepare the ganache and use the mould(s) indicated in the recipe of your choice (for example, pp.346, 348).

(1) Using a piping bag, fill the imprints with tempered chocolate.

(2) Tap the mould on the work surface to release any air bubbles in the chocolate then invert it, tipping out the excess. Lightly tap the mould with a flexible spatula so that the chocolate flows quicker.

(3) Keep the mould inverted and using a metal scraper remove the residual chocolate from the top of the mould. The surface of the mould should be clean and the chocolate should only line at the bottom and sides of the imprints (i.e. there is space in the centre). Set the mould aside at room temperature for 10 minutes, or until the chocolate hardens.

4. Fill a piping bag with ganache, cut a small opening, place the end in the centre of each imprint. Fill the imprints leaving 2 mm of empty space between the ganache and the top of the mould (to seal), being careful not to overflow. Then refrigerate for 20 minutes until hardened.

5. Cover the imprints with a layer of tempered chocolate to enclose ganache and seal the chocolate.

6. Immediately place a sheet of thick plastic, or acetate, on top; press on each imprint to push the chocolate into the imprints.

7. Scrape the surface of the mould with a plastic scraper (corne) to remove excess chocolate. Refrigerate 20 minutes until the chocolate is hardened.

8. Once the chocolate has hardened, carefully pull away the sheet of thick plastic and invert the mould and lightly tap it on the work surface to turn out the chocolates. Keep the chocolates according to the method and time indicated in the recipe.

The best way to coat sweets with chocolate

Prepare a ganache, shape it into small balls and refrigerate until hardened as indicated in the recipe of your choice (pp.344, 376, 384).

(1) Remove the ganache balls from the refrigerator and bring them to room temperature (ideally between 18–22°C). Put unsweetened cocoa powder into a large flat high-sided container. Temper a sufficient quantity of chocolate (p.314).

(2) Slide a regular or chocolate fork (ringed or pronged) under the ganache ball and dip the ball carefully into

the tempered chocolate. Then lift the ball up, letting the excess chocolate drip into the bowl. Gently shake the fork, wiping the base several times on the side of the bowl to remove the residual chocolate and obtain a smooth coating.

(3) Using the fork, roll the chocolate in the cocoa powder. Set aside to firm at room temperature. When the chocolates have hardened, place in a sieve and shake gently to remove excess cocoa.

The best way to make a small paper piping bag for decorating

Use for the quantity of chocolate specified in the recipe of your choice (p.322).

1 Cut a 25 cm square of baking parchment into 2 triangles and discard one. For ease of explanation, we will call the right angle "A", and the other two angles, "B" and "C". Curl the point of "B" around until it meets the point of the right angle "A", forming a cone. Wrap the opposite point "C", around to meet the other two points and tighten the cone. Pull all three points together tightly to create a sharp tip and fold the flap inside, creasing it firmly to hold the bag in shape.

2 Using a spoon, fill the piping bag with warm melted chocolate

3 Roll and fold over the top of the bag until the chocolate is squeezed into the nose of the cone. The parchment should be taut around the chocolate. Just before using, snip off the tip. For fine lines of piping, cut close to the tip.

Chocolate Almond Treats

MAKES 20

DIFFICULTY ★ ★ ★

PREPARE: 45 minutes

REST: 30 minutes

- 200 g yellow almond paste
- 20 blanched almonds, toasted

Chocolate Coating
- 300 g dark chocolate

◊ See pp.320-324: Tempering chocolate.

Roll the almond paste into a rope about 2 cm in diameter. Cut the rope into 20 pieces each weighing 10 g. Wearing rubber gloves roll the pieces by hand to form ovals. Lightly press a toasted almond into each oval.

Chocolate Coating: Temper the dark chocolate: Coarsely chop the chocolate. Place $^2/_3$ (200 g) in a bowl and melt over a simmering bain-marie until the temperature reaches 45°C on a digital thermometer. Remove the bowl from the heat and add the remaining chocolate stirring until the temperature cools to 27°C. Return the bowl to the bain-marie and, stirring gently, reheat the chocolate to 32°C.

Line a baking tray with baking parchment. Insert a toothpick into each almond paste oval.

Dip the bottom of the ovals into the tempered chocolate to come to the 3/4 mark and place on the baking tray. Set aside at room temperature for 30 minutes, or until the chocolate hardens.

Remove the toothpicks. Store in an airtight container at 12°C maximum; consume within 15 days.

CHEF'S TIP: It's possible to change the colour of the paste, if you prefer, by using a plain almond paste and adding food colouring to obtain the colour of your choice.

Annabella Bonbons

MAKES 30

DIFFICULTY ★ ★ ★

MACERATE: Overnight

PREPARE: 1½ hours

- 40 g raisins
- 20 ml rum
- 150 g almond paste
- Icing sugar

Chocolate Coating
- 300 g white chocolate

Decoration
- 50 g dark chocolate

◊ This recipe must be started the day before.

◊ See p.329: Making paper piping bag

◊ See pp.320-324: Tempering chocolate.

Macerate the raisins in the rum overnight.

The next day, combine the macerated raisins and the almond paste. Dust the work surface with icing sugar. Wearing rubber gloves, divide the almond paste into two equal parts and form each one into a rope. Cut the rope into pieces 1 cm thick (about 10–15 g). Roll by hand into balls and place on a plate.

Chocolate Coating: Temper the white chocolate: Coarsely chop the chocolate. Place $^2/3$ (200 g) of the chopped chocolate in a bowl; melt over a simmering bain-marie until the temperature reaches 40°C on a digital thermometer. Remove the bowl from the heat and add the remaining chocolate, stirring until the temperature cools to 25°C. Return the bowl to the bain-marie and, stirring gently, reheat the chocolate to 28°C.

Make a small paper piping bag using baking parchment. Melt the dark chocolate over a bain-marie; cool. Wearing rubber gloves, dip the almond paste balls into the tempered white chocolate, shake gently to remove the excess and set on baking parchment to harden. Fill the paper piping bag with the melted dark chocolate. Roll and fold over the top of the bag until the chocolate is squeezed into the nose of the cone. The parchment should be taut around the chocolate. Snip off the end close to the tip and streak the white chocolate with fine lines of dark chocolate.

CHEF'S TIP: You could also use a teaspoon dipped in dark chocolate to streak the white chocolates. When serving, play with colours. Here we have accompanied the Annabella Bonbons with Plain Chocolate Truffles (p. 376), rolled into log shapes before dipping into cocoa powder.

Soft Chocolate Caramels

MAKES 25

DIFFICULTY ★ ★ ★

PREPARE: 30 minutes

REFRIGERATE: 2 hours

- 80 g dark chocolate
- 250 ml whipping cream
- 250 g caster sugar
- 75 g mild honey
- 25 g unsalted butter

Chop the chocolate and place in a bowl.

Heat the whipping cream until simmering and set aside. Place 50 g of the sugar in a separate saucepan, stir from time to time with a wooden spoon and cook until it turns golden. To stop the sugar cooking, add the cream, a little at a time, stirring with the wooden spoon (the mixture will bubble violently). Add the remaining sugar and continue stirring until the mixture is thick and creamy; be careful not to let the mixture burn.

Moisten a wooden spoon and use it to blend the honey into the caramel. Return the mixture to the heat and cook until it registers 114°C on a digital thermometer; remove from the heat. Stir in a little chopped chocolate, gradually add the remainder then blend in the butter.

Place an 18 cm square dessert frame on a sheet of baking parchment and pour in the chocolate caramel; refrigerate for 2 hours.

Slide the point of a knife around the wall of the frame and lift it off. Cut the caramel as desired.

CHEF'S TIP: If you do not have a dessert frame, use an 18 cm square cake tin lined with cling film. Let the edges of the cling film hang over the sides of the tin, so that you can turn out the hardened caramel easily.

Chocolate Coated Cherries

MAKES 30

DIFFICULTY ★ ★ ★

DRAIN: Overnight

PREPARE: 30 minutes

REST: 30 minutes

• 300 g stemmed Morello or Montmorency cherries, in eau-de-vie

Chocolate Coating
• 350 g dark chocolate

◇ See pp.320-324: Tempering chocolate

◇ This recipe must be started the night before.

Drain and set the cherries aside to dry overnight.

Chocolate Coating: Temper the chocolate: Coarsely chop the chocolate. Place $2/3$ (240 g) of the chopped chocolate in a bowl; melt over a simmering bain-marie until the temperature reaches 45°C on a digital thermometer. Remove the bowl from the heat and add the remaining chocolate stirring until the temperature cools to 27°C. Return the bowl to the bain-marie and, stirring gently, reheat the chocolate to 32°C.

Holding the stem, dip each cherry into the tempered chocolate and shake gently to remove the excess; place on baking parchment. Set aside to harden at room temperature for 30 minutes.

CHEF'S TIP: To ensure that the chocolate coating is smooth and shiny, the cherries must be dry and at room temperature when dipped.

Chocolate-Orange Truffles

MAKES 30 TRUFFLES

DIFFICULTY ★ ★ ★

PREPARE: 1 hour 20 minutes

DRY: Overnight

Orange-Almond Filling
- 45 g candied orange peel
- 200 g almond paste
- 1 tbsp Kirsch
- Icing sugar

Chocolate Coating
- 350 g dark chocolate

◇ See pp.320-324: Tempering chocolate.

◇ This recipe must be started a day ahead.

Orange-Almond Filling: Finely chop the candied orange peel, then combine with the almond paste and Kirsch; mix until smooth. Dust the work surface with icing sugar. Wearing rubber gloves, divide the mixture in two equal parts and form each one into a long rope. Cut the ropes into pieces 1 cm thick (approx. 15 g). Roll by hand into balls and place on a plate. Set aside to dry out overnight.

The next day, cover a baking tray with baking parchment and set out a wire rack.

Chocolate Coating: Temper the chocolate: Coarsely chop the chocolate and place $2/3$ (230 g) in a bowl; melt over a simmering bain-marie until the temperature reaches 45°C on a digital thermometer. Remove the bowl from the heat and add the remaining chocolate stirring until the temperature cools to 27°C. Return the bowl to the bain-marie and, stirring gently, reheat the chocolate to 32°C.

Wearing rubber gloves, dip the balls, one by one, into the tempered chocolate; set on the baking parchment to harden. Then coat with chocolate again, shaking gently to remove the excess and place on the rack. When the chocolate starts to firm, roll the balls on the rack to form 'prickles'. Place on the baking tray to harden at room temperature for 20 minutes. Store the chocolates in an airtight container.

Chocolate-Pistachio Truffles

MAKES 40 TRUFFLES

DIFFICULTY ★ ★ ★

PREPARE: 1 hour 20 minutes

DRY: Overnight

Pistachio-Almond Filling
- 1 tbsp water
- 20 g caster sugar
- 5 g mild honey
- 35 g pistachios
- 200 g almond paste
- 20 g soft unsalted butter
- ½ tbsp rum
- Icing sugar, sifted

Chocolate Coating
- 400 g dark chocolate

◊ See pp.320-324: Tempering chocolate.

◊ This recipe must be started a day ahead.

Pistachio-Almond Filling: Bring the water, sugar and honey to the boil to make a syrup; set aside. Put the pistachios into a blender or food processor and grind to a fine powder; add the syrup and continue mixing to obtain a thin paste. Combine the pistachio paste with the almond paste, soft butter and rum. Dust the work surface with sifted icing sugar. Wearing rubber gloves, divide the mixture in two equal parts and form each one into a rope about 30 cm long. Cut the ropes into 2 cm pieces. Roll by hand into balls and place on a plate. Set aside to dry out overnight.

The next day, cover the baking tray with baking parchment and set out a wire rack.

Chocolate Coating: Temper the chocolate: Coarsely chop the chocolate and place $2/3$ (260 g) in a bowl; melt over a slowly simmering bain-marie until the temperature reaches 45°C on a digital thermometer. Remove the bowl from the heat and add the remaining chocolate, stirring until the temperature cools to 27°C. Return the bowl to the bain-marie and, stirring gently, reheat the chocolate to 32°C.

Wearing rubber gloves, dip the balls, one by one, into the tempered chocolate; set on the baking parchment to harden. Then coat with chocolate again, shaking gently to remove the excess and place on the rack. When the chocolate starts to harden, roll the balls on the rack to form 'prickles'. Place on the baking tray to harden at room temperature for 20 minutes. Store the chocolate-pistachio truffles in an airtight container.

Lemon Tea Chocolates

MAKES 50

DIFFICULTY ★ ★ ★

PREPARE: 1 hour

INFUSE: 15 minutes

REFRIGERATE: 50 minutes

Lemon Tea Ganache
- 50 ml water
- 2 lemon teabags
- Juice of 2 lemons
- 240 g milk chocolate
- 80 g dark chocolate
- 2 egg yolks
- 100 g caster sugar
- 50 ml whipping cream

Chocolate Coating
- 400 g dark chocolate
- Icing sugar
- Grated zest of 3 lemons

◇ See p.328: Coating sweets with chocolate.

◇ See pp.320-324: Tempering chocolate.

Lemon Tea Ganache: Bring the water to the boil, add the lemon teabags and infuse for 15 minutes. Strain about 25– 30 ml (about 2 tablespoons) of the tea, add the lemon juice and set aside. Finely chop the milk and dark chocolates and place in a bowl. Beat the egg yolks and 50 g of the sugar. Put the cream, lemon tea and the remaining sugar in a saucepan, heat until simmering and, whisking quickly, pour into the egg yolk-sugar mixture. Return the mixture to the saucepan and cook over low heat, stirring continuously with a wooden spoon, until the cream is thickened and coats the back of the spoon. (Do not allow to boil!) Remove from the heat immediately, strain over the chopped chocolate; stir until smooth. Refrigerate for 30 minutes, or until firm.

Line a baking tray with baking parchment. Use a teaspoon or a pastry bag fitted with a small round nozzle to form 50 mounds of ganache on the parchment; refrigerate until firm.

Chocolate Coating: Temper the dark chocolate: Coarsely chop the dark chocolate and place 2/3 (260 g) in a bowl; melt over a simmering bain-marie until the temperature reaches 45°C on a digital thermometer. Remove the bowl from the heat and add the remaining chocolate, stirring until the temperature cools to 27°C. Return the bowl to the bain-marie and, stirring gently, reheat the chocolate to 32°C.

Sift the icing sugar into a flat container, stir in the lemon zest. Remove the ganache balls from the refrigerator and bring to room temperature. Using a regular or a chocolate fork (ringed or pronged), dip the ganache balls one by one into the tempered chocolate. Tap the fork on the side of the bowl and shake gently to remove any excess chocolate. Roll the chocolates in the icing sugar and lemon and place on a rack to harden. Then, place in a sieve and shake gently to remove the excess icing sugar; store in an airtight container.

Matcha Green Tea Chocolates

MAKES 50

DIFFICULTY ★ ★ ★

PREPARE: 1 hour

REFRIGERATE: 50 minutes

Matcha Green Tea Ganache
- 240 g milk chocolate
- 80 g dark chocolate
- 2 egg yolks
- 100 g caster sugar
- 100 ml whipping cream
- ¼ tsp powdered matcha green tea

Chocolate Coating
- 400 g dark chocolate
- Unsweetened cocoa powder

◇ See pp.320-324: Tempering chocolate.

◇ See p.328: Coating with chocolate.

Matcha Green Tea Ganache: Finely chop the milk and dark chocolates and place in a bowl. In a separate bowl, beat the egg yolks and sugar until pale yellow and creamy. Put the cream and powdered matcha green tea into a saucepan and heat until simmering. Whisking quickly, pour a little into the egg yolk-sugar mixture. Return to the saucepan and cook the mixture over low heat, stirring continuously with a wooden spoon, until the cream is thickened and coats the back of a spoon. (Do not allow to boil!) Remove from the heat immediately, strain over the chopped chocolate; stir until smooth. Refrigerate for 30 minutes, or until firm.

Line a baking tray with baking parchment. Use a teaspoon or a pastry bag fitted with a round nozzle to form 50 mounds of ganache on the parchment; refrigerate until firm.

Chocolate Coating: Temper the dark chocolate: Coarsely chop the dark chocolate and place 2/3 (260 g) in a bowl; melt over a simmering bain-marie until the temperature reaches 45°C on a digital thermometer. Remove the bowl from the heat and add the remaining chocolate, stirring until the temperature cools to 27°C. Return the bowl to the bain-marie and stirring gently, reheat the chocolate to 32°C.

Sift the cocoa powder into a flat container. Remove the ganache balls from the refrigerator and bring to room temperature. Using a regular or a chocolate fork (ringed or pronged), dip the ganache balls one by one, into the tempered chocolate. Tap the fork on the side of the bowl and shake gently to remove any excess chocolate. Roll the chocolates in cocoa powder and set aside to harden. Then, place in a sieve and shake gently to remove the excess cocoa; store in an airtight container.

Banana Ganache Chocolates

MAKES 30

DIFFICULTY ★ ★ ★

PREPARE: 1 hour

COOK: 10 minutes

REFRIGERATE: 40 minutes

REST: 30 minutes

Banana Ganache
• 50 g mild honey
• 10 g unsalted butter
• ½ banana (approx. 75 g)
• 65 g milk chocolate
• 35 g dark chocolate
• 50 ml whipping cream

Chocolate Coating
• 400 g dark chocolate

◊ See p.326: Moulding chocolates.

◊ See pp.320-324: Tempering chocolate.

Banana Ganache: Heat the honey and butter in a saucepan. Crush the banana, add to the honey and butter mixture and cook to a smooth purée. Coarsely chop the milk and dark chocolates and place in a bowl. Heat the cream to simmering, pour over the chopped chocolate and stir until smooth. Combine the banana purée with the chocolate mixture and set aside until thickened.

Chocolate Coating: Temper the dark chocolate: Coarsely chop the chocolate and place $2/3$ (260 g) in a bowl; melt over a slowly simmering bain-marie until the temperature reaches 45°C on a digital thermometer. Remove the bowl from the heat and add the remaining chocolate, stirring until the temperature cools to 27°C. Return the bowl to the bain-marie and, gently stirring, reheat the chocolate to 32°C.

Hold a polycarbonate chocolate mould with 30 imprints at an angle over a sheet of acetate and using a small ladle, fill the imprints with tempered chocolate. Tap the mould on the work surface to release the air bubbles and invert to tip out the excess. Remove the chocolate from the surface of the mould using a metal scraper. Only the base and walls of the imprints should be chocolate coated. Set aside at room temperature for 30 minutes, or until the chocolate hardens. Fit a piping bag with a small round nozzle and fill with banana ganache. Place the nozzle in the centre of each imprint and fill to the $2/3$ mark, without touching the moulded chocolate edge; refrigerate 20 minutes, or until firm. Hold the mould at an angle again and ladle the tempered chocolate over the ganache-filled imprints. Smooth with the spatula to evenly cover and seal the imprints, scraping the excess chocolate from the surface of the mould; refrigerate 20 minutes. When the chocolate is hard, invert the mould and lightly tap it on the work surface to turn out the banana ganache chocolates.

CHEF'S TIP: To give the ganache a more intense flavour, flame the banana with rum in the honey and butter mixture before crushing it.

Blackcurrant-filled Chocolates

MAKES 40

DIFFICULTY ★ ★ ★

PREPARE: 1½ hours

REFRIGERATE: 40 minutes

EQUIPMENT: 2 polycarbonate chocolate moulds with 20 imprints

Blackcurrant Ganache
- 40 g dark (70%) chocolate
- 70 ml whipping cream
- 8 g honey
- 70 g unsalted butter
- 35 g blackcurrant purée

Coating
- 400 g dark chocolate
- 20 g red coloured cocoa butter
- Edible gold powder

◇ See p.326: Moulding chocolates.

◇ See pp.320-324: Tempering chocolate.

Blackcurrant Ganache: Melt the chocolate over a bain-marie.

Gently heat the cream, honey and butter in a saucepan. Stir in the blackcurrant purée, leave to cool, and pour over the melted chocolate. Mix well.

Coating: Temper the dark chocolate by closely following each of the steps below to achieve a good crystallisation of the chocolate: Coarsely chop the dark chocolate. Melt $^2/_3$ over a bain-marie until it reaches 45°C on a digital thermometer. When the chocolate reaches this temperature, remove from the bain-marie. Add the remaining $^1/_3$ of the chocolate and mix until it cools to 27°C. Reheat again over the bain-marie and stir until it reaches 32°C.

Place a plastic sheet on the work surface. Brush the imprints of the mould with red cocoa butter, then dust with gold powder. Use a piping bag to fill the imprints with the tempered chocolate. Immediately tap the mould on the work surface to release any air bubbles, then invert it tipping out the excess chocolate. Leave the mould inverted and scrape the surface with a metal scraper. Only the walls of the imprints should be coated in chocolate, the surface of the mould should be perfectly clean. Leave to harden at room temperature for 10 minutes.

Use a piping bag to fill the imprints with the blackcurrant ganache, leaving 2 mm between the ganache and the top of the mould. Leave to harden in the refrigerator for 20 minutes. Cover the imprints with a layer of tempered chocolate. Immediately place a thick plastic sheet on top, and scrape again to remove any excess chocolate.

Refrigerate to harden for a further 20 minutes or set aside at room temperature for 4 hours. As soon as the chocolates have hardened, invert the mould and tap it on the work surface to turn out the blackcurrant chocolates.

Chocolate Rum and Raisin Bites

MAKES 20

DIFFICULTY ★ ★ ★

MACERATE: Overnight

PREPARE: 30 minutes

REFRIGERATE: 2 hours

- 30 g raisins
- 50 ml rum
- 170 g caster sugar
- 60 g glucose (or mild honey)
- 140 ml whipping cream
- 15 g unsalted butter
- 80 g dark chocolate

◇ This recipe must be started the night before.

Macerate the raisins in rum overnight.

The next day, line a 20 x 16 cm cake tin with baking parchment. Put the sugar, glucose (or honey), cream and butter into a saucepan. Heat the mixture until the temperature registers 120°C on a digital thermometer; remove from the heat. Drain the raisins and add to the sugar mixture; cool to 60°C without stirring.

Coarsely chop the chocolate and melt over a bain-marie; remove from the heat. When the sugar mixture has cooled, blend in the melted chocolate. Stir slowly until the mixture thickens and becomes opaque (if you stir too quickly, crystals could form). Pour a uniform layer into the prepared cake tin. Refrigerate for 2 hours, or until firm.

Turn out the chocolate and, using a knife dipped in hot water, cut in 4 cm squares; store in an airtight container at room temperature.

CHEF'S TIP: Glucose is a liquid sugar, which does not crystallise and makes preparations such as this one smooth and moist. If it's not available in your local supermarket, you can purchase it from specialist cook shops or on the Internet.

Crunchy Praline Chocolates

MAKES 20

DIFFICULTY ★ ★ ★

PREPARE: 1¼ hours

COOL: 10 minutes

Crunchy Praline Filling
• 30 ml water
• 150 g caster sugar
• 75 g blanched almonds
• 75 g blanched hazelnuts
• 75 g milk chocolate
• 50 g crêpes dentelles, lightly crushed

Caramelised Almonds
• 2 tbsp water
• 10 g sugar
• 35 g blanched almonds
• 5 g unsalted butter

Chocolate Coating
• 400 g milk chocolate

◊ See p.325: Making praline paste.

◊ See pp.320-324: Tempering chocolate.

Crunchy Praline Filling: Put the water and sugar into a saucepan over low heat, stirring until the sugar dissolves. Increase the heat and boil for 2 minutes without stirring; stir in the blanched nuts using a wooden spoon. Remove from the heat, and continue stirring until the sugar crystallises, covering them with a white powder. Return the saucepan to low heat until the sugar melts and the nuts turn golden brown. Immediately spread on an oiled baking tray; set aside until cold. Break the praline in pieces, place in a food processor and grind, first to a powder then to a creamy paste. It will be necessary to stop the food processor often, and mix with a spatula. (Or, to avoid overworking the food processor, grind the praline in several batches.) Place the praline paste in a bowl. Melt the milk chocolate over a bain-marie, pour it over the praline paste and add the crushed crêpes dentelles. Spread the mixture in an 18 x 14 cm cake tin using a spatula; refrigerate until required.

Caramelised Almonds: Put the sugar and water into a small saucepan over low heat, stirring until the sugar is completely dissolved. Remove from the heat, add the almonds and stir until the syrup crystallises, covering them with a white powder. Return the saucepan to low heat and cook until the sugar melts and the nuts turn golden; incorporate the butter. Spread on baking parchment, roll with a spatula to separate and cool the caramelised almonds.

Chocolate Coating: Temper the milk chocolate (see pp.320-324).

Turn out the praline filling and cut in 2 x 3 cm rectangles using a knife dipped in hot water. Use a fork to dip the rectangles, one by one, into the tempered milk chocolate. Then, shake gently and scrape on the side of the bowl to remove the excess. Transfer to parchment paper. Dip the bases of the caramelised almonds, one by one, in the melted chocolate and place on each crunchy praline chocolate.

CHEF'S TIP: If you do not have an 18 x 14 cm cake tin, use a rectangular plastic container of the dimensions noted.

Chocolate-Dipped Fruit

SERVES 4–6

DIFFICULTY ★ ★ ★

PREPARE: 20 minutes

REFRIGERATE: 15 minutes

- 250 g strawberries
- 2 clementines or satsumas
- 185 g dark chocolate, chopped
- 1 tbsp vegetable oil

Cover a baking tray with baking parchment. Wash and dry the strawberries, keeping them whole. Peel and separate the clementine or satsuma segments; dry with kitchen paper.

Melt the dark chocolate slowly over a simmering bain-marie. Add the vegetable oil and stir until smooth; remove from the heat. Place the bowl on a folded tea towel to keep the chocolate warm.

Holding the strawberries by their stem dip, one by one, into the chocolate so it comes to the ¾ mark. Carefully wipe off the excess on the side of the bowl and transfer to the baking tray. Repeat the operation for the clementine segments.

Refrigerate the dipped fruit for 15 minutes. Serve at room temperature to enhance the fruit flavour and allow the chocolate to soften.

CHEF'S TIP: When you are dipping the fruit, if the chocolate becomes too thick, reheat the bain-marie and place the bowl of chocolate over it, being careful not to cook the chocolate. All types of fruit can be used for this recipe. The important thing to remember is that the surface of the fruit must be dry before dipping.

White Chocolate-Pistachio Fudge

MAKES 36 PIECES

DIFFICULTY ★ ★ ★

PREPARE: 20 minutes

REFRIGERATE: 2 hours

- 200 g white chocolate
- 20 g unsalted butter
- 150 ml whipping cream
- 50 g mild honey
- 125 g caster sugar
- 80 g chopped pistachios

Line an 18 cm square cake tin with baking parchment.

Chop the white chocolate and place in a bowl with the butter. Heat the cream, honey and sugar until the temperature of the mixture registers 112°C on a digital thermometer. Pour the mixture over the chopped chocolate and butter; stir until smooth. Then blend in the chopped pistachios.

Pour the white chocolate-pistachio fudge mixture into the prepared cake tin and refrigerate for 2 hours. When the fudge is firm, cut in 3 cm squares; serve.

CHEF'S TIP: The fudge can be kept for one week in an airtight container lined with parchment to stop it sticking. Store at room temperature in a cool dark place.

Creamy Chocolate-Caramel Parcels

MAKES 10 PARCELS

DIFFICULTY ★ ★ ★

PREPARE: 30 minutes

COOK: 6-8 minutes

REFRIGERATE: 15 minutes

- 300 g dark chocolate
- 300 ml whipping cream
- 100 ml milk
- 300 g caster sugar
- 100 g salted butter
- 150 g unsalted butter
- Filo pastry sheets

Line a 20 cm square cake tin with cling film.

Chop the chocolate and place in a bowl. Heat the cream and milk until simmering; set aside. In a separate saucepan, cook 100 g of the sugar, stirring from time to time with a wooden spoon until it becomes an amber-coloured caramel. Stop the sugar cooking by stirring in a little of the creamy milk (the mixture will bubble violently!); add the remainder of the creamy milk a little at a time. Then add the rest of the sugar, continue stirring and cook until smooth; be careful not to let it burn. Cook until the temperature of the mixture registers 114°C on a digital thermometer; remove from the heat. Stir in a little chopped chocolate, adding the remainder gradually. Blend in the salted butter and 100 g of the unsalted butter.

Pour the mixture into the prepared cake tin and refrigerate for at least 15 minutes, or until completely cold.

Preheat the oven to 200°C (400°F). Line 2 baking trays with baking parchment. Melt the remaining unsalted butter. Cut the filo into 10 rectangles (20 x 15 cm); cover with a damp tea towel so they don't dry out.

Divide the cold caramel chocolate in 10 equal portions; form into 'logs' (about 4 x 10 cm). Place one 'log' on each filo pastry rectangle, and wrap to form a parcel similar to a Christmas cracker. Place wooden clothes pegs dipped in water at each end of the filling to enclose it and brush the parcel with the melted butter. Place on the baking trays, transfer to the oven and cook for 6–8 minutes, or until lightly coloured. Serve hot.

CHEF'S TIP: French chefs use feuilles de brick, a Tunisian flaky pastry, which is occasionally available from some UK supermarkets.

Chocolate Caramel-Coated Chestnuts

MAKES **12**

DIFFICULTY ★ ★ ★

DRAIN: Overnight

PREPARE: 30 minutes

COOL: 15 minutes

- 12 whole tinned chestnuts in syrup
- 50 g dark chocolate
- 250 g caster sugar
- 60 ml water
- 50 g mild honey

◊ This recipe must be started a day ahead.

Place a rack over a bowl and drain the chestnuts overnight.

The next day, chop the dark chocolate. Line a baking tray with baking parchment.

Straighten 12 paper clips, leaving a hook at one end. Insert the straight part of the paper clips into the drained chestnuts.

Place the sugar, water and honey in a saucepan and cook until the temperature of the mixture registers 114°C on a digital thermometer; remove from the heat. Add the chopped chocolate gradually; stir until smooth.

Cover a work surface with baking parchment and position a rack 20 cm above it. Dip the chestnuts into the chocolate caramel and hook them onto the rack for about 15 minutes until cold. When cooling, the caramel will drip forming a tail..

Chocolate Fruit and Nut Wafers

MAKES 30 WAFERS

DIFFICULTY ★ ★ ★

PREPARE: 1 hour

REST: 30 minutes

- 500 g dark chocolate
- 30 g hazelnuts
- 60 g dried apricots, diced
- 60 g pistachios
- 30 g dried cranberries

◇ See pp.320-324: Tempering chocolate.

Line a baking tray with baking parchment.

Temper the dark chocolate: Coarsely chop the dark chocolate and place $^2/_3$ (330 g) in a bowl; melt over a simmering bain-marie until the temperature reaches 45°C on a digital thermometer. Remove the bowl from the heat and add the remaining chocolate, stirring until the temperature cools to 27°C. Return the bowl to the bain-marie and, stirring gently, reheat the chocolate to 32°C.

Fit a pastry bag with a 4 mm round nozzle and fill with the tempered chocolate. Pipe discs of chocolate, about 3 cm in diameter, on the baking tray.

Before the chocolate starts to harden, arrange the nuts and dried fruits on each disc. Set the wafers aside for about 30 minutes, or until the chocolate is hard; store in an airtight container.

CHEF'S TIP: You can use other types of dried fruit, such as dried figs, on the wafers. In the traditional French (normally Christmas) confection, known as mendicants, the dried fruits and nuts represent the four monastic orders of the Dominicans (raisins), Augustinians (hazelnuts), Franciscans (figs) and Carmelites (almonds).

Milk Chocolate Rolls

MAKES 40 ROLLS

DIFFICULTY ★ ★ ★

PREPARE: 1 hour

REFRIGERATE: 20 minutes

Milk Chocolate Ganache
- 200 g milk chocolate
- 80 ml whipping cream
- 25 g mild honey
- 20 g praline paste (p.325)

Milk Chocolate Coating
- 350 g milk chocolate

Decoration
- Icing sugar

◇ See p.328: Coating sweets with chocolate.

◇ See pp.320-324: Tempering chocolate.

Line a baking tray with baking parchment.

Milk Chocolate Ganache: Chop the milk chocolate and place in a bowl. Heat the cream and honey until simmering and pour over the chopped chocolate. Stir gently with a spatula until smooth then blend in the praline paste; set aside until cold. Once it has cooled, whip to emulsify and fit a pastry bag with a 12 mm round nozzle and fill with the cold ganache. Pipe two long ropes of ganache on the baking tray; refrigerate for 20 minutes. Dip a knife in hot water, dry it and cut each rope into 3 cm long pieces.

Milk Chocolate Coating: Temper the chocolate: Coarsely chop the chocolate and place 2/3 (230 g) in a bowl; melt over a simmering bain-marie until the temperature reaches 45°C on a digital thermometer. Remove the bowl from the heat and add the remaining chocolate, stirring until the temperature cools to 26°C. Return the bowl to the bain-marie and stirring gently, reheat the chocolate to 29°C.

Sift the icing sugar into a flat container. Using a fork, dip the ganache pieces, one by one, into the tempered milk chocolate. Shake gently and scrape the fork on the side of the bowl to remove the excess chocolate. Roll in the icing sugar; set aside until hardened. Then, place the rolls in a sieve and shake gently to remove the excess icing sugar.

Store in an airtight container at 12°C maximum; consume within 10 days.

CHEF'S TIP: If desired, replace the praline paste with a chocolate hazelnut spread. Use the same quantity as noted in the recipe.

Chocolate Nougats

MAKES 50

DIFFICULTY ★ ★ ★

PREPARE: 45 minutes

COOK: 15 minutes

REFRIGERATE: 2 hours

• 350 g hazelnuts
• 500 g glacé cherries
• 300 g dark chocolate

Italian Meringue
• 300 g mild honey
• 2 egg whites
• 1 pinch salt
• 10 g caster sugar

Sugar Paste
• 280 g caster sugar
• 100 ml water
• 50 g mild honey

Preheat the oven to 140°C (285°F).

Place the hazelnuts on a baking tray, transfer to the oven and toast for 15 minutes. Chop the glacé cherries. Finely chop the chocolate and melt over a simmering bain-marie; stir from time to time. Set the toasted hazelnuts, chopped cherries and melted chocolate aside.

Italian Meringue: Place the honey in a saucepan and heat until the temperature registers 118–120°C on a digital thermometer. While the honey is heating, put the egg whites and salt into a metal bowl and beat with an electric beater until foamy. Beating continuously, gradually pour the boiling honey into the egg whites. Continue beating until the Italian meringue becomes very firm and cold.

Line a baking tray with baking parchment.

Sugar Paste: Combine the sugar, water and honey in a saucepan, stirring over low heat until the sugar dissolves. Increase the heat and cook until the mixture registers 145°C on a digital thermometer.

Beat the sugar paste gradually into the meringue. Continue beating and rotate the bowl, heating it with a blow torch to dry out the mixture. Add the melted chocolate, chopped cherries and hazelnuts, mixing with a spatula to combine the ingredients. Pour a layer of the chocolat nougat, 1.5 cm thick, onto the prepared oven tray; refrigerate for 2 hours.

Remove from the refrigerator and cut the chocolate nougat in small squares or rectangles. They can be kept for 2 or 3 weeks in an airtight container.

CHEF'S TIP: If you do not have a blow torch, use a hair dryer to dry the Italian meringue mixture. Also, the pieces of nougat could be coated with tempered dark chocolate (pp.320-324).

Gold-Flecked Palettes

MAKES 30

DIFFICULTY ★ ★ ★

PREPARE: 1 hour

REFRIGERATE: 1 hour

Ganache
• 170 g dark chocolate
• 85 ml whipping cream
• 20 g mild honey
• 40 g soft unsalted butter

Chocolate Coating
• 400 g dark chocolate

Decoration
• Edible gold flakes or dust

◊ See pp.320-324: Tempering chocolate.

Line a 14 x 12 cm oven tray or cake tin with baking parchment. Draw 30 small squares about 3 x 3 cm on a thick sheet of plastic.

Ganache: Chop the dark chocolate and place in a bowl. Heat the cream and honey until simmering, pour over the chopped chocolate and stir gently until smooth using a spatula; blend in the butter. Pour the ganache into the cake tin in a layer 6– 7 mm thick; refrigerate for at least 1 hour. When cold, turn the ganache out onto a clean work surface, then cut into rounds with a 3 cm in diameter cutter. Refrigerate them until use.

Chocolate Coating: Temper the dark chocolate: Coarsely chop the chocolate and place $2/3$ (260 g) in a bowl; melt over a simmering bain-marie until the temperature reaches 45°C on a digital thermometer. Remove the bowl from the heat and add the remaining chocolate, stirring until the temperature cools to 27°C. Return the bowl to the bain-marie and stirring gently, reheat the chocolate to 32°C.

Using a fork, dip the ganache rounds one by one into the tempered chocolate. Shake gently and scrape the fork on the side of the bowl to remove any excess chocolate. Place them on a sheet of baking parchment, put a small plastic square on each palette and press lightly. Leave to harden for 30 minutes at room temperature. Once they have hardened, remove the plastic squares and turn the palettes over. Carefully decorate the flat surface of the palettes with the edible gold leaf.

Store the chocolates in an airtight container, in a cool place (12°C maximum); consume within 10 days.

CHEF'S TIP: If you do not have a round, plain cutter, cut square shapes with a knife. Similarly, if you do not have a 14 x 12 cm oven tray with edges to spread the ganache, replace it with the lid of an airtight box covered with parchment paper.

Chocolate Praline Truffles

MAKES 30

DIFFICULTY ★ ★ ★

PREPARE: 1 hour

Praline Ganache
- 100 g chopped almonds
- 60 g (55-70%) dark chocolate
- 120 g praline paste

Chocolate Coating
- 250 g dark chocolate

◊ See p.325: Making praline paste.

◊ See p.320-324: Tempering chocolate.

Praline Ganache: Place the chopped almonds in a non-stick frying pan over low heat and toast until fragrant and evenly golden brown. Chop the chocolate and melt over a bain-marie; remove from the heat. Blend in the praline paste and 50 g of the chopped toasted almonds. Set the mixture aside until it can be rolled easily. Wearing rubber gloves, divide the mixture in two equal portions and form each one into a long rope. Cut each rope into pieces weighing approx.10 g; roll by hand into balls and place on a plate.

Chocolate Coating: Temper the chocolate: Coarsely chop the dark chocolate and place 2/3 (160 g) in a bowl; melt over a simmering bain-marie until the temperature reaches 45°C on a digital thermometer. Remove the bowl from the heat and add the remaining chocolate, stirring until the temperature cools to 27°C. Return the bowl to the bain-marie and, stirring gently, reheat the chocolate to 32°C.

Wearing rubber gloves, dip the ganache balls, one by one, into the tempered chocolate, shaking gently to remove any excess; set on baking parchment to harden. When the chocolate starts to harden, gently roll each ball in the remaining chopped toasted almonds; set aside. The truffles will keep about 15 days; store in an airtight container, in a cool place (12°C maximum).

Crunchy Almond Wafers

MAKES 30 WAFERS

DIFFICULTY ★ ★ ★

PREPARE: 1½ hours

Caramelised Almond Sticks
• 250 g slivered almonds
• 60 ml water
• 150 g caster sugar

Chocolate Coating
• 150 g dark chocolate

◊ See pp.320-324: Tempering chocolate.

Caramelised Almond Sticks: Heat the water and sugar stirring to dissolve the sugar; bring to the boil and cook for about 5 minutes (do not stir!) until the syrup registers 117°C on a digital thermometer. Remove from the heat, add the slivered almonds and stir until the sugar crystallises coating them with a white powder. Return the saucepan to low heat until the sugar melts and the almonds turn golden brown. Remove from the heat immediately and spread on baking parchment; roll to cool then place in a bowl.

Chocolate Coating: Temper the dark chocolate: Coarsely chop the dark chocolate and place $2/3$ (100 g) in a bowl; melt over a simmering bain-marie until the temperature reaches 45°C on a digital thermometer. Remove the bowl from the heat and add the remaining chocolate, stirring until the temperature cools to 27°C. Return the bowl to the bain-marie and, stirring gently, reheat the chocolate to 32°C.

Line a baking tray with baking parchment. As soon as the chocolate reaches 32°C, pour it over the caramelised almonds. Use a tablespoon to make small piles of the mixture on the parchment. Harden at room temperature for 30 minutes.

CHEF'S TIP: The almonds could be replaced with pine nuts.

Hazelnut Clusters

MAKES 25

DIFFICULTY ★ ★ ★

PREPARE: 1½ hours

Caramelised Hazelnuts
• 40 ml water
• 100 g caster sugar
• 100 g hazelnuts
• 5 g unsalted butter

Milk Chocolate Coating
• 300 g milk chocolate

◊ See pp.320-324: Tempering chocolate.

Caramelised Hazelnuts: Bring the water and sugar to the boil, swirling the saucepan to dissolve the sugar; cook for about 5 minutes until the syrup registers 117°C on a digital thermometer. Remove from the heat, add the hazelnuts and stir until the sugar crystallises, coating the hazelnuts with a white powder. Return the saucepan to low heat until the sugar melts and the hazelnuts turn golden brown, add butter. Remove from the heat immediately and spread on baking parchment. Using a fork, immediately arrange the hazelnuts into groups of three bonded by the caramel; set aside to harden for about 10 minutes.

Milk Chocolate Coating: Temper the milk chocolate: Coarsely chop the chocolate and place $^2/_3$ (200 g) in a bowl; melt over a simmering bain-marie until the temperature reaches 45°C on a digital thermometer. Remove the bowl from the heat and add the remaining chocolate, stirring until the temperature cools to 26°C. Return the bowl to the bain-marie and, stirring gently, reheat the chocolate to 29°C.

Using a fork, dip the hazelnut clusters into the tempered chocolate. Shake gently to remove any excess chocolate and place on a baking parchment. Set aside to harden for 30 minutes before serving.

Plain Chocolate Truffles

MAKES 50 TRUFFLES

DIFFICULTY ★ ★ ★

PREPARE: 40 minutes

REFRIGERATE: 50 minutes

Ganache
- 300 g dark chocolate
- 100 ml whipping cream
- 1 tsp vanilla extract

Coating
- Unsweetened cocoa powder

Ganache: Finely chop the chocolate and place in a bowl. Heat the cream until simmering and pour over the chopped chocolate; add the vanilla extract. Whisk lightly until the mixture is smooth and thick. Refrigerate for 30 minutes until the ganache is set.

Line a baking tray with baking parchment. Using a teaspoon, or a pastry bag fitted with a round nozzle, make small balls of ganache on the sheet; refrigerate for 20 minutes.

Coating: Sift the cocoa powder into a flat container. Wearing rubber gloves, roll the balls in the cocoa powder, coating them evenly. Then transfer to a sieve and shake gently to remove any excess cocoa; put each truffle into a small paper baking case.

Place in an airtight container and store in a cool place (12°C maximum). Consume the chocolate truffles within 15 days.

CHEF'S TIP: You can keep the truffles refrigerated for 1 week on a plate filled with cocoa powder, before rolling them completely in cocoa and placing in paper baking cases. Children will like this recipe, too, because it contains no alcohol.

Lemon Truffles

MAKES 50 TRUFFLES

DIFFICULTY ★ ★ ★

PREPARE: 1 hour

REFRIGERATE: 50 minutes

Lemon Ganache
- 240 g milk chocolate
- 80 g dark chocolate
- 2 egg yolks
- 100 g caster sugar
- 100 ml whipping cream
- Zests of 2 lemons, finely chopped

Coating
- 400 g dark chocolate
- Icing sugar

◊ See pp.320-324: Tempering chocolate.

Lemon Ganache: Finely chop the milk and dark chocolates and place in a bowl. In a separate bowl, beat the egg yolks and sugar until pale yellow and creamy. Heat the cream until simmering; whisking quickly, pour a little into the egg yolk-sugar mixture. Return to the saucepan and cook the mixture over low heat for 2 minutes, stirring continuously with a wooden spoon, until the cream is thickened and coats the back of a spoon. (Do not allow to boil!) Remove from the heat immediately and strain over the chopped chocolate; stir until smooth and thick. Stir in the chopped lemon zest; refrigerate for 30 minutes until firm.

Line a baking tray with baking parchment. Using a teaspoon or a pastry bag fitted with a round nozzle, make small balls of lemon ganache on the baking tray; refrigerate for 20 minutes.

Coating: Temper the chocolate: Coarsely chop the dark chocolate and place 2/3 (260 g) in a bowl; melt over a simmering bain-marie until the temperature reaches 45°C on a digital thermometer. Remove the bowl from the heat and add the remaining chocolate, stirring until the temperature cools to 27°C. Return the bowl to the bain-marie and, stirring gently, reheat the chocolate to 32°C.

Sift the icing sugar into a flat container. When the ganache balls are firm, remove from the refrigerator. Wearing rubber gloves, dip the ganache balls one by one, into the tempered chocolate, shaking gently to remove any excess. Roll the lemon truffles in icing sugar and set aside to harden at room temperature. Then place in a sieve and shake gently to remove any excess icing sugar.

Consume the lemon truffles within 7 days; store in an airtight container, in a cool place (12°C maximum).

Cointreau Truffles

MAKES 50 TRUFFLES

DIFFICULTY ★ ★ ★

PREPARE: 1 hour

REFRIGERATE: 1 hour approx.

Two-Chocolate Ganache
- 150 g milk chocolate
- 150 g dark chocolate
- 150 ml whipping cream
- 50 g mild honey
- 30 ml Cointreau

Chocolate Coating
- 500 g dark chocolate
- 100 g unsweetened cocoa powder

◊ See p.328: Coating sweets with chocolate.

◊ See pp.320-324: Tempering chocolate.

Line a baking tray with baking parchment.

Two-Chocolate Ganache: Chop the milk and dark chocolates and place in a bowl. Heat the cream and honey until simmering and pour over the chopped chocolate, stir until smooth; add the Cointreau. Refrigerate the ganache for 30 minutes. Fit a piping bag with a plain round nozzle. When the ganache is completely cold, remove from the refrigerator and gently stir. Pour it into the piping bag and pipe 50 mounds on the baking tray; refrigerate for 20 minutes. Wearing rubber gloves, roll the ganache by hand to form round balls; refrigerate again for 10– 16 minutes.

Chocolate Coating: Temper the chocolate: Coarsely chop the dark chocolate and place 2/3 (330 g) in a bowl; melt over a simmering bain-marie until the temperature reaches 45°C on a digital thermometer. Remove the bowl from the heat and add the remaining chocolate, stirring until the temperature cools to 27°C. Return the bowl to the bain-marie and, stirring gently, reheat the chocolate to 32°C.

Sift the cocoa powder into a flat container. Slide a fork under the ganache balls, and carefully dip, one by one, into the tempered chocolate; shake gently to remove any excess. Using the fork, roll in the cocoa powder. Set aside to firm at room temperature. When firm, place in a sieve and shake gently to remove any excess cocoa.

The truffles will keep about 15 days stored in an airtight container in a cool place (12°C maximum).

CHEF'S TIP: You can replace the Cointreau with a different liqueur or alcohol, using the same quantity. If you have leftover tempered chocolate, use it to make a sauce.

Rum Truffles

MAKES 30 TRUFFLES

DIFFICULTY ★ ★ ★

PREPARE: 1 hour

REFRIGERATE: 30 minutes

Chocolate-Rum Ganache
- 170 g dark chocolate
- 150 ml whipping cream
- 15 g soft unsalted butter
- 1 tsp rum

Chocolate Coating
- 500 g dark chocolate
- 100 g unsweetened cocoa powder

◇ See pp.320-324: Tempering chocolate.

Line a baking tray with baking parchment.

Chocolate-Rum Ganache: Chop the chocolate and place in a bowl. Heat the cream until simmering and pour over the chopped chocolate, let it melt for a couple of seconds then stir until smooth; blend in the butter and rum. Refrigerate the ganache for 10 minutes. Fit a piping bag with a plain round nozzle. When the ganache is cold, remove from the refrigerator and gently stir with a spatula. Pour it into the piping bag and pipe 30 small mounds on the baking tray; refrigerate for 20 minutes. Wearing rubber gloves roll the ganache by hand to form round balls; refrigerate until required.

Chocolate Coating: Temper the chocolate: Coarsely chop the dark chocolate and place 2/3 (340 g) in a bowl; melt over a simmering bain-marie until the temperature reaches 45°C on a digital thermometer. Remove the bowl from the heat and add the remaining chocolate, stirring until the temperature cools to 27°C. Return the bowl to the bain-marie and, stirring gently, reheat the chocolate to 32°C.

Sift the unsweetened cocoa powder into a flat container. Slide a fork under each ganache ball, and carefully dip, one by one, into the tempered chocolate; shake gently to remove any excess. Use a teaspoon to roll the rum truffles in the cocoa powder. Set aside to firm at room temperature for 30 minutes. When firm, place in a sieve and shake gently to remove any excess cocoa.

The truffles will keep about 15 days stored in an airtight container in a cool place (12°C maximum).

Mini Mocha Truffles

MAKES 45–50 TRUFFLES

DIFFICULTY ★ ★ ★

PREPARE: 1 hour

REFRIGERATE: 1 hour approx

Two-Chocolate Ganache
- 120 g milk chocolate
- 180 g dark chocolate
- 200 ml whipping cream
- 45 g mild honey
- 15 g instant coffee
- 150 g caster sugar

Chocolate Coating
- 400 g dark chocolate
- 40 g almonds, chopped and toasted

◊ See p.328: Coating sweets with chocolate.

Line a baking tray with baking parchment.

Two-Chocolate Ganache: Coarsely chop the milk and dark chocolates and place in a bowl. Heat the cream, honey and coffee until simmering. Put the sugar in a separate saucepan and cook until it becomes a dark caramel colour. Slowly add the hot cream mixture to stop the sugar cooking (be careful, the mixture will bubble violently). Return to the heat until simmering. Pour the caramel cream over the chopped chocolate and stir gently until smooth; cool. Refrigerate for 30 minutes. When the ganache is completely cold, remove from the refrigerator and gently stir with a spatula. Fit a piping bag with a small round nozzle and fill with the ganache. Pipe 45–50 tiny mounds on the prepared baking tray; refrigerate for 20 minutes. Wearing rubber gloves roll the ganache mounds by hand to form balls; refrigerate again for 10–15 minutes.

Chocolate Coating: Temper the chocolate: Coarsely chop the dark chocolate and place 2/3 (260 g) in a bowl; melt over a simmering bain-marie until the temperature reaches 45°C on a digital thermometer. Remove the bowl from the heat and add the remaining chocolate, stirring until the temperature cools to 27°C. Return the bowl to the bain-marie and, stirring gently, reheat the chocolate to 32°C.

Slide a fork under each ganache ball and carefully dip, one by one, into the tempered chocolate; shake gently to remove any excess. Place on baking parchment to harden. As soon as the chocolate starts to harden, roll the truffles in the chopped toasted almonds.

The mocha truffles will keep about 15 days; store in an airtight container in a cool place (12°C maximum).

Chocolate decorations

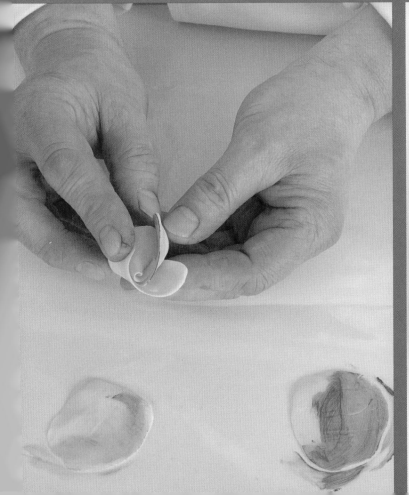

The best way to make chocolate honeycomb

Temper the chocolate as indicated on pages 320 to 324.

1 Place a sheet of bubble wrap on the work surface. Use a ladle to pour a small amount of tempered chocolate over it.

2 Use a stainless-steel palette knife to spread out a thin layer of tempered chocolate. Leave to harden in the refrigerator for 20 minute.

3 As soon as the chocolate hardens, carefully remove the bubble wrap. If the chocolate does not come away easily, return to the refrigerator for a few more minutes.

4 Cut the honeycombs into the desired shape to decorate cakes or entremets.

The best way to make chocolate leaves

Temper the chocolate as indicated on pages 320 to 324.

(1) Place a sheet of baking parchment on the work surface. Place shiso and cabbage leaves on the baking parchment. Brush the inside of the leaves with the tempered chocolate. Leave a 0.5 cm border around the edge of the shiso leaves, and a 1 cm border around the edge of the cabbage leaves to make it easier to detach the chocolate. Leave to harden in the refrigerator for 20 minutes.

(2) Carefully remove the chocolate leaves from the shiso and cabbage leaves.

(3) Put some red, yellow and orange powdered food colouring onto a plate. Brush the top of the chocolate leaves with each colour.

Chocolate leaves can be stored for one month in an air-tight container.

The best way to make chocolate flowers

Temper the chocolate as indicated on pages 320 to 324.

(1) Cut a strip of thick plastic or acetate sheet to the same width and length as a log tin and place on the work surface. Dip a knife in the tempered chocolate, then lay the knife on the plastic, chocolate side down, to make long petals.

(2) Place the plastic strip with the petals inside the log tin to curve them.

(3) Leave to harden in the refrigerator for 20 minutes, then remove the plastic strip from the log tin. Gently remove the petals from the plastic.

(4) Put a small amount of tempered chocolate onto a small piece of thick plastic. Attach 6 petals to form the centre of the flower.

5 Put a small amount of tempered chocolate onto a second piece of thick plastic. Shape a larger flower by sticking the petals together, leaving enough space in the middle for the centre of the flower.

6 Remove the centre of the flower from the plastic and attach it to the middle of the large flower with tempered chocolate.

7 For a velvety finish, spray the flower with cocoa butter using a spray gun.

8 Gently lift the edible gold leaf from its backing and decorate the flower.

Chocolate flowers can be kept in an airtight container for two weeks.

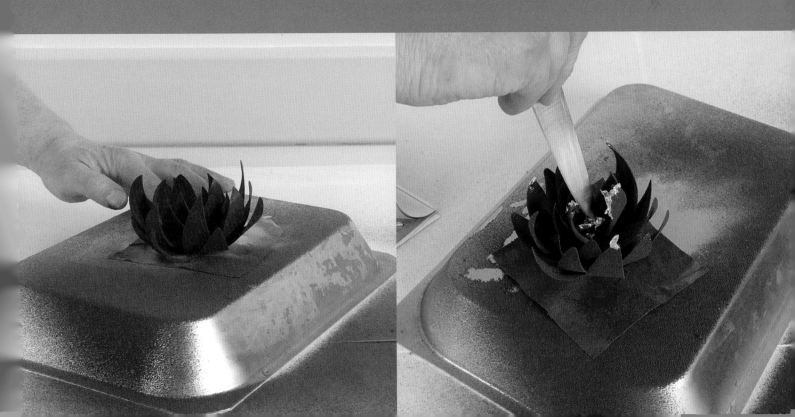

The best way to make chocolate roses

1. Put 250 g of icing sugar into a bowl and pour 250 g of melted cocoa butter and 150 g of glucose over it.

2. Mix with a flexible spatula to obtain a smooth dough called modelling chocolate. Leave to cool.

3. Make a thick roll with the dough, around 3 cm in diameter, then cut into slices about 0.5 cm thick.

4. Place a thick plastic or acetate sheet on the work surface. Put the dough rounds on it and cover with a second thick plastic sheet. Flatten each round with the back of a spoon, applying more pressure on the edge (and keep thicker at the base) and form a petal-like shape.

5. Remove the top plastic sheet. Put a small amount of liquid red food colouring in a container and dip the tip of your index finger in the liquid. Lightly dab the petals to give them a rose-like colour.

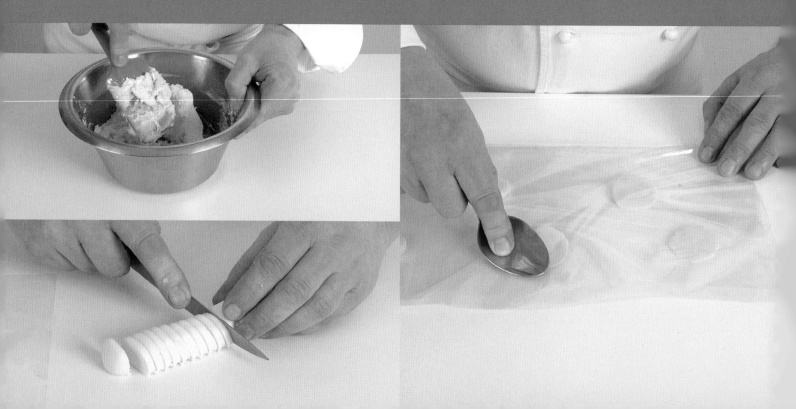

6 Form the central bud by making a cone shape with the modelling chocolate. Detach the petals from the plastic and arrange them one by one, overlapping around the cone, to cover the bud.

7 One by one, arrange the petals by staggering them a little each time to form the rose and making them overlap. As the rose grows, the more you gently open out the petals. Once you have finished shaping the rose, cut off the base with a knife.

Chocolate roses can be kept in an airtight container for two weeks and are perfect for decorating cakes or entremets.

The best way to make traditional French chocolate fish for Easter

Temper the chocolate as indicated on pages 320 to 324 and pour into a piping bag.

1 Melt a little coloured cocoa butter to a temperature of about 30°C in a small saucepan. Place a sheet of baking parchment on the work surface. Brush the imprints of the mould with the melted cocoa butter.

2 Lightly dust the imprints with edible gold powder.

3 Use a piping bag to fill the imprints with tempered chocolate.

4 Gently tap the moulds on the work surface to remove any air bubbles.

5 Leave to harden in the refrigerator for 20 minutes.
Invert the moulds on the work surface to turn out.

Chocolate fish can be stored for 1 month in an
airtight container.

The best way to decorate chocolates

Temper the chocolate as indicated on pages 320 to 324. Make the chocolates according to your chosen recipe and place in the refrigerator to harden.

① Place a chocolate transfer sheet on the work surface. Take the chocolates out of the refrigerator and let them come to room temperature (ideally around 18 to 22°C). Use a chocolate fork or a normal fork. Slide the fork under the chocolate, gently dip in the chocolate, lift out and allow the chocolate to drip back into the bowl.

② Gently tap the fork on the side of the bowl to let the chocolate drip off. Then, wipe the underside of the fork on the rim of the bowl several times to remove the excess chocolate and achieve a smooth coating. Lay the coated bonbon on the transfer sheet and repeat the process for all the chocolates.

③ Leave to harden in the refrigerator for 30 minutes, then remove from the transfer sheet. Put the chocolates in a box or on a sheet of baking parchment.

The best way to make chocolate shavings

Chocolate shavings are ideal to decorate your desserts (see p.214). You will need 200 g chocolate. There are 2 different methods you can use. The first one produces shorter shavings.

① First method: Stand a block of chocolate, smooth side out, on a piece of baking parchment and use a hair dryer to soften the surface. Wait 2 minutes for the chocolate to return to room temperature. Hold the chocolate block at a slight angle and scrape off shavings using a fixed-blade vegetable peeler. Refrigerate until required.

② Second method (professional): Temper the chocolate (pp.320-324). Use a palette knife and spread it out thinly on a marble work surface or a sheet of acetate or thick plastic; cool.

③ Holding a long-bladed knife at an angle, scrape up the chocolate, keeping the pressure steady along the blade to form curls. Refrigerate until required.

The best way to make chocolate spirals

Prepare a cake or entremets according to your chosen recipe. Temper the chocolate as indicated on pages 320 to 324 and pour into a piping bag.

1. Cut a 20 x 6 cm strip from a sheet of acetate. Pipe a line of tempered chocolate along the strip.

2. Hold the edge of the strip down and use a stainless steel palette knife to spread the chocolate thinly across the entire surface.

3. Scrape the chocolate with a chocolate comb to create thin strips of chocolate.

4. Place a strip of baking parchment over the chocolate.

5. Wrap around a rolling pin and leave to harden in the refrigerator for 30 minutes.

6. Carefully remove from the rolling pin by first unwrapping the baking parchment from the chocolate. Next, gently remove the acetate from the chocolate.

7. Detach the spirals, one by one, and decorate the cake or entremets.

The best way to make chocolate teardrops

Prepare a cake or entremets according to your chosen recipe. Temper the chocolate as indicated on pages 320 to 324 and pour into a piping bag.

①　Cut a 12 x 6 cm strip from a sheet of acetate. Pipe a line of tempered chocolate along the strip.

②　Hold the edge of the strip down and use a stainless steel palette knife to spread the chocolate thinly across the entire surface.

③　Carefully lift the chocolate strip and place it on a clean work surface.

④　Scrape the chocolate with a chocolate comb to create thin strips of chocolate.

⑤　Bring the ends of the strip together and use a clip to hold them in place. Leave to harden in the refrigerator for 30 minutes.

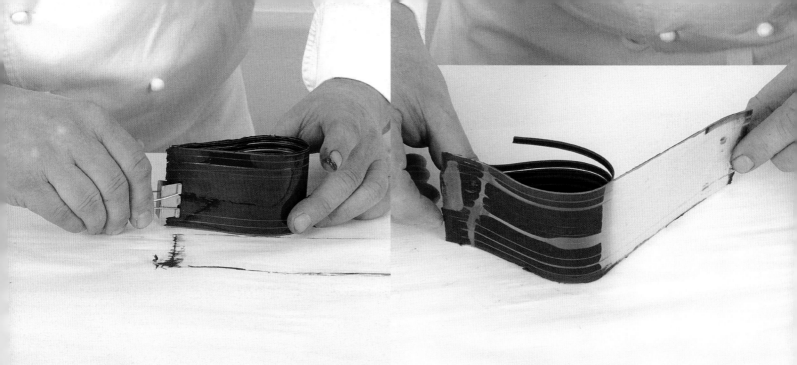

⑥ Remove the clip and gently peel the acetate from the thin chocolate teardrops.

⑦ Trim the ends of the chocolate teardrop damaged by the clip.

⑧ Separate each chocolate teardrop and use to decorate a cake or entremets.

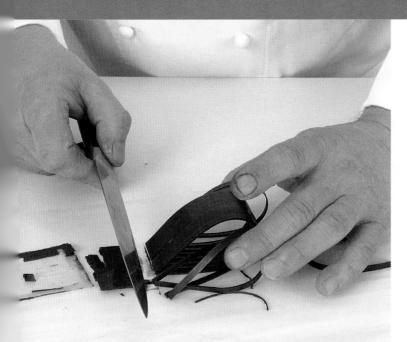

The best way to make a chocolate collar

Prepare a cake or entremets according to your chosen recipe. Temper the chocolate as indicated on pages 320 to 324.

(1) Freeze a clean baking tray and place it upside down on the work surface. Use a ladle to pour a line of tempered chocolate along the length of the tray.

(2) Spread the chocolate with a stainless steel palette knife so to obtain a thin layer that it is about the same length as the circumference of the cake or entremets but slightly higher.

(3) Use a knife to cut an even band of chocolate to the desired height.

(4) Before the chocolate starts to harden, remove the band from the baking tray and gently wrap it around the cake or entremets.

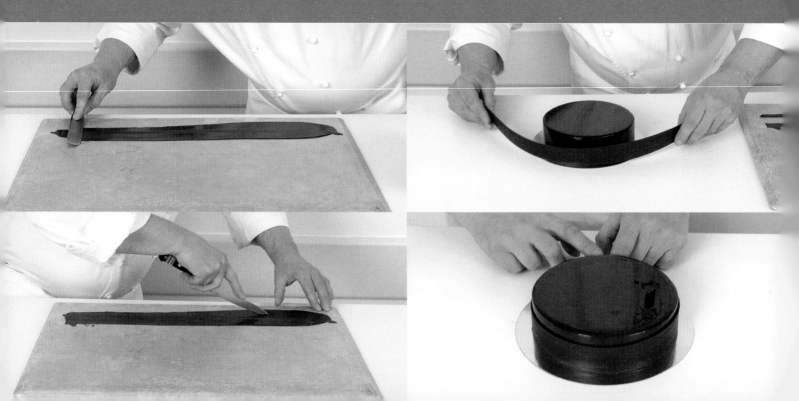

The best way to make a collar using cocoa butter

Prepare a cake or entremets according to your chosen recipe.

① Cut a strip of thick plastic or acetate sheet to the same length and height as the circumference of the cake or entremets. Place the strip on a sheet of baking parchment and make a wave pattern with melted red cocoa butter (or another colour) along the length of the plastic strip. Make another wave pattern over it using melted yellow cocoa butter (or another colour).

② Gently blend the colours together with a pastry brush.

③ Carefully lift up the strip and place the cocoa butter side around the cake or entremets.

④ Refrigerate the cake or entremets for 15 minutes, then carefully remove the plastic strip before serving.

The best way to make a chocolate gold leaf collar

Prepare a cake or entremets according to your chosen recipe. Temper the chocolate as indicated on pages 320 to 324, and pour into a piping bag.

① Cut a strip of acetate to the same length and height as the circumference of the cake. Pipe a line of tempered chocolate along the strip.

② Hold the edge of the strip down and use a stainless steel palette knife to spread the chocolate thinly across the entire surface.

③ Scrape the chocolate with the tines of a fork to create grooves.

④ Use a spatula to mix 20 g of melted cocoa butter with a little gold powder to make a golden liquid. Gently pour the golden liquid in the chocolate grooves.

 Use a palette knife to spread the gold liquid to fill the grooves.

6 Pipe another line of chocolate along the entire strip.

7 Hold down the edge of the strip and use a stainless steel palette knife to once again spread the chocolate thinly across the surface to cover the gold.

8 Carefully lift up the acetate and wrap the chocolate side around the cake or entremets.

9 Refrigerate the cake or entremets for 15 minutes; and remove the acetate strip before serving.

GLOSSARY

BAIN-MARIE: The French term for a hot water bath. Can be bought as a specialist piece of equipment or improvised by sitting a bowl containing the dessert in a larger pan of simmering water. Used for cooking or warming food (particularly delicate sauces), melting chocolate and for preparations such as a Génoise or sabayon, which must not be placed on direct heat.

BAKE: To cook food uncovered in an oven at a required temperature.

BAKING PARCHMENT: A non-stick paper that is particularly useful for lining baking tins.

BAKING POWDER: A dry chemical raising agent used to increase volume and lighten the texture of baked goods such as cakes.

BEAT: To mix ingredients using a quick, regular motion until smooth and evenly blended. Can be performed using a wire whisk, spoon, hand beater or an electric mixer. Also used for incorporating air into soufflés and batters, which need to rise.

BEURRE EN POMMADE: Softened (not melted) butter, beaten until it becomes creamy and smooth.

BEURRE NOISETTE: Nut-brown butter; obtained by heating butter until it liquefies, turning golden brown and the milk solids colour and stick to the bottom of the saucepan.

BISCUIT: 1. Type of small sweet cake or pastry. 2. A specific type of sponge similar to a Génoise sponge.

BOIL: To heat a liquid until bubbles break on the surface. To boil a food item is to cook it in boiling liquid (usually water). The boiling point of water is 100°C but varies for other liquids.

BRÛLÉE: A sugar topping melted under a hot grill until it caramelises. A crisp crust will form when it cools.

BUTTER/OIL: To lightly coat a recipient with soft or melted butter, or oil, using a pastry brush, to prevent foods sticking.

CARAMEL: Sugar melted and cooked to 180°C; it changes from a light golden to a dark brown syrup during the cooking process. When cooled, it is very brittle and breaks easily.

CARAMELISE: To coat food or line a mould with caramel. Sugar can also be caramelised when sprinkled on a dessert and melted under a hot grill (see brûlée).

CHANTILLY CREAM: Whipped cream with the addition of icing sugar.

CHILL: To place food in a refrigerator or a bath of iced water or cubes to make or keep it cool or firm.

CHINOIS: A conical metal strainer or sieve.

CHOP: To cut food into small pieces using a knife or food processor.

CHURN/FREEZE: The process of converting a liquid mixture into ice cream or sorbet using an ice-cream or sorbet machine.

CLARIFIED BUTTER: A process of gently melting butter in which the whey (or milk solids) sinks to the bottom of the pan and the impurities float to the top of the liquefied butter. When clarified, butter can be kept refrigerated for longer than non-clarified butter without becoming rancid and it burns less quickly when heated.

COAT: To completely cover an ingredient with another, such as chocolate.

COCOA NIBS: Chocolate or cocoa nibs are roasted cocoa beans separated from their husks and broken into small bits.

COMPOTE: A preparation of fresh or dried fruit cooked in sugar syrup until soft.

CORE: To remove the central core from fruit such apples and pears.

COULIS: A sieved purée of sweetened fruit combined with a small amount of lemon juice.

CREAM: To beat ingredients together until they have blended into a light, fluffy and smooth consistency. The term is usually applied to creaming sugar with a fat, such as butter.

CREAM, WHIPPED: Whipping cream whisked until firm peaks cling to the whisk.

CRÈME ANGLAISE: A vanilla custard cream sauce made with milk, eggs and sugar and served with a variety of desserts. The vanilla can be replaced with other flavours such as chocolate and pistachio. It is the base preparation for ice cream.

CRÈME PÂTISSIÈRE: French for pastry

cream, it is a thick cream made with milk, egg yolks, sugar and flour and traditionally flavoured with vanilla. Used as the base preparation in many desserts and also as a filling for éclairs.

CRUSH: To reduce a solid ingredient to small pieces using a food processor or a rolling pin.

CRYSTALLISED: Describes fruit or flower petals, generally used for decoration, that have been coated in lightly beaten egg white then sugar.

DÉTREMPE: A French term describing the mixture of flour and water. It is the first step in the preparation of puff pastry.

DICE: To cut food into small cubes.

DOUGH: A mixture based on flour and water that is soft and malleable, yet firm enough to hold its form.

DROPPING CONSISTENCY: Describes the consistency of a mixture that can be dropped by the spoonful on to a baking sheet, yet holds its shape once dropped.

DUST: To lightly sprinkle food or a work surface with a powdery ingredient such as flour, cocoa powder or icing sugar.

ENRICH: To add cream, egg yolks or butter to a preparation giving it a richer texture or flavour.

FLOUR: To dredge or sprinkle pans with flour, usually over butter, to prevent food sticking.

FOLD: To blend a light ingredient with a heavier one. Usually, the lighter is placed on the heavier one. The two are combined using a spatula or metal spoon in a figure-of-eight motion, to retain air in the mixture.

FRITTER: Food coated in batter and deep-fried. The batter coating varies according to the food.

FRY: To cook food in hot fat. Deep-fried foods are submerged in fat. Sautéed or pan-fried foods are cooked in a small amount of fat – just enough to coat the bottom of the pan and prevent sticking.

GANACHE: A mixture obtained by pouring hot cream over chopped chocolate. It is used for garnishing desserts and as a filling for cakes and chocolates.

GELATINE: A colourless solid, in powder or leaf form used as a thickening agent. When mixed in hot liquid it becomes viscous and turns to jelly, solidifying when the mixture is cold.

GÉNOISE: A whisked yellow sponge made with eggs, sugar and flour.

GLAZE: 1. To coat the surface of a dessert with a thin sweet liquid such as ganache, or icing that will set to a smooth, glossy finish. 2. To brush uncooked dough with beaten egg to give it a sheen when cooked.

GREASE: To coat an item of equipment with a fat such as butter or oil, to prevent foods from sticking to it.

GRIND: To reduce dry foods to a powder or into tiny grains using either a pestle and mortar or a food processor.

HULL: To remove the stalk and core from fruit such as strawberries.

ICE-BATH: To immerse the base of a hot pan of ingredients in a bowl of water and ice cubes to suddenly arrest the cooking process.

IMBIBE: To use a flavoured syrup or liqueur to soak a cake, adding flavour

and increasing moisture.

INFUSE: To steep herbs, spices or citrus zests, etc. in a hot liquid giving the liquid flavour and aroma.

JULIENNE: To cut fruit, citrus peel or vegetables into very fine shreds or strips.

KNEAD: To manipulate dough by hand pushing it and pulling it across the work surface to obtain a perfect mixture of all the ingredients.

LINE: 1. To cover a baking sheet or the inside of a mould with baking parchment to prevent the finished product from sticking during cooking. 2. To cover the interior wall and/or bottom of a tart or flan tin with pastry dough, for example, before baking or adding a filling.

MACERATE: To soak food, often fruit, in sugar syrup, liqueur or alcohol to flavour it.

MARBLING: A decorative effect achieved by partially mixing a cake batter or chocolate of two different colours.

MERINGUE: A mixture of whisked egg whites and sugar. There are three types of meringue: 1. French—egg whites into which sugar is beaten progressively until stiff peaks form. 2. Italian—whisked egg whites with a cooked sugar syrup added. 3. Swiss meringue—egg whites and sugar whisked over a bain-marie until firm.

MIX: The technique of combining two or more ingredients.

MOULD: 1. To shape a dessert by placing a soft malleable preparation in a mould to set into that shape either by chilling or using a setting agent such as gelatine. 2. A container available in a variety of shapes and sizes.

MOUSSE: A French term used to describe a preparation with a light, airy texture, obtained by the addition of whisked egg whites.

NAP: To lightly coat a dessert with a coulis or cream.

NOZZLE: Piping nozzles are hollow and conical and made from steel or plastic. They can be plain or fluted and used in a piping bag to pipe cream, choux paste or meringue.

PASTE: Food ground to a fine texture and moistened slightly to make a stiff spreadable mixture.

PASTRY CIRCLE: A metal circle of various diameters and heights used for assembling desserts. Pastry chefs prefer this tool over the traditional round mould.

PASTRY CUTTER: A metal or plastic tool in a variety of shapes and sizes used to cut pastry dough into even shapes.

PÂTE: The French term used to describe a pastry mixture: pâte sucrée (sweet pastry); pâte brisée (shortcrust pastry); pâte sablé (shortbread pastry).

PÂTON: The French term used to describe uncooked puff pastry dough.

PINCH: A very small quantity of an ingredient such as salt or sugar taken using the thumb and the forefinger.

PITH: The bitter white layer of skin between the coloured outer skin (the zest) and flesh of citrus fruit.

POACH: To immerse food and cook it in a slowly simmering liquid such as water or a sugar syrup.

PRALINE: Almonds and/or hazelnuts cooked in boiling sugar until caramelised. The mixture is then cooled and

ground to a powder. If continued to be ground, it becomes praline paste.

PRICK: To make small holes in pastry dough with a fork to prevent air pockets forming during baking.

PURÉE: Fruit or vegetables, cooked or raw, liquidised in an electric blender or mouli and sieved to a smooth pulp which can be used as a sauce or as a base in other preparations.

QUENELLES: Ovals of a soft preparation such as ice cream or whipped cream, shaped with two spoons and often used decoratively.

REDUCE: To boil a liquid at a high heat in an uncovered pan, evaporating it and concentrating the flavour.

RIBBON: When a beaten egg and sugar preparation falls from a spoon or whisk in a smooth, unbroken flow, it is said to be at ribbon consistency.

SIEVE (OR STRAIN): To pass a liquid through a sieve (or strainer) to remove any solids.

SIFT: To sieve dry ingredients such as flour or icing sugar, adding air and separating lumps from the fine powder.

SIMMER: To maintain a liquid just below boiling point, so that the surface bubbles gently. The term also refers to cooking food gently in a liquid (see poaching).

SKIM: To remove impurities or foam from the surface of a preparation using a ladle or large spoon.

SLICE: To cut fruit, for example, using a knife into thin or fine regular slices.

SOUFFLÉ: A French term used to describe a light, airy preparation based on

whisked egg whites. Cooked versions rise.

SWEAT: To gently cook fruit or vegetables in a little butter or oil without colouring to bring out the flavour.

SYRUP: A liquid made by heating sugar and water. Syrups have a variety of uses depending on the ratio of sugar to water and the temperature to which they are heated.

TEMPER: To heat, cool and reheat chocolate to three precise temperatures (p. 315), giving it a glossy, streak-free and crisp finish.

TURN/FOLD: A technique used to blend the butter into puff pastry dough.

VANILLA ESSENCE/EXTRACT: Products made from pure vanilla to obtain a reliable flavour, and can be used to replace a vanilla pod.

WELL: A large hollow made in the centre of a quantity of flour, either in a bowl or on the work surface, to hold liquid ingredients.

WHISK: To blend ingredients using a wire whisk in a circular motion, incorporating air into a mixture. Mostly used with liquid rather than dry ingredients.

ZEST: The coloured outer skin of citrus fruit.

RECIPE INDEX A–Z

INDEX OF INGREDIENTS

ACKNOWLEDGEMENTS

Le Cordon Bleu and Larousse wish to thank the teams of Chefs around the globe, located in almost 20 countries and more than 35 schools, who helped to write this book through their know-how and creativity.

We wish to express our gratitude to the **Paris school**, with the Chefs Xavier Cotte, Jean-François Deguignet, Patrick Lebouc, Franck Poupard, Jean-Jacques Tranchant, Nicolas Jordan (MOF), Frederic Lesourd, Olivier Mahut, Patrick Caals, Williams Caussimon, Christian Monk, Marc Vaca, Pascal Quéré and Olivier Boudot.

At the **London School**, with the Chefs Alan Swinson, Loïc Malfait, Eric Bédiat, Anthony Boyd, Tom Birks, Daniel Hardy, David Duverger, Reginald Ioos, Colin Westal, Julie Walsh, Graeme Bartholomew, Matthew Hodgett, Nicolas Houchet, Javier Mercado, Dominique Moudart, Olivier Mourelon, Ian Winton and Jerome Pendaries.

At the **Tokyo School**, with the Chefs Guillaume Siegler, Yuji Toyonaga, Stéphane Reinat, Dominique Gros, Katsutoshi Yokoyama, Hiroyuki Honda, Robert Manuel, Kazuki Ogata and Jean-Francois Favy.

At **Kobe School**, with the Chefs Patrick Lemesle, Tsuyoshi Kawamichi, Philippe Koehl and Jullian Pekle.

At the **Ottawa School**, with the Chefs Didier Chantefort, Aurélien Legué, Herve Chabert, Yannick Anton, Jocelyn Bouzenard, Khushroo Kambata, Julie Vachon, Frederic Rose, Xavier Baudy and Jason Desjardins.

At the school of **Korea**, with the Chefs Fabrice Huet, Laurent Reze, Julien Favario, Alain Heuze and Alain Sanchez.

At the **Peruvian school**, with the Chefs Torsten Enders, Paola Espach, Clet Laborde, Eric Germanangues, Jeremy Peñaloza, Javier Ampuero, Hajime Kasuga, Gregor Funke, Elena Braguina, Giovanna De Rivero, Angelo Ortiz, Fabian Beelen, Gloria Hinostroza, Annamaria Dominguez, Daniel Punchin, Olivier Roseau, Andrea Winkelried, Christophe Leroy, Patricia Colona, Samuel Moreau, Raul Cenzano and Martin Tufro.

At the **Mexico City School**, with Chefs Arnaud Guerpillon, Alberto Acero, Carlos Barrera, Carlos Santos, Omar Morales, Malik Meghezi, Denis Delaval, Richard Lecoq, Sergio Torres and Cedric Carême.

At the school of **Thailand**, with the Chefs Fabrice Danniel, Christian Patrice Ham, Lisa Thorsen Barker, Pruek Sumpantaworaboot, Marc Champiré, Willy Pierre Daurade, Niruch Chotwatchara, Guillaume Francois Lucien Ancelin, Rapeepat Boriboon, Supapit Opatvisan, Jérémy Gilles and Julien Laurent.

At schools in **Australia**, under the responsibility of Chef Andre Sandison.

At the **Shanghai School**, with Chefs Philippe Clergue and Nicolas Serrano.

At the **Istanbul School**, with the Chefs Gilles Company, Olivier Pallut, Christopher Gauci and Christophe Bidault.

At the school of **Madrid**, with the Chefs Yann Barraud, Victor Pérez, Erwan Poudoulec, Franck Plana, David Millet, José Enrique Gonzalez, Jean-Charles Boucher, Amandine Finger, Carlos Collado and Natalia Vázquez.

At the school in **Taiwan**, with the Chefs Nicolas Belorgey and Sébastien Graslan.

At the **New Zealand School**, with the Chefs Sebastian Lambert, Paul Dicken, Francis Motta, Michel Rocton, Thomas Holleaux and Michael Arlukiewicz.

At the **Malaysian School**, with the Chefs Rodolphe Onno, David Morris and Thierry Lerallu.

The publication of this book would not have been possible without the professionalism and the enthusiasm of the coordination teams and administration, nor without the photographer and participation 'testers' under the leadership of Chef Daniel Walter: Catherine Baschet, Kaye Baudinette, Isabelle Beaudin, Émilie Burgat, Robyn Cahill, Marie-Anne Dufeu, Christian Lalonde (PhotoluxStudio), Charlotte Madec, Leanne Mallard, Sandra Messier, Kathy Shaw and Lynne Westney.

We especially thank Isabelle Jeuge-Maynard (President and CEO and Ghislaine Stora (Deputy Chief Executive Officer) of Larousse and their team; Brigitte Courtillet, Anne-Charlotte Diverres, Camille Durette, Véronique Finance-Shoemaker, Colette Hanicotte, Aude Mantoux and for this edition Agnès Busière, Coralie Benoit and Olivier Ploton (photographer).

For this edition in English, Le Cordon Bleu wishes to thank Grub Street Publishing directed by Anne Dolamore.

OVEN TEMPERATURES

CELSIUS	FAHRENHEIT	GAS	DESCRIPTION
110°C	225°F	$1/4$	Cool
120°C	250°F	$1/2$	Cool
140°C	275°F	1	Very low
150°C	300°F	2	Very low
160°C	325°F	3	Low
170°C	335°F	3	Moderate
180°C	350°F	4	Moderate
190°C	375°F	5	Moderate/hot
200°C	400°F	6	Hot
220°C	425°F	7	Very hot
230°C	450°F	8	Very hot

VOLUME

METRIC	IMPERIAL	METRIC	IMPERIAL
25 ml	1 fl oz	500 ml	18 fl oz
50 ml	2 fl oz	568 ml	20 fl oz/1 pint
75 ml	$2^1/2$ fl oz	600 ml	1 pint milk
100 ml	$3^1/2$ fl oz	700 ml	$1^1/4$ pints
125 ml	4 fl oz	850 ml	$1^1/2$ pints
150 ml	5 fl oz/$1/4$ pint	1 litre	$1^3/4$ pints
175 ml	6 fl oz	1.2 litres	2 pints
200 ml	7 fl oz/$1/3$ pint	1.3 litres	$2^1/4$ pints
225 ml	8 fl oz	1.4 litres	$2^1/2$ pints
250 ml	9 fl oz	1.5 litres	$2^3/4$ pints
300 ml	10 fl oz/$1/2$ pint	1.7 litres	3 pints
350 ml	12 fl oz	2 litres	$3^1/2$ pints
400 ml	14 fl oz	2.5 litres	$4^1/2$ pints
425 ml	15 fl oz/$3/4$ pint	2.8 litres	5 pints
450 ml	16 fl oz	3 litres	$5^1/4$ pints

SPOONS

METRIC	IMPERIAL
1.25 ml	$1/4$ tsp
2.5 ml	$1/2$ tsp
5 ml	1 tsp
10 ml	2 tsp
15 ml	3 tsp/1 tbsp
30 ml	2 tbsp
45 ml	3 tbsp
60 ml	4 tbsp
75 ml	5 tbsp
90 ml	6 tbsp

US CUPS

US CUPS	METRIC
$1/4$ cup	60 ml
$1/3$ cup	70 ml
$1/2$ cup	125 ml
$2/3$ cup	150 ml
$3/4$ cup	175 ml
1 cup	250 ml
$1^1/2$ cups	375 ml
2 cups	500 ml
3 cups	750 ml
4 cups	1 litre
6 cups	1.5 litres

WEIGHT

METRIC	IMPERIAL
5 g	$1/8$ oz
10 g	$1/4$ oz
15 g	$1/2$ oz
20 g	$3/4$ oz
25 g	1 oz
35 g	$1^1/4$ oz
40 g	$1^1/2$ oz
50 g	$1^3/4$ oz
55 g	2 oz
60 g	$2^1/4$ oz
70 g	$2^1/2$ oz
75 g	$2^3/4$ oz
85 g	3 oz
90 g	$3^1/4$ oz
100 g	$3^1/2$ oz
115 g	4 oz
125 g	$4^1/2$ oz
140 g	5 oz
150 g	$5^1/2$ oz
175 g	6 oz
200 g	7 oz
225 g	8 oz
250 g	9 oz
275 g	$9^3/4$ oz
280 g	10 oz
300 g	$10^1/2$ oz
315 g	11 oz
325 g	$11^1/2$ oz
350 g	12 oz
375 g	13 oz
400 g	14 oz
425 g	15 oz
450 g	1 lb
500 g	1 lb 2 oz
550 g	1 lb 4 oz
600 g	1 lb 5 oz
650 g	1 lb 7 oz
700 g	1 lb 9 oz
750 g	1 lb 10 oz
800 g	1 lb 12 oz
850 g	1 lb 14 oz
900 g	2 lb
950 g	2 lb 2 oz
1 kg	2 lb 4 oz
1.25 kg	2 lb 12 oz
1.3 kg	3 lb
1.5 kg	3 lb 5 oz
1.6 kg	3 lb 8 oz
1.8 kg	4 lb
2 kg	4 lb 8 oz
2.25 kg	5 lb

MEASURES

METRIC	IMPERIAL
2 mm	$1/16$ in
3 mm	$1/8$ in
5 mm	$1/4$ in
8 mm	$3/8$ in
10 mm/1 cm	$1/2$ in
1.5 cm	$5/8$ in
2 cm	$3/4$ in
2.5 cm	1 in
3 cm	$1^1/4$ in
4 cm	$1^1/2$ in
4.5 cm	$1^3/4$ in
5 cm	2 in
5.5 cm	$2^1/4$ in
6 cm	$2^1/2$ in
7 cm	$2^3/4$ in
7.5 cm	3 in
8 cm	$3^1/4$ in
9 cm	$3^1/2$ in
9.5 cm	$3^3/4$ in
10 cm	4 in
11 cm	$4^1/4$ in
12 cm	$4^1/2$ in
12.5 cm	$4^3/4$ in
13 cm	5 in
14 cm	$5^1/2$ in
15 cm	6 in
16 cm	$6^1/4$ in
17 cm	$6^1/2$ in
18 cm	7 in
19 cm	$7^1/2$ in
20 cm	8 in
22 cm	$8^1/2$ in
23 cm	9 in
24 cm	$9^1/2$ in
25 cm	10 in
26 cm	$10^1/2$ in
27 cm	$10^3/4$ in
28 cm	11 in
29 cm	$11^1/2$ in
30 cm	12 in
31 cm	$12^1/2$ in
33 cm	13 in
34 cm	$13^1/2$ in
35 cm	14 in
37 cm	$14^1/2$ in
38 cm	15 in
39 cm	$15^1/2$ in
40 cm	16 in
42 cm	$16^1/2$ in
43 cm	17 in
44 cm	$17^1/2$ in